Gerry Daly's

GARDENING BOOK

Gill and Macmillan

Published in Ireland by
Gill and Macmillan Ltd
Goldenbridge
Dublin 8
with associated companies in
Auckland, Budapest, Gaborone, Harare, Hong Kong,
Kampala, Kuala Lumpur, Lagos, London, Madras,
Manzini, Melbourne, Mexico City, Nairobi,
New York, Singapore, Sydney, Tokyo, Windhoek
© Gerry Daly 1986, 1992
First published 1986 by Gerry Daly and Associates
Photographs by the author, except pages 51 and 52
from the Harry Smith Photographic Collection
Printed by Colour Books, Dublin

A catalogue record for this book is available from the British Library.

CONTENTS

Introduction to the Revised Edition

Introduction to the Revised Edition

To my great satisfaction, readers of the first edition of this book found it easy to follow, and helpful in their gardening. This Revised Edition updates the original and it has even more information, particularly in the area of labour saving.

The book is divided into twenty Sections. The first nine of these relate to the growing of plants. Advice is offered on the use of the various kinds of plants in the garden; their site and soil preferences, planting, training, pruning, weed control, harvesting, and pests and diseases.

The Sections on Soils, Nutrients and Fertilisers; Tools and Equipment; and Garden Skills are intended for the new gardener, or those who wish to get back to first principles on basic aspects.

The Sections on the Principles of Labour Saving; Labour-intensive Garden Features; and Labour-saving Garden Features are intended to allow planning for reduced effort in the garden with better overall results. The Lists of plants for various site and soil conditions, and for less pruning and staking, will enable better plant choice.

The Section on Weeds is a brief outline of the main techniques of weed control. Details of specific strategies are given separately in each Section.

The Sections on Pests and Diseases contain a fuller treatment of the pests and diseases mentioned in the previous sections, together with advice on control based on the needs of gardeners. A range of control options is presented in each case with the non-chemical approach as first choice. The chemical solution is presented as an option of last resort to be used with reluctance and caution.

Finally, the Calendars follow the various plant categories through the seasons, giving appropriate dates for a wide range of gardening operations. The page on Weather and Timing should be read in conjunction with the Calendars.

Good gardening!

Trees and Shrubs

Types

Trees carry their branches on a single stem, or trunk. **Shrubs** have a number of stems at ground level. Trees are generally larger than shrubs, but there are exceptions. Dwarf trees — still truly trees — may be only a few feet tall.

Trees and shrubs are either **evergreen** — retaining their leaves all year round — or **deciduous** — dropping their leaves each autumn. Trees which bear cones instead of flowers are called **conifers**. Evergreens may be **broad-leaved evergreens** such as Holly and Laurel; conifers with needles such as Spruce and Pine; or conifers with soft foliage such as Lawson's cypress and Thuya.

Flame of the forest
Pieris formosa 'Forrestii'
striking red, young foliage in spring.

Uses

Trees and shrubs are used in gardens for ornamental purposes. Trees fill some of the space of the garden, taking the flat, bare look off it. They give privacy and provide a backdrop for smaller plants. Shrubs are more ornamental and provide variety of interest. Trees and shrubs are best planted in combination, to create a pleasing, decorative effect.

Particularly beautiful trees or shrubs may be planted as single specimens in a lawn area where their special qualities are put on show. Use only one specimen in a small lawn, or a small number of isolated specimens in a large lawn. Otherwise the effect is lost.

Climbers are used to decorate walls and fences. These woody plants make good use of vertical space which is often wasted.

Some trees and shrubs make good hedges and screens. They provide privacy and respite from noise and dust. Evergreens are best against noise. Deciduous trees are best against dust.

Low-growing shrubs may be used as ground-cover plants to hide the soil surface and help to keep weeds under control.

Summer-flowering clematis
Clematis 'Comtesse de Bouchaud'
masses of bright pink into autumn.

Site factors

●**Shelter.** Trees and shrubs are relatively tall plants and, therefore, prone to wind damage — Ireland has a very windy climate! Western and southern coastal areas suffer particularly from strong gales. Eastern and northern areas often get cold, dry winds in spring. The midlands, being flat, can be very windy too.

In exposed gardens, shelter is the first essential. Even where exposure is not great, trees and shrubs grow better with some shelter. Certain species of trees and shrubs tolerate strong winds and even salty gales. These species may be used to protect their more finicky cousins. Young plants especially need protection, but it must be remembered that too much shelter makes a garden cold and dark.

A useful shelter effect is achieved for a distance of 10 times the height of the shelter. *(See Shelter Belts later in this Section. Page 14).* In a very exposed situation, consider using artificial shelter to allow natural shelter to become established. Porous wooden fencing, or plastic netting, may be used to reduce wind — not to block it. Solid windbreaks may increase the problem by forcing wind upwards, only to have it come down behind the barrier with even greater force. Note that these effects are often created around and between houses and, although the locality may not be exposed, parts of the garden may be very windy. *(See the List of Wind-Resistant Trees. Page 98).*

●**Size.** The size of the garden has a big influence on the size of trees and shrubs that may be grown. Tall, broad trees are not suitable for small gardens. Narrow trees, weeping forms and standards (trees with a clear stem) take up less space.

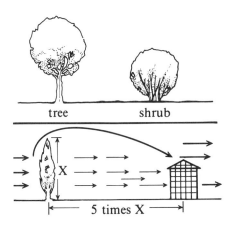

The effect of shelter is considerable for a distance of at least five times the height of the windbreak.

●**Wires.** Check the position of drains underground and wires overhead. Do not plant trees with vigorous root action, such as Poplar and Willow, over drains. Do not plant tall, fast-growing trees beneath overhead wires.

●**Views.** Observe the view from the garden and the main windows. Position trees and shrubs so that they block unsightly views, but frame and emphasise pleasant views. A tree planted close to the observer will more quickly block an unsightly view than if it is planted close to the object to be hidden.

●**Soil.** Trees and shrubs need good, fertile, moist — but well-drained — soil. Some types tolerate wet, heavy soil and some enjoy warm, dry soil. Thus a choice may be made for any soil type. It is not practical to improve the soil for trees and large shrubs, but proper planting will greatly help establishment. Soil for smaller plants may be improved by digging in well-rotted manure, compost or peat and some general fertiliser, before planting.

The acidity of soil may affect trees and shrubs. Very acid, peaty soil causes poor growth and limy soil causes some of the best garden shrubs — Rhododendrons, Camellias and Heathers — to fail. Slightly acid conditions, pH 6.5, are ideal. Hydrangeas are good indicator plants. They are pink on limy soils, blue on acid and pale purple on neutral soils. Reasonably accurate test kits are available.

Choosing trees and shrubs

●**Size.** Find out the eventual size of a tree or shrub before planting. Use the larger plants to provide the framework of the planting and the smaller ones to complement and contrast with these. Generally, the tall plants are put to the back, the smaller ones to the front. An occasional exception might be made, to provide contrast.

●**Shape.** Every tree and shrub has its individual shape. The main types of shape are columnar, conical, round, flat or 'weeping' and there are innumerable variations. A good variety of these should be planted. There is often plenty of rounded shapes, but not enough of the others. Many garden trees are grown as standards, with a clear stem of up to 6 feet (2m), which allows planting beneath.

●**Colour.** This may be provided by leaves, flowers, berries or bark. Flower colour is usually taken into account, but foliage colour, though at least as important, is often ignored. Aim to provide variety of foliage colour through spring, summer, autumn and winter by choosing trees and shrubs which change colour with the seasons. Those which vary from green — yellow, red, blue and grey foliage plants — deserve special consideration.

●**Texture.** This feature of trees and shrubs is a little less obvious than the others. The distinctive size, shape and density of foliage, and the way the plant holds its branch framework, define texture. For example, Japanese maple is soft and ferny, Chestnut is bold and strong, Scots pine is rugged and untamed. Choose plants for variety of texture. This is as important as shape or colour.

The Lists of Trees and Shrubs may be used to make choices for small to medium or large gardens. A large garden is greater than 1,200 square yards (about 1,000m²). Not nearly enough large gardens have good-sized trees, although there is often plenty of space. The Lists are just a small sample of the trees and shrubs available, but they include some of the best choices.

Spacing

●**How far apart?** How far apart and how many plants should occupy any particular piece of ground is a difficult question. It will depend on the eventual size and shape of the tree or shrub and its rate of growth. It will also depend on soil conditions and, to a considerable extent, it is a matter of taste. Dense planting fills the space quickly, hiding the soil and helping to control weeds. However, planting at close spacing is expensive, because more plants are used. After a while, they begin to interfere with each other's development too.

St. John's wort
Hypericum 'Hidcote'
good late summer flowering shrub.

Purple smokebush
Cotinus coggygria 'Royal Purple'
Potentilla 'Tangerine' growing through.

Chusan palm
Trachycarpus fortunei
hardy enough for most parts.

Purple plum
Prunus cerasifera 'Nigra'
replaces Copper beech in small
gardens.

Forsythia
Forsythia intermedia 'Lynwood'
spectacular colour without fail.

Juneberry
Amelanchier canadensis
white flowers, good autumn tints.

Variegated weigela
Weigela florida 'Variegata'
pink flowers and cream foliage.

Bottle brush
Callistemon citrinus
a bit risky inland unless sheltered.

Variegated poplar
Populus candicans 'Aurora'
spectacular variegation in mid-summer.

Rock rose
Helianthemum nummularium
a low-growing shrub, it likes dry soil.

Chilean holly
Desfontainea spinosa
hardy enough for most parts.

Hydrangea
Hydrangea macrophylla
may be pink or blue.

● **Guidelines.** To space two large trees, add together the eventual heights of the trees and divide by two. To space small trees and shrubs, add together the eventual widths of the two plants and divide by two. Dividing by three will give a closer spacing, with the plants meeting more quickly.

● **Using guidelines.** Use these guidelines to space trees, and shrubs, of similar size. Obviously it makes no sense to add together the heights of a large tree and a small shrub and space them accordingly. Space all trees of similar size first, then the shrubs. Remember that most trees will have to be underplanted, while most shrubs will not. These guidelines also hold good when planting new plants in an established planting.

● **Thinning.** The spacing guidelines may give a planting which looks sparse, but this will not last long. To avoid an initial sparse look, overplanting and subsequent thinning might be carried out. Quick-growing shrubs may be used as colourful, temporary fillers. Broom, Cistus, Escallonia, Weigela, Ceanothus and Lavatera are examples. Some of these are short-lived anyway, so thinning is almost automatic.

● **Specific rules.** When planting near boundary walls, keep large trees about 10 feet (3m) away and plant small trees and shrubs the height of the wall away. Plant wall shrubs and climbers between 6 inches and 18 inches (15-45cm) away. When planting near a house, keep large trees at a distance equal to half their eventual height plus 20 feet (6m). Plant small trees and large shrubs no closer than 10 feet (3m), unless they are of narrow, columnar shape.

Planting

Trees and shrubs are sold either as container-grown plants or in the traditional way as field-grown, bare-root plants. Deciduous bare-root plants are planted from the beginning of November to the end of March. Evergreen bare-root plants are planted in October or April. Container-grown plants can be planted at any time of year, even in high summer. However, they establish best if planted during the traditional planting months.

Before planting, soak the roots of the plants in water. Allow container-grown plants to drain for a while afterwards. Make up a planting mix of moist peat with a handful of general fertiliser or Tree and Shrub Fertiliser added to each bucketful.

— Completely remove any grass or weeds.
— Dig over the area where the planting hole will be, breaking down the soil lumps.
— Dig out the hole. Place the soil on polythene sheeting if planting in a lawn, to save messing up the grass.
— Make the hole deep enough and wide enough to take the roots or rootball.
— Break up the soil in the bottom of the hole.
— Add a 2 inch (5cm) layer of the planting mix and mix it with the soil in the bottom of the hole.
— Drive in a support stake at this stage, if a tree is being planted.
— Place the plant in the hole, spread the roots.
— Check that it is at the same depth as it was previously planted. Avoid deep planting.
— Add some fine soil and planting mix. Work this in around the roots.
— Firm gently. Add more soil and firm again.
— Leave the soil surface neat. Water after planting.

If staked, tie in the tree using two ties, one near the top and one half way down.

Be patient. Do not expect results immediately after planting. Many shrubs take a few years before starting to flower. Although the shrub may be flowering at planting, or in its first year, this can be deceptive. It is caused by the restriction of the nursery container. When its roots gain the liberty of the open soil the plant often skips flowering for a few seasons. Do not prune plants which have done this. It further delays flowering.

Norway maple
Acer platanoides
a beautiful big tree for large gardens.

Boston ivy
Parthenocissus tricuspidata
a vigorous creeper for large walls.

Parrotia
Parrotia persica
a spreading tree, lovely in autumn.

Silver birch
Betula jacquemontii
colourful bark in winter.

A good planting of shrubs showing how to use shape, size, colour and texture.

1. *Juniperus 'Pfitzeriana'* 4. *Skimmia japonica*
2. *Mahonia japonica* 5. *Fuchsia* (standard)
3. *Eleagnus 'Maculata'* 6. *Cotoneaster 'Variegatus'*

Watering

The water needs of trees and shrubs are often overlooked. Young, newly-planted trees are particularly vulnerable. For the first two summers after planting, any tree or shrub may suffer, especially conifers. During dry spells of more than one week, a close watch should be kept. Plants showing signs of shortage should get a good watering — about 5 gallons (23 litres) per plant. The danger signs are a listless appearance and a dullness of leaf colour, especially with conifers. Even big established trees may come under moisture stress.

Root disturbance, or a change in ground water level caused by building or roadworks, may cause this. Affected trees have small, sparse foliage and dead twigs. Foliage may appear on the main branches. It is possible to water a large shrub or tree by allowing a slight trickle of water from a hose to percolate down into the root zone over a period of one day or more. This delivers a very large quantity of water without waste.

Feeding

To become really well established, young trees and shrubs should be fed each year for the first five or six years. On good, fertile soils, this feeding need only be a 2 inch (5cm) layer of well-rotted manure or compost, in April. On poorer soils, or if manure is not available, one ounce per square yard ($30g/m^2$) of general fertiliser or Tree and Shrub Fertiliser should be applied, in spring. Feeding encourages good strong growth. Quick establishment enables the plant to resist diseases and pests.

Older trees and shrubs need no fertiliser unless they look unhealthy following pest or disease attack. Feeding as above aids recovery. Established plants may fail to provide good displays on poor soil and should be fed every year.

Even in summer, dwarf conifers look well, a nice mix of shape and colour.

List of Twenty Spring/Early Summer Flowering Shrubs

Name	Latin Name	Height	Spread	Colour	Flowers	Remarks
Barbary	*Barberis darwinii*	3m	3m	orange	April	enjoys dry soil
Camellia	*Camellia japonica*	2.5m	1.8m	pink	April	acid soil only
Californian lilac	*Ceanothus impressus*	2.5m	1.8m	blue	May	needs staking
Japanese quince	*Chaenomeles*	1.8m	3m	red	March	enjoys shelter
Sunrose	*Cistus* (various)	1.2m	1.2m	pink	May	enjoys sunshine
Early broom	*Cytisus praecox*	1.5m	1.5m	yellow	April	enjoys sunshine
Broom	*Cytisus scoparius*	2.5m	2.5m	red	May	enjoys sunshine
Heather	*Erica carnea*	.3m	1m	pink	Spring	lime tolerant
Escallonia	*Escallonia* (various)	1.8m	1.8m	pink	June	good seaside plant
Forsythia	*Forsythia* (various)	2.5m	2.5m	yellow	March	dull in summer
Genista	*Genista lydia*	.6m	1.2m	yellow	May	enjoys sunshine
Rock rose	*Helianthemum*	.2m	.6m	yellow	June	enjoys sunshine
Winter jasmine	*Jasminum nudiflorum*	1.8m	3m	yellow	February	train onto a wall
Beauty bush	*Kolkwitzia*	2.5m	2.5m	pink	May	plant in full sun
Mock orange	*Philadelphus*	3m	3m	white	June	tolerates some shade
Rhododendron	*Rhododendron*	1.5m	1.2m	pink	May	acid soil only
Bridal wreath	*Spirea arguta*	1.8m	1.8m	white	May	plant in sun
Lilac	*Syringa* (various)	3m	2.5m	lilac	May	may produce suckers
Viburnum	*Viburnum bodnantense*	2.5m	1.8m	pink	February	flowers early
Weigela	*Weigela variegata*	1.5m	1.5m	pink	May	plant in full sun

List of Twenty Summer/Autumn Flowering Shrubs

Name	Latin Name	Height	Spread	Colour	Flowers	Remarks
Abelia	*Abelia grandiflora*	1.8m	1.5m	pink	July-Oct.	a bit unusual
Butterfly bush	*Buddleia davidii*	3m	3m	purple	July-Oct.	enjoys sunshine
Heather	*Calluna vulgaris*	.3m	.6m	purple	July-Oct.	acid soil only
Californian lilac	*Ceanothus* 'Autumnal Blue'	2.5m	2.5m	blue	July-Oct.	needs staking
Fuchsia	*Fuchsia magellanica*	2.5m	2.5m	red	July-Oct.	tolerates some shade
Veronica	*Hebe* (various)	1.2m	1.2m	purple/white	June-Oct.	good seaside plants
Hydrangea	*Hydrangea macrophylla*	1.5m	2.5m	pink/blue	July-Sept.	enjoys light shade
St. John's wort	*Hypericum* 'Hidcote'	1.8m	1.8m	yellow	July-Oct.	enjoys sunshine
Lavander	*Lavandula* 'Hidcote'	.6m	.6m	purple	July-Aug.	enjoys sunshine
Daisybush	*Olearia* (various)	2.4m	2.4m	white	July-Aug.	good seaside plants
Potentilla	*Potentilla fruticosa*	1.2m	1.8m	yellow	June-Oct.	tolerates some shade
Senecio	*Senecio greyii*	1.2m	1.8m	yellow	June-July	good seaside plants
Spanish broom	*Spartium junceum*	3m	2.4m	yellow	July-Oct.	enjoys sunshine
Spirea	*Spirea* 'Anthony Waterer'	1.2m	1.2m	pink	July-Aug.	tolerates some shade
Summer tamarisk	*Tamarix pentandra*	3.5m	2.5m	pink	August	good seaside plant
Ceratostigma	*Ceratostigma*	1m	1m	blue	July-Sept.	needs a warm spot
Teucrium	*Teucrium fruticans*	1.2m	1.2m	blue	June-Sept.	needs a warm spot
Blue spirea	*Carypoteris*	1.2m	1.2m	blue	Aug.-Sept.	needs shelter
Russian sage	*Perovskia*	1.2m	1.5m	blue	Aug.-Sept.	good seaside plant
Pheasant berry	*Leycesteria formosa*	1.8m	1.8m	purple	July-Oct.	good for poor soil

'Remarks' refer mainly to site or soil conditions, or to some peculiarity of the plant.

Weeds

Weed competition can seriously impair the growth of young trees and shrubs by robbing them of moisture and nutrients. Weeds around young trees may be controlled by hoeing carefully, by applying a mulch of compost or grass clippings, or by using chemical weedkillers. Mulching feeds the young tree and conserves moisture, as well as keeping weeds down.

Chemical weed control is very successful but must be used properly. Contact weedkillers, such as Weedol or Basta, will deal with grass and soft weeds. Tough perennial weeds should be spot-treated, with Tumbleweed, Nettlex Brushwood Killer or Casoron G granules, in spring. Simazine, applied to weed-free ground in spring and/or autumn, gives good weed control but must not be used in the first year after planting. Certain trees and shrubs, such as Flowering cherry and Rhododendron, may be damaged by Simazine, so be careful — read the label for details. *(See the Section on Weeds. Page 110).*

Spanish broom
Spartium junceum
tends to get leggy, prune in March.

Training

Training means tying-in and/or judicious pruning to make a plant take a shape or fill a position. It applies mainly to climbing plants and wall shrubs such as Pyracantha, Cotoneaster and Winter jasmine.

Where possible, tie in young shoots to the required position. Use wires about 10 inches (25cm) apart. These should be fixed to masonry nails driven into the wall. Wooden trellis makes an attractive support for climbing shrubs. Nail the trellis to wooden battens fixed to the wall. If necessary, this allows the trellis to be easily taken down. Use soft string to tie in plants. It breaks down and rots eventually and there is no danger of constricting the branches. Tie in the new shoots as they grow. If young shoots cannot be tied in to a suitable position, or if there are too many suitable shoots, prune out the excess at source, during the summer.

Outdoor yucca
Yucca filamentosa
hardy but likes a sunny position.

Pruning

This is a science in itself but there are a few general guidelines. The only essential pruning is the removal of dead, damaged or diseased branches. Trees and shrubs will get on fine without further pruning: however the shape of a tree, or the flowering display of a shrub, may be enhanced by pruning. Get to know the plant's shape and flowering habit before attempting pruning. Note also the difference between **pruning** and **cutting-back.** *(See this Section. Page 13).*

● **Young deciduous trees.** These may or may not need pruning. Small garden trees are generally left alone to develop. The larger trees, such as Oak, Beech, Chestnut should be inspected to ensure that two lead shoots are not developing. This 'forking' leads to weakness in later life. Apart from removing such rivals, no other pruning is necessary. Some of the lower branches may be removed if they are in the way of lawn mowing or people walking beneath.

● **Mature deciduous trees.** These may need considerable pruning for safety reasons if large, heavy limbs pose a hazard. This dangerous and highly skilled work is best left to a qualified, fully insured tree surgeon.

If a smaller branch has to be removed, to let in light, for example, it should first be cut half way through on the underside, about 18 inches (45cm) from the trunk. This cut prevents the branch tearing away the bark of the trunk. Next, cut through from the top. Finally, cut off the 'snag', leaving the all-important branch collar undamaged.

● **Conifers.** These are best left unpruned. Conifers are grown as much for their shape as for their foliage. Any pruning beyond light foliage trimming will spoil their shape. If they get too big for their position, take them out completely. 'Topped' conifers are an eyesore! *(See also Hedges and Screens below).*

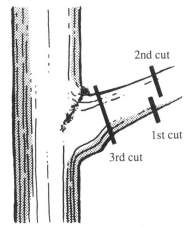

2nd cut

1st cut

3rd cut

Removing a large branch the correct way. Paint the wound immediately afterwards.

List of Twenty Trees for Small to Medium Gardens

Name	Latin Name	Foliage	Height	Spread	Feature	Remarks
June berry	Amelanchier	deciduous	3.5m	3m	flowers/autumn tints	likes moist soil
Maple	Acer (various)	deciduous	1.8m	3m	foliage colour	need shelter
Sea buckthorn	Hippophae	evergreen	4m	3m	grey foliage	good seaside plant
Holly	Ilex aquifolium	evergreen	6m	3m	foliage colour	good seaside plant
Garrya	Garrya elliptica	evergreen	4m	3m	grey catkins	needs shelter
Witchhazel	Hamamelis mollis	deciduous	3m	3m	yellow flowers, Jan.	needs shelter
Magnolia	Magnolia soulangiana	deciduous	4m	3.5m	white flowers, April	needs shelter
Pittosporum	Pittosporum	evergreen	6m	3m	green/grey foliage	good seaside plant
Flowering cherries	Prunus (various)	deciduous	7m	7m	flowers/foliage	enjoy limy soil
Sumach	Rhus typhina	deciduous	3.5m	3.5m	foliage/autumn tints	likes sunshine
Palm	Cordyline australis	evergreen	6m	1.8m	spiky foliage	good seaside plant
Judas tree	Cercis siliquastrum	deciduous	6m	4m	purple flowers, May	needs shelter
False acacia	Robinia 'Frisia'	deciduous	6m	4m	golden foliage	needs shelter
New Zealand holly	Olearia macrodonta	evergreen	6m	4m	grey foliage	good seaside plant
Hawthorn	Crataegus (various)	deciduous	6m	6m	flowers/berries	grows anywhere
Laburnum	Laburnum vossii	deciduous	6m	4m	yellow flowers	poisonous
Flowering crab	Malus (various)	deciduous	6m	4m	flowers/fruits	grows anywhere
Weeping pear	Pyrus salicifolia	deciduous	3.5m	4m	grey foliage	needs staking
Mountain ash	Sorbus (various)	deciduous	6m	3.5m	flowers/berries	grows anywhere
Parrotia	Parrotia persica	deciduous	4m	4m	autumn colour	enjoys sunshine

List of Twenty Conifers for Small to Medium Gardens

Name	Latin Name	Height	Spread	Shape	Colour
Golden yew	Taxus fastigiata aurea	3.5m	1.5m	columnar	golden
Irish juniper	Juniperus 'Compressa'	1m	.3m	columnar	blue-green
Lawson cypress	Chamaecyparis 'Lane'	6m	2.5m	conical	yellow
Lawson cypress	Chamaecyparis 'Columnaris'	3.5m	1.2m	columnar	grey-green
Dwarf cypress	Chamaecyparis 'Boulevard'	2m	2m	conical	blue-green
Dwarf spruce	Picea albertiana 'Conica'	1.2m	1m	conical	light green
Koster's spruce	Picea 'Koster'	6m	3m	conical	grey-blue
Lawson cypress	Chamaecyparis 'Minima Glauca'	1m	1.2m	rounded	blue-green
Dwarf cypress	Chamaecyparis 'Nana Gracilis'	2m	1.2m	bushy	green
Dwarf cypress	Chamaecyparis 'Filifera Aurea'	1.2m	1.5m	rounded	golden
Japanese cedar	Cryptomeria 'Elegans'	3.5m	3m	bushy	bronze (winter)
Mountain pine	Pinus mugo 'Gnome'	1.2m	1.2m	bushy	dark green
Dwarf thuya	Thuya 'Rheingold'	1.5m	1.2m	conical	bronze (winter)
Dwarf thuya	Thuya 'Aurea Nana'	1.2m	1m	egg-shaped	gold-green
Korean fir	Abies koreana	4m	2.5m	conical	green, cones
Dwarf spruce	Picea 'Nidiformis'	.6m	1.2m	spreading	dark green
Canadian juniper	Juniperus 'Depressa Aurea'	.6m	1.8m	spreading	golden
Creeping juniper	Juniperus 'Blue Carpet'	.3m	2.5m	flat	dark green
Column juniper	Juniperus 'Skyrocket'	3m	.3m	columnar	green
Prostrate yew	Taxus 'Repens Aurea'	.6m	3m	spreading	gold-green

'Shape' means the approximate shape of the mature plant.

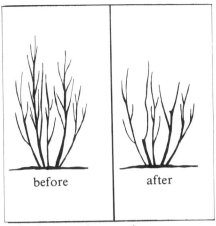

A simple approach to pruning shrubs— completely remove one or two old branches, shorten others.

Laburnum
Laburnum anagyroides
one of the best flowering garden trees.

Flowering cherry
Prunus 'Kanzan'
a large sucker is taking over.

●**Shrubs.** Flowering shrubs generally benefit from a little careful pruning. It helps to maintain a good display of flower and prevents the shrubs getting too big or too dense. The aim is to encourage the replacement of old shoots by new ones which carry more flowers. Remove a few old shoots each year. Take these out completely, from where they arise.

Prune spring and early summer flowering shrubs such as Forsythia, Flowering Currant and Philadelphus immediately after flowering. Shrubs which flower after the end of July should be pruned in March. These include Hydrangea, Hypericum and Fuchsia.

Very many flowering shrubs need no pruning — Rhododendron, Camellia, Pernettya, Winter sweet, Magnolia. Make sure that any pruning carried out is to a purpose. The flowering shrubs which benefit are generally twiggy and bushy with many stems at ground level. Evergreen shrubs are grown for foliage and are not pruned usually. *(See the List of Shrubs That Need No Pruning. Page 106).*

Cutting back

Careful pruning enhances a tree or shrub. Cutting back usually spoils a plant, at least temporarily, but it may become necessary if a plant has outgrown its space. Before cutting back consider removing some shrubs or trees completely from a planting to allow room for the development of the remainder.

The best method of cutting back trees or shrubs is to reduce the number of branches. Completely remove, at source, half of the plant's branches. Careful selection of the branches for removal will allow the plant to retain its shape. This thinning process may achieve enough size reduction. If not, shorten the remaining branches by one-third of their length.

Another method, for shrubs only, is to cut down the plant to ground level. The cut stumps will sprout again and the shrub regenerates itself. This rather drastic treatment may occasionally cause a shrub to die off.

To actually kill off tree stumps and prevent sprouting, paint the cut surfaces with Nettlex Brushwood Killer diluted with diesel or home heating oil, or Root-Out.

Suckers

Some of the most popular garden trees are grafted on to rootstocks. Flowering cherry, Flowering crab-apple, Flowering hawthorn, Mountain ash and Whitebeam are examples. Any of these may produce suckers at ground level or at the top of the trunk — wherever the graft union is located. Suckers usually have smaller leaves, are more vigorous and have white flowers. They should be removed as soon as they are noticed, or they will take over.

A few other plants, although not grafted, produce suckers, for example Stagshorn Sumach, Poplar, Kerria, Snowberry. These suckers arise from the roots of the tree or shrub and are the same plant. If they arise from trees such as Stagshorn Sumach or Poplar, they should be removed. If they arise from shrubs which spread outwards by suckering, such as Kerria or Snowberry, they may be left if they are not a nuisance.

Hedges and Screens

A hedge, or screen, is just a line of trees or shrubs planted close together and trimmed to shape. Apart from providing shelter, privacy and boundaries, hedges may be used as a backdrop for the shapes and colour of ornamental plants. A disadvantage is their tendency to draw moisture and nutrients from the surrounding soil. They cast shade too, and provide a haven for slugs and snails.

●**Planting.** Follow the same procedure as for planting trees and shrubs. Planting into a trench the full length of the hedge, instead of into individual holes, is a good way to achieve uniform soil conditions. Use small plants — they are cheaper and generally establish better.

●**Spacing.** Trees which achieve large size need not be planted as closely as small shrubs. Hedges planted at close spacing thicken up more quickly, but cost a bit more. Competition between the plants at closer spacing means they are more easily kept to the desired size. Most common hedges, including evergreens, are best planted 2 feet (60cm) apart. Smaller types, such as Berberis, should be planted at 18 inches (45cm) apart.

●**Formal training.** For a formal hedge, training begins at planting, when the top 6 inches (15cm) of all leading shoots are removed. This makes the plants bush out low down. Continue this tipping-back process during the first two seasons. Don't forget strong side-shoots. Start clipping the sides first, to prevent the hedge becoming too wide. Clip the hedge to a wedge shape to let light get at the lower part. Otherwise the foliage dies and the bottom of the hedge goes bare.

●**Informal training.** For an informal hedge, such as Forsythia or Escallonia, and for tall screens, simply let the plants develop naturally for a couple of years. Then trim the sides with a secateurs, shortening all strong side-shoots. Flowering hedges should get this treatment after flowering. Avoid using hedge-clippers on informal hedges or screens because it eventually makes them formal.

●**Clipping.** Regular clipping follows on the initial training period. Begin regular clipping before a hedge has reached its desired final size. Never let a hedge get beyond its ideal height and then, too late, try to bring it under control, particularly with the Cypresses. Stop the plants one foot (30cm) short of the ideal height and let them reach it over five or six years, thickening up in the process.

The amount of clipping depends on the vigour of the hedge. Privet and Lonicera need four or five clips each year. Griselinia needs two, in May and August. Most others need only one. July is a good month — most of the season's growth being over, but the shoots not yet woody and hard.

●**Overgrown hedges.** Badly overgrown hedges can be cut back to within a few inches of the ground, and they will sprout again. Hedges which have become too broad can have one side cut off. The second side may be cut off, two years later, if desired. April is the month for these operations.

●**Conifer hedges** cannot be cut back in this way, as they do not regenerate. Never cut them back beyond the green part of the shoots or they will stay bare.

Shelter Belts

Shelter belts perform the same functions as hedges or screens, but on a larger scale. Very many large gardens, rural houses and farmyards would benefit from more shelter planting.

●**Planting.** The best shelter belts are porous. They allow the wind through, but reduce its speed. Dense conifers on their own do not make ideal shelter. They are better mixed with deciduous trees. Mixed shelter belts are better to look at, too, especially in winter when coniferous shelter can be depressingly dull. Plant shelter belts across the direction of the wind which is to be slowed down. Where possible, plant two or more lines in a shelter belt, mixing at random a number of types such as Poplar, Alder, Pine, Spruce, Cypress, Beech, Larch and Birch.

●**Spacing.** In single rows, plant shelter trees about 5 feet (150cm) apart. Space double rows about 4 feet (120cm) apart and plant the trees about 6 feet (180cm) apart in the rows. For multiple rows, space the rows about 5 feet (150cm) apart and the trees 8 to 10 feet (240-300cm) apart in the rows. Stagger the trees in each row.

●**After planting care.** Fence off shelter belts. Keep grass and weeds down for a few seasons with Gramoxone or Roundup. Give a little general fertiliser in the early years. If shelter becomes bare at the base, try underplanting with Laurel.

Peat Beds

Where the soil is limy, a peat bed is necessary to grow Rhododendron, Camellia, Azalea, Pernettya and other lime-haters. It may be any size, even small enough for just one plant.

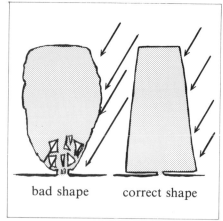

bad shape   correct shape

The correct shape for a hedge is achieved by training from the early stages. Note how the light gets in at the base.

A handsome example of a well-grown hawthorn hedge, straight, dense and correctly clipped.

The effect of salty gales on an Ash tree, shelter is vital in exposed places.

The natural beauty of big trees allowed to develop where there is space, there should be more of this.

List of Twenty Trees for Large Garden or Country Planting

Name	Latin Name	Foliage	Soil	Exposure
Alder	*Alnus glutinosa*	deciduous	any soil	tolerates wind
Chestnut	*Aesculus*	deciduous	any fertile soil	dislikes wind
Birch	*Betula pendula*	deciduous	any soil	tolerates wind
Beech	*Fagus sylvatica*	deciduous	good soil	dislikes wind
Sweet chestnut	*Castanea sativa*	deciduous	good soil	needs good conditions
Eucalyptus	*Eucalyptus gunnii*	evergreen	good, moist soil	dislikes wind
Ash	*Fraxinus excelsior*	deciduous	any soil	tolerates sea wind
Oak	*Quercus robur*	deciduous	good soil	tolerates wind
Poplar	*Populus nigra*	deciduous	good in wet soil	tolerates wind
Willow	*Salix alba*	deciduous	good in wet soil	tolerates wind
Lime	*Tilia platyphyllos*	deciduous	good, moist soil	tolerates wind
Japanese larch	*Larix kaempferi*	deciduous	well-drained soil	withstands wind
Sitka spruce	*Picea sitchensis*	evergreen	damp soil	withstands wind
Scot's pine	*Pinus sylvestris*	evergreen	well-drained soil	withstands wind
Lodgepole pine	*Pinus contorta*	evergreen	any soil	withstands sea wind
Whitebeam	*Sorbus aria*	deciduous	any soil	withstands sea wind
Sycamore	*Acer pseudoplatanus*	deciduous	any soil	withstands sea wind
Norway maple	*Acer platanoides*	deciduous	good soil	dislikes wind
Blue Atlas cedar	*Cedrus atlantica*	evergreen	good soil	dislikes wind
Walnut	*Juglans regia*	deciduous	good soil	needs good conditions

●**Sunken peat bed.** The usual way to set about making a peat bed is to remove 10 inches (25cm) of soil. Line the hole with polythene, punctured in three or four places for drainage. Fill with a mixture of 2 parts acid soil and one part peat, or a lime-free compost such as Shamrock Brown Gold. Be careful to select a site in the garden where limy water will not drain into the bed and destroy it.

●**Raised peat bed.** This is a more simple approach and likely to be more successful. The acid soil/peat mixture, or lime-free compost, is simply heaped on to the existing soil surface, to a depth of 10 inches (25cm). The sides are retained by stones, turf sods or timber. The peat bed actually acidifies the soil beneath over time. A raised bed is ideal for a grouping of lime-haters, but would look bad for a single plant. Peat beds need ample watering in drought periods and occasional topping up with peat or well-rotted, organic material.

Pests

Rabbits and hares cause very serious damage in rural areas. Fencing is the complete answer. Wrapping the stems of young trees with heavy polythene is effective too.

Greenfly feed off many trees and shrubs, especially Honeysuckle, Viburnum, Privet, Beech, Lime, Flowering cherry. Control is usually not necessary.

Caterpillars of many kinds eat the leaves of trees and shrubs, usually leaving holes. Damage is slight and control not necessary.

Leaf miners attack many trees, notably Holly, leaving twisting tracks and blisters on the leaves. Though unsightly, control is not necessary.

Red spider mite attacks many trees and shrubs. Control is not necessary, except on Dwarf spruces, which could lose all their leaves. Spray in April or May. *(See the Section on Pests for more on control measures. Page 112).*

Diseases

Honey fungus, or **bootlace fungus** *(Armillaria)* is a widespread and serious root disease. Privet, Griselinia, Cypress, Lilac, Birch, Willow and Pine are very susceptible. The fungus grows in the roots just below the bark, producing white fluffy growth, black bootlace-like strings and yellow mushrooms.

Butt rot is a similar root disease of conifers, common near old shelter belts and forest plantations. There is no control. Remove stumps.

Phytophthora root rot has become a common disease since the advent of container-grown plants. Lawson's cypress, Rhododendron, Heather, Flowering cherry, Yew, Beech and Lime are susceptible. The affected plants wilt and die slowly over a period of time, especially in summer. Avoid nurseries where there are dead and dying Lawson's cypress.

Heart rots. These are diseases of the heart wood of large trees. Fungi enter the trunks through broken branches, and rot the heartwood. Brackets appear on the tree and release spores. Oak, Beech, Chestnut, Ash, Walnut and Birch are often attacked and seriously weakened.

Silverleaf is a disease mainly of Flowering cherry. The leaves on one or two branches go silvery and the tree eventually dies.

Bacterial canker is another serious disease of the Plum and Cherry family, including Laurel. Gum usually exudes from a main branch, and little holes (Shot-hole) may appear in the leaves. The tree usually dies.

Die-back is a general name for the damage caused by a variety of fungi on small twigs and branches of many different trees and shrubs. Cut out dead shoots.

Dutch Elm disease is a very specific disease of Elm which starts by killing a few small branches, and eventually the tree itself. Almost all Ireland's Elms are dead.

Leafspot and **Powdery mildew** diseases, caused by a variety of fungi, attack a wide range of trees and shrubs. Usually harmless, if a plant is weakened, give it some fertiliser to speed recovery. *(See the Section on Diseases. Page 117).*

Fireblight affects apples, pears, Cotoneaster, Pyracantha, Hawthorn, Mountain-ash and Japanese quince. It first kills a few branches; these retaining their leaves as though scorched by fire. If suspected, notify the Dept. of Agriculture.

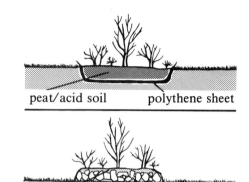

peat/acid soil   polythene sheet

peat/acid soil   stones

Two ways of setting up a peat bed, the raised type is less work and more effective.

Deciduous azaleas
Rhododendron (hybrids)
brilliant colour, sometimes scented.

Mountain ash
Sorbus aucuparia
white flowers, red berries.

List of Twenty Shrubs grown for Colourful Fruit, Leaves or Bark

Name	Latin Name	Height	Spread	Feature	Remarks
Bamboo	*Arundinaria*	2.5m	1.2m	grassy foliage	likes moist soil
Berberis	*Berberis atropurpurea*	1.8m	1.8m	purple foliage	tolerates poor soil
Dogwood	*Cornus* (various)	1.8m	2.5m	coloured bark	tolerates shade
Purple hazel	*Corylus purpurea*	3m	3m	purple foliage	tolerates shade
Smokebush	*Cotinus 'Royal Purple'*	2.5m	2.5m	purple foliage	enjoys sunshine
Eleagnus	*Eleagnus maculata*	3m	3m	variegated leaves	tolerates poor soil
Cotoneaster	*Cotoneaster* (various)	1.8m	1.8m	red berries	tolerates poor soil
Chinese spindle	*Euonymus elatus*	2.5m	1.8m	red autumn leaves	any soil
Japanese spindle	*Euonymus radicans*	1m	2m	variegated leaves	tolerates shade
Castor oil plant	*Fatsia*	3m	3m	big, green leaves	tolerates shade
Hypericum	*Hypericum 'Elstead'*	1.2m	1.8m	red fruits	likes dry soil
Pernettya	*Pernettya*	1m	1m	pink/white fruits	acid soil only
Forest flame	*Pieris* (various)	2.5m	1.8m	young red foliage	acid soil only
Firethorn	*Pyracantha* (various)	2.5m	2.5m	red berries	enjoys sunshine
Willow	*Salix lanata*	1.2m	1.2m	grey foliage	likes moist soil
Golden elder	*Sambucus aurea*	2.5m	2.5m	golden foliage	any soil
Skimmia	*Skimmia 'Foremanii'*	1.2m	1.8m	red berries	tolerates shade
Snowberry	*Symphoricarpus*	1.5m	1.5m	white berries	tolerates shade
New Zealand flax	*Phormium tenax*	1.5m	1.5m	spiky effect	good seaside plant
Santolina	*Santolina*	.6m	1.2m	grey/white foliage	good seaside plant

'Feature' means the principal feature for which the plant is grown.
'Remarks' mainly refer to site or soil conditions.

List of Twenty Shrubs and Trees for Special Uses

Name	Latin Name	Soil	Site	Remarks
Climbers				
Clematis	*Clematis* (various)	moist, limy	top in sun	needs support
Climbing hydrangea	*Hydrangea petiolaris*	any soil	any wall	self-supporting
Honeysuckle	*Lonicera* (various)	moist, humus	top in sun	needs support
Virginia creeper	*Parthenocissus*	any soil	any wall	self-supporting
Russian vine	*Polygonum*	poor soil	needs space	needs support
Wisteria	*Wisteria chinensis*	moist, rich	face south	needs support
Ivy	*Hedera* (various)	any soil	any wall	self-supporting
Hedges/Screens				
Beech	*Fagus*	good soil	open sunshine	good rural hedge
Yew	*Taxus baccata*	any dry soil	sun or shade	best conifer hedge
Griselinia	*Griselinia*	any soil	sun	good seaside hedge
Spotted laurel	*Aucuba*	any soil	sun or shade	good shade hedge
Olearia	*Olearia traversii*	any soil	sunshine	tough seaside screen
Lauristinus	*Viburnum tinus*	any soil	sun or shade	good shade hedge
Hawthorn	*Crataegus*	any soil	sun or shade	good rural hedge
Purple Plum	*Prunus cerasifera*	good soil	open sunshine	an unusual hedge
Holly	*Ilex aquifolium*	any soil	sun or shade	good seaside hedge
Ground Cover				
Ivy	*Hedera* (various)	any soil	sun or shade	slow-growing
Periwinkle	*Vinca minor*	any soil	sun or shade	medium
St. John's wort	*Hypericum calycinum*	dry soil	sun or shade	invasive
Rubus	*Rubus tricolor*	any soil	sun or shade	vigorous

Annual mallow
Lavatera trimestris 'Silver Cup'
growing through New Zealand flax.

Tuberous begonia
Begonia multiflora
good summer bedding, over-winter
inside.

Bearded iris
Iris 'Gay Head'
provides early summer colour.

Border phlox
Phlox paniculata
invaluable late summer flower.

Day lily
Hemerocallis (hybrids)
easy to grow, flower all summer.

Oriental poppy
Papaver orientale 'Goliath'
eye-catching colour in early summer.

Aubrietia
Aubrieta deltoidea
a mainstay in springtime.

Star of the veldt
Osteospermum ecklonis
loves a dry, sunny spot

Crane's bill
Geranium psilostemon
very striking colour in early summer.

Flowers

Types

Flower plants which germinate, grow and flower in one growing season are called **annuals.** Some of these tolerate frost and they may be sown outdoors — these are **hardy annuals.** Annuals which cannot tolerate frost must be sown indoors and planted out when the danger of frost has passed — these are **half-hardy annuals.**

Flower plants which grow leaves and stems one season, and flower the next, are called **biennials.** Plants which flower each year, and then die down over winter are called **perennial flowers.** The taller types — from one to eight feet (30cm-240cm) — are used as border perennials. Those which grow to less than about 12 inches (30cm) are used as rockery perennials. Bulbs are a special category of perennial flowers, and deserve special mention. *(See the Lists of the various flowers in this Section).*

Summer bedding — half-hardy annuals

● **Uses.** The most general use of summer bedding plants is in flower beds, to give a mass display in July, August and September. They are also extensively used as container plants : in tubs, planters, window boxes and hanging baskets. Very effective use may be made of these colourful plants for filling gaps between shrubs, or between border perennials. This is particularly useful in the early years of a garden when a lot of bare ground must be covered quickly and cheaply. Quite a few summer bedding plants make excellent flowering pot plants for the greenhouse, or the home itself. *(See the Section on Greenhouse Growing. Page 53).*

● **Plant raising.** Most of the plants used for summer bedding are half-hardy annuals, but a few are perennials. The half-hardy annuals are raised by sowing seed in pots, or in trays of good seed compost in the second week of March. A few slow developers, such as Geraniums, Busy Lizzies and Snapdragons should be sown about one month earlier. These three are, in fact, perennials, but are treated as annuals.

Use clean trays and purchased seed compost to avoid damping-off disease of the seedlings. Sow the seed as directed on the seed packet. Cover with a sheet of glass and brown paper. Place the tray in a warm place — a warm greenhouse, a heated room, or a special propagator. Do not place seed trays on top of the television, as this is dangerous. Do not place seed trays in the hot-press — it is too hot. Watch the trays and remove the paper when the seedlings emerge. Remove the glass a few days later. At this stage, the temperature may be lower and they will be fine in a frost-protected greenhouse or on a window-sill indoors.

Prick out the seedlings, at 2 inches by 2 inches, in trays or boxes of fresh compost, about two weeks after emergence. *(See also Seed sowing in the Section on Garden Skills. Page 71).* Harden off the young plants about ten days before planting out, by placing them outside by day and taking them in at night. This procedure applies to the perennials used as summer bedding too, such as Dahlias, Begonias and Geraniums, which may exist as tubers or plants stored from the previous year, or newly purchased. Start these into growth in March, in trays or pots of moist compost. Alternatively, plant them out, unsprouted, in late April.

● **Planting.** Remove spring bedding plants about the third week of May. Dig the ground, working in about 2 ounces per square yard ($70g/m^2$) of general fertiliser, Vegyflor or Growmore. If the soil is dry, give it a heavy soaking and let it settle for a day. Summer bedding needs good, fertile soil to develop quickly, and

Nemesia
Nemesia 'Sutton's Mixed'
easy to grow, quick to flower.

Lobelia
Lobelia 'Cascade Mixed'
excellent in hanging baskets, as here.

Verbena
Verbena 'Showtime'
good as bedding or in containers.

List of Twenty Summer Bedding Plants — Half-hardy Annuals

Name	Latin Name	Height	Flowers	Colour	Soil	Position
Petunia	Petunia	30cm	July-Oct.	various	any	sunny
Phlox	Phlox	30cm	July-Sept.	various	any	sunny
Dahlia	Dahlia	45cm	July-Nov.	various	good	sunny
Nemesia	Nemesia	30cm	June-Sept.	various	any	sun/shade
Tobacco flower	Nicotiana	60cm	June-Sept.	various	any	sun/shade
Spider flower	Cleome	75cm	July-Oct.	pink	good	sunny
Musk	Mimulus	20cm	June-Sept.	yellow/red	moist	light shade
Livingstone daisy	Mesembryanthemum	10cm	June-Sept.	orange/red	light	sunny
Lobelia	Lobelia	15cm	June-Sept.	blue	good	sun/shade
Ageratum	Ageratum	15cm	June-Sept.	blue	good	sunny
Alyssum	Alyssum	15cm	June-Sept.	white	any	sunny
Snapdragon	Antirrhinum	40cm	July-Sept.	various	any	sunny
Busy lizzie	Impatiens	20cm	June-Oct.	pink/white	good	sun/shade
Annual aster	Callistephus	45cm	Aug.-Oct.	various	limy	sunny
Cosmos	Cosmea	75cm	July-Oct.	pink/red	light	sunny
Begonia	Beg. semperflorens	30cm	June-Oct.	pink/red	good	sun/shade
Annual carnation	Dianthus	45cm	July-Oct.	pink/red	any	sunny
Marigold	Tagetes	25cm	June-Oct.	yellow/orange	any	sunny
Verbena	Verbena	30cm	July-Sept.	red/lilac	good	sunny
Zinnia	Zinnia	45cm	July-Oct.	various	good	sunny

'sun/shade' means the plant will grow in sun or partial shade.
'any soil' means any, ordinary, well-drained garden soil.
'good soil' means ordinary soil enriched with organic material.

List of Twenty Hardy Annuals — Summer Colour

Name	Latin Name	Height	Flowers	Colour	Soil	Position
Godetia	Godetia	40cm	June-Sept.	pink/red	any	sunny
Pot marigold	Calendula	45cm	June-Sept.	orange	poor	sunny
Baby's breath	Gypsophila	40cm	June-Sept.	white	limy	sunny
Virginia stock	Malcolmia	20cm	July-Aug.	lilac/white	any	sunny
Candytuft	Iberis	30cm	June-Aug.	pink/lilac	any	sunny
Baby blue eyes	Nemophila	15cm	June-Aug.	blue	good	sunny
Californian poppy	Eschscholzia	40cm	June-Aug.	orange/red	poor	sunny
Love-in-a-mist	Nigella	40cm	July-Sept.	blue	any	sun/shade
Flax	Linum	40cm	June-Aug.	various	any	sunny
Bee flower	Limnanthes	15cm	June-Aug.	yellow	any	sunny
Strawflower	Helichrysum	45cm	July-Sept.	red/yellow	any	sunny
Clarkia	Clarkia	45cm	July-Sept.	red/pink	any	sunny
Tickseed	Coreopsis	40cm	July-Sept.	yellow/brown	any	sunny
Viscaria	Viscaria	25cm	June-Aug.	lilack/pink	any	sun/shade
Larkspur	Delphinium	75cm	June-Aug.	various	any	sun/shade
Annual mallow	Lavatera	75cm	July-Sept.	pink/white	any	sun/shade
Sunflower	Helianthus	200cm	July-Sept.	yellow	any	sunny
Nasturtium	Tropaeolum	30cm	June-Oct.	yellow/red	poor	sun/shade
Cornflower	Centaurea	45cm	July-Sept.	blue/pink	any	sun/shade
Sweet pea	Lathyrus	150cm	June-Sept.	various	any	sunny

'Sun/shade' means the plant will grow in sun or shade.
Note. Most of these plants flower for 6 to 8 weeks during the months indicated depending on sowing date.

flower well. All types enjoy sunshine, and some must have it to get good results. *(See the List of Twenty Summer Bedding Plants. Page 20).* Using a line to keep the rows straight, plant the summer bedding plants at a spacing of about one foot (30cm) each way — a bit more for large types, less for edging and small types. If planting time is not dictated by the removal of Wallflowers or such like, summer bedding may be planted in early to mid-May in the south and coastal areas, mid to late May in the midlands and north. Do not be in any rush to plant out, because bedding plants may get a severe shock from cold weather, and be disappointing later on. Water the plants immediately after planting, to settle them in.

●**Aftercare.** If the weather is dry, water the plants to ensure continued growth. Watch carefully for slugs and snails, and use slug-killer if necessary. Hoe lightly between the rows as soon as weed seedlings appear. Do not let weeds get beyond the two-leaf stage.

Summer bedding plants are discarded after flowering finishes in October, except for the few perennial types which are retained. Dahlias and Tuberous begonias are lifted and allowed to dry off in boxes. Store them in a dry shed. Geraniums may be discarded, if cuttings were taken in August. Otherwise, lift and pot up the plants, or simply shake off all the soil and hang the plants in bundles in a cool shed or garage.

●**Containers.** Plant up containers in early May, if a greenhouse is available. Grow them on, and harden them off in the container. In this way the plants will already be well established when the containers are put outside. Otherwise, plant containers in mid to late May and place them on the ground, close to a sunny wall, until established. Use trailing types for containers, along with some Fuchsias, Miniature roses, Cordylines or small Conifers, to give bulk.

Ordinary soil is not good enough for containers. Use half soil, half peat, and add a small fistful of general fertiliser to each bucketful. Keep containers, especially hanging baskets, well watered. To this purpose, line hanging baskets with polythene.

Summer colour — hardy annuals

●**Uses.** Being informal plants, hardy annuals are not suitable for use in formal flower beds. Their tendency to have a single burst of flower rules them out for containers too. Traditionally, they were used in a hardy annual border where a whole range of them would give an extended display. Their main use, nowadays, is as colourful fillers-in, ideal for odd corners and gaps between other plants. They give a 'cottage-garden' look to a bed or border—a jumble of types of different heights and colours flowering over a period in mid-summer.

●**Plant raising.** Hardy annuals are raised from seed sown directly where the plants are to flower. They may be sown in March, April or May. March sowings may be affected by cold, wet weather. May sowings may be affected by dry conditions and, anyway, they tend to flower late. Early April is usually a good time. Seed of some types may be sown in September, too. These over-winter as young plants and flower earlier the following summer than the spring sowings do.

Dig the ground, working in general fertiliser at 2 ounces per square yard (70g/m²). Break up all lumps and rake the surface fine. Some peat might be worked in too if the soil is poor. *(See Seed sowing in the Section on Garden Skills. Page 71).* Make little drills with a stick about 6 inches (15cm) apart and ½ inch (1cm) deep. Sow the seed thinly and cover with soil. If the area being sown is larger than about 10 square feet (1m²) divide the space into areas of about this size and sow a few different types. Seed may be sown scattered about too, but sowing in lines makes it easier to distinguish flower seedlings from weeds. Hardy annuals grow best in good, fertile, but not over-rich soil. Some, such as California poppy and Pot marigold, can tolerate poor, dry soil.

●**Aftercare.** When the rows of seedlings can be distinguished, lightly run the hoe between them to kill weed seedlings. Weeds should never be allowed to get

Busy lizzie
Impatiens 'Zig-Zag'
grows in light shade, as here.

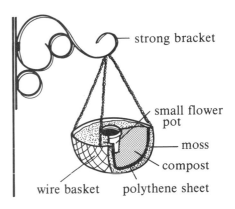

strong bracket

small flower pot

moss

compost

wire basket   polythene sheet

Good preparation of a hanging basket gives best results and makes it easier to look after.

Candytuft
Iberis umbellata
one of the best hardy annuals.

List of Twenty Rockery Perennials

Name	Latin Name	Height	Flowers	Colour	Soil	Position
New Zealand burr	Acaena	8cm	July-Aug.	brown	any	sun or shade
Aethionema	Aethionema	20cm	April-May	pink	any	sunny
Gold dust	Alyssum saxatile	20cm	April-June	yellow	any	sunny
Arabis	Arabis	20cm	March-April	white/pink	any	sunny
Thrift	Armeria	25cm	May-July	pink	any	sunny
Aubrietia	Aubrieta	10cm	March-June	pink/blue	any	sunny
Bellflower	Campanula	20cm	June-Aug.	blue	any	sun or shade
Pink	Dianthus	20cm	May-July	pink/white	dry	sunny
Erinus	Erinus	10cm	April-June	pink	dry	sunny
Candytuft	Iberis	20cm	May-June	white	any	sunny
Creeping jenny	Lysimachia	8cm	June-July	yellow	moist	sun or shade
Oxalis	O. adenophylla	8cm	May-July	pink	dry	sunny
Dwarf phlox	Phlox subulata	8cm	April-May	pink	any	sunny
Draba	Draba	8cm	April	yellow	dry	sunny
Raoulia	Raoulia	3cm	June-July	yellow	dry	sunny
Saxifrage	Saxifraga	20cm	Feb.-June	pink/yellow	dry	sunny
Stonecrop	Sedum	8cm	June-July	yellow/pink	dry	sunny
Houseleek	Sempervivum	8cm	July	pink	dry	sunny
Pigroot	Sisyrynchium	15cm	June-Sept.	yellow/blue	any	sunny
Thyme	Thymus serpyllum	8cm	June-July	pink	dry	sunny

Note: Most of these rockery plants spread to between 30 and 100cm.

List of Twenty Perennial Flowers for Mixed Borders

Name	Latin Name	Height	Flowers	Colour	Soil	Position
Lady's mantle	Alchemilla	45cm	June-Aug.	lime green	any	sun or shade
Evening primrose	Oenothera	45cm	July-Sept.	bright yellow	dry	sunny
Japanese anemone	Anemone hybrida	50cm	Aug.-Oct.	pink/white	any	sun or shade
Michaelmas daisy	Aster amellus	60cm	Aug.-Sept.	pink/blue	not dry	sunny
Columbine	Aquilegia	75cm	May-June	pink/blue	any	sun or shade
Astilbe	Astilbe	60cm	June-Aug.	pink/red	moist	sun or shade
Elephant ears	Bergenia	40cm	March-May	pink	any	sun or shade
Pampas grass	Cortaderia	180cm	Aug.-Sept.	silver	any	sunny
Bleeding heart	Dicentra	45cm	May-June	red	any	some shade
Day lily	Hemerocallis	90cm	June-Aug.	yellow/orange	any	sun or shade
Coral flower	Heuchera	40cm	June-Aug.	pink/red	any	sun or shade
Plaintain lily	Hosta	45cm	July-Aug.	lilac/white	any	some shade
Red hot poker	Kniphofia	100cm	July-Sept.	red/yellow	any	sunny
Yellow loosestrife	Lysimachia	90cm	July-Aug.	yellow	moist	sun or shade
Phlox	Phlox	90cm	July-Oct.	pink/purple	moist	sun or shade
Polygonum	Polygonum	60cm	July-Sept.	pink	moist	sun or shade
Primula	Primula	60cm	April-July	pink/yellow	moist	sun or shade
Lungwort	Pulmonaria	30cm	April-May	pink/blue	moist	sun or shade
Stonecrop	Sedum spectabile	45cm	Aug.-Oct.	pink	any	sunny
Thalictrum	Thalictrum	90cm	May-June	pink/white	any	sun or shade

Brompton stock
Matthiola incana
late-flowering spring bedding.

Wallflower
Cheiranthus cheiri 'Persian Carpet'
the mainstay of spring bedding.

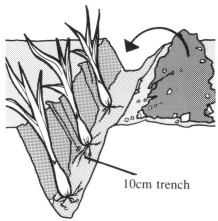

10cm trench

Lining out Tulips after lifting gives
them a chance to die back gradually.

established. Watch for slugs and snails, too. When the seedlings are about one inch (2.5cm) high, a first thinning may be carried out, though, if the seeds were sown thinly enough, this will not be necessary. When the seedlings are 2 inches (5cm) high, they may be thinned to their final spacing. This varies from a couple of inches for small types to 12 inches (30cm) apart for large types. If there are gaps, they may be filled by lifting and transplanting excess seedlings carefully. Some of the taller types may flop about when grown on good soil. Bushy twigs might be used for support. Hardy annuals often self-seed, so a corner might be set aside for this to occur.

Spring bedding — biennials

●**Uses.** Spring bedding plants may be used in the same ways as summer bedding, namely, in flower beds, in containers, as 'spots' of colour between shrubs and border perennials, and even as pot plants, for example, Polyanthus and Double daisy. Spring bedding used in hanging baskets is prone to damage by the more severe winter weather. The baskets should be hung in a sheltered position, or left on the ground in a bright spot until spring.

●**Plant raising.** Although most spring bedding plants are actually perennials, they are treated as biennials. The seed is sown in late May or early June, outdoors, in a good seedbed. *(See Seed sowing in the Section on Garden Skills. Page 71).* Water the seed-bed, if necessary, in dry weather. When the seedlings are about 2 inches (5cm) high, lift them, and carefully transplant them to a nursery bed, at a spacing of 8 inches (20cm) each way. Water them if they show any signs of wilting. Protect Wallflowers and Stocks from cabbage root fly. *(See the Section on Pests. Page 113).*

●**Planting.** In October or November, when summer bedding is removed, dig the ground, incorporating some organic material. Rake in some general fertiliser, at 2 ounces per square yard (70g/m²). Plant spring bedding at a spacing of about 12 - 15 inches (30 - 37.5cm) apart. Tulips and Daffodils are planted when the other plants are in place. They are planted from 6 to 12 inches (15 - 30cm) apart and about 3 inches (7.5cm) deep. Ground for spring bedding must not get waterlogged — the organic material will help drainage.

●**Aftercare.** Remove any weeds which appear. Firm the plants if they are loosened by the wind. After flowering finishes, in late May, spring bedding is usually discarded to make way for summer bedding plants. Polyanthus and Double daisy may be lifted and planted elsewhere until planting time again. Daffodils and Tulips may be lifted and lined out in shallow 4 inch (10cm) deep trenches until the foliage dies off when they are lifted and stored in brown paper bags or boxes until autumn. If only a few Stocks or Pansies were planted intermittently for 'spot' colour, they may be left to give some flower into the summer. Even Wallflowers may be treated as a small shrub, and left in position for a few years — only trim off the seed-heads.

Border perennial flowers

●**Uses.** Border perennial flowers are used in mixed plantings with shrubs, or on their own in herbaceous borders. Traditionally, the non-woody border perennials were restricted to the herbaceous border, which can be stunning, but demands a lot of attention. The mixed border of herbaceous perennials and shrubs has several advantages. Its shrub content demands little attention, and provides interest in winter, when the border perennials have died down. The border perennials provide colour and lush foliage in summer to soften the harsher outline of the woody plants. The shrubs provide valuable shelter, and shade on occasion, for the herbaceous perennials which fill in around, between and underneath them. In large gardens, where there is space, island beds of border perennials and shrubs may be planted. Many border perennials provide good cut flowers.

●**Plant raising.** Border perennials may be raised from seed sown indoors in April, or in seed-beds outdoors in May or June. Time and method of sowing vary with the type. The seed-packets give good instructions. *(See also Seed sowing in the Section on Garden Skills. Page 72)*. Lift and transplant the seedlings into nursery beds at 12 inches (30cm) apart until they are large enough for planting into their permanent positions. Raising plants from seed is the cheapest way to acquire a stock of border perennials. Alternatively, plants may be purchased, or divisions exchanged. Division, by pulling the crowns apart, or by cutting with a spade, is the main method of plant raising. Plants may be divided at any time during the dormant season, but the usual months are October/November and March/April.

●**Planting.** Plant border perennials in good, well-prepared soil, with no perennial weeds. *(See Ground Preparation in the Section on Garden Skills. Page 71)*. Dig the site and work in plenty of well-rotted manure, compost, straw or peat. About 3 ounces of general fertiliser per square yard ($100g/m^2$) should be applied. The site should be sunny for most types, and the soil moist, but well-drained. Some types, however, enjoy damp conditions, some like shade, and a choice may be made for hot, dry, conditions too *(See the List of Twenty Border Perennial Flowers. Page 22)*.

Planting time is October/November or March/April, when the soil is moist but not wet. Place the crowns about one inch (2.5cm) deeper than they were before lifting. Plant in uneven-numbered groups for best informal effect.

●**Aftercare.** Hoe around the plants in spring, to prevent weeds becoming established. Mulches of well-rotted manure or compost, or grass clippings assist greatly in weed control, and conserve moisture too. Dig out, or paint 'Tumbleweed' on to, perennial weeds when they appear.

As the plants grow, some types need to be staked. Place 3 or 4 sticks or canes close to the plant and run twine around and through the clump of shoots for support. Put support in place in time to prevent plants flopping around. Some plants will need watering when young, and in dry summers. Watch for signs of drought, then water heavily. When the flowers fade, the plants begin to die back for winter. By October, most of the nutrients in the flower stalk and foliage will have been re-absorbed by the plant. The tops may be cut away and the area tidied up. Every few years, the more vigorous plants will have to be lifted, divided and re-planted to keep them to a reasonable size. *(See the List of Flowers That Need No Staking. Page 108)*.

Rockery perennials

●**Uses.** Rockery perennial flowers are mainly used in rockeries, but the smaller ones may also be grown in alpine beds, and the trailing types are suitable for planting in a dry stone wall. The larger ones may be used at the very front of borders, or as edging near pathways and paved areas. *(See the Section on Garden Skills for Rockery Construction. Page 78)*.

●**Plant raising.** Many types are raised from seed sown indoors in April or September. However, the range of seed available is not great. Most plants are raised by dividing existing plants in October or March, or by taking cuttings of the spreading types. Cuttings are usually taken between June and September. *(See Seed sowing and Cuttings in the Section on Garden Skills. Page 71)*.

●**Planting.** Being mountain plants, the majority of them like open, sunny conditions. They are smaller than their lowland cousins because they have adapted to the shortage of soil, moisture and nutrients. Provide them with conditions of very free drainage, and adequate, but not very rich, soil. The top few inches of a rockery should be mixed specially — 2 parts soil, 1 part peat and 1 part sand or grit. Plant in October or March/April. Watch for snails.

●**Aftercare.** Keep rockery plants free of weeds — they just cannot compete. A layer of gravel, grit or chippings prevents weeds, and sets off the plants well. Although rockery plants like free drainage, they are used to regular rainfall and will need to be watered in prolonged dry spells. Many rockery perennials self-seed. This may not be desirable, and can be prevented by trimming off the flower heads after flowering. *(See the Section on Labour-Intensive Garden Features. Page 87)*.

Red hot poker
Kniphofia 'Royal Standard'
an old favourite, easy to grow.

Japanese anemone
Anemone hybrida
trouble-free, grows in light shade.

A natural rock garden beautifully planted with rockery perennials and some dwarf conifers.

The beauty of herbaceous perennials in high summer — the double border in the National Botanic Gardens.

List of Twenty Bulbs, Corms and Tubers

Name	Latin Name	Height	Flowers	Colour	Position	Uses
Anemone	*Anemone*	30cm	March-April	red/blue	any	border/rockery
Tuberous begonia	*Begonia*	40cm	July-Sept.	red/orange	shady	border
Montbretia	*Crocosmia*	35cm	July-Sept.	orange	sunny	border
Crocus	*Crocus*	10cm	Feb.-March	various	any	rockery/natur.
Dwarf cyclamen	*Cyclamen*	10cm	Sept. or March	pink	shady	rockery/natur.
Dahlia	*Dahlia*	75cm	Aug.-Oct.	various	sunny	border
Bluebell	*Endymion*	25cm	May-June	blue	shady	naturalise
Winter aconite	*Eranthis*	10cm	Feb.-March	yellow	any	naturalise
Crown imperial	*Fritillaria*	75cm	April	yellow/red	any	border
Snowdrop	*Galanthus*	15cm	Jan.-April	white	shady	naturalise
Gladiolus	*Gladiolus*	75cm	July-Sept.	various	sunny	border
Hyacinth	*Hyacinthus*	25cm	April-May	various	any	border
Iris	*Iris*	60cm	June-July	various	sunny	border
Snowflake	*Leucojum*	20cm	Feb.-March	white	any	naturalise
Lily	*Lilium*	75cm	June-Aug.	various	any	border
Daffodil	*Narcissus*	30cm	Feb.-April	yellow	any	border/natur.
Nerine lily	*Nerine*	50cm	Sept.-Oct.	pink	sunny	border
Scilla	*Scilla*	15cm	March-April	blue	sunny	rockery
Tulip	*Tulipa*	50cm	March-May	various	sunny	border
Flowering onion	*Allium*	60cm	June	pink	sunny	border

Bulbs

● **Uses.** Included here are corms, tubers, rhizomes and true bulbs — all storage organs. Plants in this group find many uses in the garden. Earlier in this Section, bulbs were described for use as spring and summer bedding plants. *(See Page 19)*. They may also be used to bring colour to herbaceous and mixed borders in spring, summer and autumn. Certain bulbs may be used in semi-wild conditions — 'naturalised' under trees or shrubs, in grass or ground cover.

● **Plant raising.** Bulbs are usually raised as offsets from the mother bullb, and will, in time, grow to flowering size. Some types may be grown from seed too.

● **Planting.** Bulbs like well drained, fairly rich soil. Plenty of organic material is important. Water-logging rots most types, so avoid damp spots. Plant the spring-flowering types in October and the summer and autumn-flowering types in spring/early summer. As a general rule, plant bulbs at a depth equal to twice their height. This helps to support the stems.

For naturalising, plant the bulbs at random, but not too far apart. Bulbs in pots or bowls are potted up in early September, for flowering at Christmas. They should be kept in a cool, dark place indoors, or buried outdoors — bowl and all — until early November when they are brought into a warm room to flower.

● **Aftercare.** Bulbs generally need little attention. Keep them reasonably weed-free for best results. Some fertiliser, every few years, helps to maintain flowering. Frost-prone plants, such as Dahlia, Begonia and Gladiolus, will have to be lifted in autumn and stored indoors for the winter. They might be risked outdoors by covering them with a 3 inch (7.5cm) layer of peat or ashes. Bulbs naturalised in grass must not have their foliage mown off until it goes yellow and begins to die. This is usually in late June and a lawn may look very ragged by then. Naturalise bulbs in lawn areas which would not be conspicuous if left unmown, such as under trees. Otherwise, naturalise the bulbs in ground cover, such as Ivy, Ajuga or Acaena, and the mowing problem does not arise.

Pests

Slugs and **snails** are the most serious pests of flower plants of all types. Most damage is done in summer to young plants and new shoots. Precautions will often be necessary.

Greenfly cause curling and stunting of foliage, and pass on virus diseases. Control may be necessary.

Caterpillars of various types eat holes in the leaves of many flower plants. Unless the damage is extensive, which is unusual, control is not necessary.

Capsid bugs are little beetles which eat the very young leaves as they push out of the 'bud'. Dahlias and Annual asters are especially vulnerable.

Earwigs and **woodlice** are usually responsible for 'mystery' damage to foliage and flowers. No pest can be found because feeding is often nocturnal.

Leatherjackets, vine weevils and **cutworms** are soil inhabitants which attack the flower plant roots or stems at ground level.

Eelworm are microscopic pests of flowers. If plants are stunted, 'bloated' in the stem, or fail to flower, eelworm may be the cause. *(See Pests, Page 112)*.

Diseases

Root-rot and **damping-off** sometimes occur if plants are over-watered as seedlings or, later, as plants. The roots die and rot sets in. Avoid over-watering and injury during pricking-out. Use clean trays and compost.

Virus diseases attack many perennial flowers and bulbs, causing mottling or streaking of the foliage, stunting and reduced flowering. Affected plants should be destroyed.

Leaf spot diseases of various types sometimes cause red or brown spots on the leaves of many flowers. These are rarely serious.

Powdery mildew attacks some flowers, especially Michaelmas daisies. Spraying is not worthwhile and if the trouble is persistent, grow something else. *(See the Section on Diseases. Page 117)*.

Narcissi
Narcissus 'February Gold'
dainty, early flowering type.

Spring anemone
Anemone blanda
early flowering, small type.

Dahlia
Dahlia 'Coltness Hybrids'
bright late summer colour.

Lawns

An excellent lawn, uniform in colour, level, dense, weed-free, the perfect foil for colourful plants.

Site

The ideal site for a lawn is a level piece of ground which gets full sunshine. A slight slope will not matter but steep slopes are awkward to mow. If there is a slope with a fall of greater than one foot (30cm) in three (100cm) put in a retaining wall and a terrace, or make a rockery. *(See Construction in the Section on Garden Skills. Page 78).*

Choose the lawn area for as much sun as possible. Lawns in the shade of trees, tall hedges and buildings take longer to dry out and tend to be moss-infested. Near hedges and under trees, they suffer from drought in summer as well. In the shade of trees, use ground-cover shrubs or herbaceous plants instead.

Think of the lawn as a distinct area of the garden. Do not consider the entire garden as a lawn with trees, shrubs and flower beds plonked into it. The lawn should be a feature in itself. It should be bordered by trees, shrubs, borders, flower beds, pathways and paved areas — not contain them, except perhaps for one or two specimen trees or shrubs. Otherwise the impression of space is lost. Choose a favourable area for the lawn and use trees, shrubs, flowers or paving as appropriate for the rest of the garden. The lawn will look better, and will be easier to keep. *(See the Section on Labour-Intensive Garden Features. Page 84).*

A lot of obstacles make for awkward mowing, and extra lawn edging!

Soil

A lawn needs 6 inches (15cm) of good top-soil. If the quality of the soil is poor, or if there is not enough of it, the grass will always struggle. Additional top-soil is well worth getting, and it is not too expensive. The ideal soil should not be too heavy, or growth will be slow in spring and moss will have a field day; nor should it be sandy, or it will dry out in summer and clover will be a problem. These are points to watch when buying top-soil.

Soil preparation

The key to success in laying a lawn is careful soil preparation. If soil conditions vary a lot, the lawn will not be uniform, therefore, take some time over soil preparation.

●**Drainage.** Drainage should be such that water does not stand in pools for longer than one day at a time. Large stones, tree roots and other rubbish should be removed.

●**Weeds.** A weed-free start is essential. Use Tumbleweed or Roundup to control existing grasses and weeds, including perennial weeds. Repeat applications may be necessary. *(See the Section on Garden Skills for Ground Preparation and Drainage. Page 71).*

●**Timing.** Sowing is done in spring or autumn. Prepare for spring sowing during the previous autumn and winter. Prepare for autumn sowing during the summer.

●**Levelling.** Level the humps and fill in the hollows before digging or adding extra top-soil. This helps to ensure an even depth of good top-soil. Dig the ground with a spade or use a rotavator if the area is large. Let the soil settle for a few weeks.

●**Conditioning.** Tread the area when dry, to firm the soil and break up lumps. Rake over the area to even out small bumps and hollows. Apply Moss Peat at the rate of one Giant Bale per 15 or 20 square yards (13-18m^2). Work this into the top 2 inches (5cm) during subsequent raking. The peat will give body to sandy soils and help to lighten heavy soils.

A weed-free start is essential. Tumbleweed will kill existing weeds before cultivation.

●**Raking.** Continue raking the ground at intervals of three weeks or so. Suspend operations during the months when the soil is wet. Serious compaction may result from walking over wet soil. Repeated raking levels the ground, settles it, makes it fine and controls small weed seedlings. If a flush of weed seedlings gets a start, use Weedol or Basta to burn them off before they get too big.

●**Fertiliser.** Apply a general fertiliser at 3 ounces per square yard ($100g/m^2$), about a fortnight before sowing is planned. Rake this in. At that stage, stones more than one inch across should not exist in the top inch (2.5cm) of soil. If they do, rake the ground until they are removed.

Sowing

The best sowing months are September and April. In September wait until a spell of rain has moistened the soil. In April, wait until the ground has dried out after the rainy months.

●**Seed mixtures.** For very good quality lawns which will get little wear, and full care, use a Number One seed mixture. This contains fine, low-growing grasses. For an average lawn with reasonable wear, and adequate maintenance, use a Number Two mixture. This contains both fine grasses and tough grasses and it is ideal for most gardens. A Number Three mixture contains tough, hard-wearing, vigorous grasses. It is suitable for heavy wear situations, but remember that if it does not get heavy wear it will need more cutting. Buy enough seed to sow one ounce per square yard ($35g/m^2$). Do not use 'hayseed' — it contains weed seeds.

●**Sowing.** Choose a still day after a few warm days when the soil is moist but not wet. Rake the soil. Scatter seed in two directions to get an even spread. *(See Spreading in the Section on Garden Skills. Page 75).* Using a yardbrush, or rake, gently cover the seed with soil.

●**Watering.** If there is no rain and the soil has dried out before the seed sprouts, water the soil with a fine sprinkler. Coarse spray droplets wash the seed away. Give a single heavy soaking rather than several light ones.

Mowing the new lawn

When the grass reaches 3 inches (7.5cm), it should get its first cut. This is just a trim to encourage the young plants to thicken up. Set the mower high. Do not cut too tightly because it weakens the new grass. There will be no need for rolling if the ground has been firmed and allowed to settle before sowing.

Some soft weeds may appear with the new grass. There is no cause for alarm because the mower will soon control them. These are usually annual weeds such as groundsel, fumitory and chickweed. They have no storage roots and soon die out. If ground preparation has been thorough, there will be no perennial weeds. Mow the new lawn each week through its first growing season.

Feeding

The first secret of a good lawn is feeding. Fertiliser encourages healthy grass growth, allowing it to compete with weeds and moss.

●**Spring feeding.** The most important feed is the first of the year because the grass will be hungry and weak after winter. Apply fertiliser in March or April, to set it up for the growing season. Use a spring lawn feed, such as Lawn Feed Special, Velvas, Fison's Lawn Food, Lawnsman Spring Feed or Special Lawn Fertiliser. These contain nitrogen which the grass badly needs but, also, phosphorus and potash for balanced growth. General fertilisers such as 10:10:20 or 7:6:17 are not really suitable as they do not contain enough nitrogen. But they may be used, being better than nothing.

Ideally, feeding should be repeated a couple of times, at two-month intervals. The cheaper sulphate of ammonia (containing nitrogen only) may be used for the repeat applications. CAN (NET Nitrate) may also be used if large areas are involved. Use fertilisers at the rate recommended on the pack. Do not use more fertiliser than advised, nor apply it when the grass is already growing strongly, as

This is how fine the soil should be at sowing, do not sow the seed too thickly.

Soft weeds — chickweed, fathen, groundsel and shepherd's purse — will appear, as here. Do not worry, regular mowing kills them.

White clover
a common weed of lawns that have not been fed, especially on poor soil.

it only increases mowing. Apply fertilisers evenly to moist soil when rain is expected, or else water them in. Scorching of the grass is caused by uneven application, particularly in dry conditions. *(See Spreading in the Section on Garden Skills. Page 75).*

●**Autumn feeding.** Good quality lawns may be fed in autumn as well. The idea is to supply phosphorus and potash to toughen the grass before winter. Autumn lawn feeds, such as Autumn Toplawn, or Lawnsman Winterizer, should be applied in September or October. Sulphate of iron may be used in autumn and winter to toughen grass, give it a good green colour and reduce mowing. Apply 8 ounces per 100 square yards ($280g/100m^2$) every 6 to 8 weeks from the end of August to April. Spray it on, or apply it dry mixed with sand.

●**Top dressing.** In September/October, or March/April, very good lawns should get a top-dressing of fine soil mixed 50:50 with peat. One bucketful per 4 square yards ($4m^2$) will give the grass new rooting material, and boost growth. Very good lawns should get this each year, but it may also be used to boost a thin lawn, especially on poor soil. Some fertiliser and seed may be added to the mixture in the latter case.

Top-dressing with peat/soil mixture makes a good lawn even better.

Mowing

The second secret of a good lawn is correct mowing. This means frequent, regular mowing, starting early in the year and finishing late.

●**How often?** Start in late February or early March. Around that time there is usually a dry spell when the ground is firm enough and the grass dry enough to cut. Continue mowing at fortnightly intervals until May, when weekly mowing will become necessary. Mow frequently and there will be less grass to remove each time. Continue weekly mowing through the summer, except in hot, dry weather, when growth eases off. Fortnightly mowing is adequate in September and October. Continue into November if the ground is still firm. Even in winter, if there is a dry, mild spell, it is a good idea to 'top' the grass. Above all, avoid irregular mowing — it weakens the grass and encourages weeds and moss.

●**How close?** The first mowing in early spring should just be a trim with the blades set high. Gradually lower the blades until the desired height is reached. Do not be tempted to mow very tightly. Very tight mowing weakens the grass unless it is well fed and cared for. An inch (2.5cm) to an inch and a half (3.75cm) is ideal for most Irish lawns. The higher level is ideal for rougher lawns and those getting a lot of wear. The lower level is suitable for good quality lawns. The desired height of cut should be maintained once weekly mowing starts. Raise the blades during drought spells, and towards the end of the season. Any winter 'topping' should be done at the highest setting.

Daisy common in lawns which are too tightly mown. These have just been sprayed.

●**Grass boxes.** The grass-box, or grass-bag, should always be used. Mowing is easier, faster and safer, and weed control is improved by collecting seed heads instead of spreading them.

Weeds

A few weeds in a lawn is no great problem — indeed it can be quite attractive with a few daisies! However, a heavy infestation by weeds, such as daisies, clover or speedwell can squeeze out the grass and spoil the look of the lawn.

●**Conditions for weeds.** Weeds cope better than grass with low levels of soil fertility. Starved grass is susceptible to competition from weeds, so feeding the lawn is essential. Irregular 'scalping' of the lawn opens the grass sward and allows weeds to become established. Too tight mowing weakens the grass and this also gives weeds a chance. Daisies can grow flatter than lawn grass and thrive on tight mowing. Regular mowing, using the grass-bag, prevents existing weeds from seeding and spreading.

Baby's tears, Mind-your-own business a very difficult weed of shady, damp corners.

●**Lawn weedkillers.** When weeds have made too much progress, a chemical lawn weedkiller may be used to help restore the balance. A variety of products is available — Verdone 2, Supertox, Clovercide, Bio Lawn-Weedkiller, Hygeia Lawn Weedkiller and Murphy Lawn Weedkiller. These contain similar active ingredients and are best applied in fine, warm weather when growth is active. April, May and June are ideal, but they may be applied between March and September. Feeding the grass two weeks before application improves results.

Combined feed and weed products, such as Feed and Weed, Green-up Evergreen and Toplawn, work well but may be expensive if a large area has to be treated. Lawn sand is a traditional lawn tonic combining feeding and weed suppression. Twenty parts clean sand, 3 parts sulphate of ammonia and one part sulphate of iron is the formula. Ready made lawn sand products such as Goulding's, Golden Vale or Velvas, are convenient to use.

● **Difficult weeds.** Speedwell has pale blue flowers in April. It is quite difficult to control. Weedkillers containing ioxynil or mecoprop, such as Speedotox, Clovotox or Verdone, will give some control but must be applied before the flowers appear. Mind-your-own-business or Baby's Tears (Helxine) is a common weed of shady, damp corners. It spreads over the surface of the soil swamping grass and will even climb over damp stones. There is no reliable chemical control, but tar oil winter wash, at half rate, may be used to scorch it, giving it a set-back. However, the grass may suffer too.

Speedwell
another difficult weed to control. It is really only vulnerable in early spring.

Moss

Moss thrives where there is dampness. Poor drainage, compacted soil, heavy soil and shade encourage moss. Avoid siting the lawn where there is dampness or shade. Consider planting such areas with suitable shrubs. *(See the Section on Trees and Shrubs. Page 5).*

Starved grass, and grass weakened by too tight or irregular mowing, cannot compete with moss. Feed the lawn and mow correctly, as the first step to control. Scarifying, by heavy raking or a scarifying machine, encourages the grass and dries the soil surface. This may be carried out in autumn or spring.

Chemical mosskillers, such as Bio Mosskiller, Hygeia Mosskiller, Super Moss Killer, Mosskil, Lawnsman Moss Killer, Green Up Mossfree and Mercurised Lawnsand will control moss, but if the conditions remain the same, it recolonises the area. Mosskillers are useful for giving the grass a once-off chance to recover while correct mowing and feeding are carried out. On chronically mossy areas, repeat applications will be necessary every year, or every few years, depending on the extent of the problem.

Moss
shade, poor drainage, compaction, lack of feeding are the main causes.

Bare patches

Bare patches are generally caused by wear, disease, dogs, petrol spillage or they may be left when weeds and moss are killed off. In a new lawn, uneven sowing or bad germination may leave bare spots.

In March/April, or September/October, fork the soil surface until the top inch or two (5cm) is loose. Add a thin layer of moist peat and/or fine soil. Level this out. Sow seed at one ounce per square yard ($35cm/m^2$). Criss-cross the patch with string on pegs, to give it a chance to recover. Thin patches may be treated in the same way.

Bumps and hollows

Cut and lift the sod. Add, or take away soil, as necessary. Replace the sod and firm it down. The sod re-establishes better if this is done in autumn. For minor hollows, the top-dressing technique described in this section under Feeding (Page 29) is an adequate solution. Repeated over a few years, the hollows will fill up.

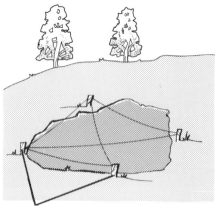

pegs with bright string

Bare patches may be re-seeded in spring or autumn, fence them off to give the new grass a chance.

Restoring neglected lawns

If a lawn was laid level originally, and the level is still good, it is not worth digging it up to make a new lawn. It can be restored. Clear any debris. Use a rotary mower without a grass-bag, or a strimmer, to cut the heavy growth. Rake off the mown grass. Tear out old grass and moss with a rake. Mow again. Apply a spring lawn feed.

Begin regular mowing. Apply lawn weedkiller two or three weeks after feeding. A repeat application of lawn weedkiller will be necessary, and feeding should also be repeated. Moss control may be necessary. Top-dressing and re-seeding overall will help to restore the sward. Then simply maintain routine lawn care.

Pests

Leatherjackets often eat grass roots and may cause thin patches. Treading on the affected patches when the soil is reasonably dry helps to control them. In a bad attack, chemical control may be necessary, but this is unusual.

Birds, such as **starlings** and **crows,** often pull out bits of grass to get at the leatherjacket grubs. This damage is minimal and the birds help to control the grubs.

Earthworms are not a pest in gardens — as they can be on golf greens. If casts are considered unsightly, just brush them away.

Dogs may foul lawns and cause scorched patches. *(See the Section on Pests. Page 112).*

Scalping caused by the mower going over a bump. Proper levelling before sowing avoids this problem.

Diseases

Fairy rings are rings of green, vigorous grass which sometimes produce small brown mushrooms as well. They are caused by a fungus in the soil. Often, the grass inside the ring goes patchy, and dies. Fairy rings are usually only a problem on good lawns. Control is difficult. Sterilise the affected area with Basamid and re-seed that part of the lawn. Alternatively remove the top 12 inches (30cm) of soil from the affected area, taking care not to drop contaminated soil on other parts of the lawn, drench the hole with Jeyes Fluid or Clean-up solution and re-fill with fresh soil. Applying fertiliser, except on the ring itself, masks the problem.

Inkcaps and other **toadstools** arise from bits of rotten timber and other organic material in the soil. When this material finally rots away the toadstools no longer appear. They are not, strictly speaking, a disease.

Other diseases sometimes cause yellow, brown or dead patches in the lawn. They are worst on fine grass mixtures and damp, starved lawns. If there is a reddish tinge on the dying grass, when examined closely, a spray with Benlate, Fungus Fighter or Murphy's Systemic Fungicide will help. *(See the Section on Diseases. Page 117).*

To remove bumps or fill hollows, peel back the sod and remove, or add, soil.

Correct, regular mowing and the use of a grass-bag to collect the mowings are essential for a good quality lawn.

Be careful with the spray drift of lawn weedkillers, here a Lavander bush has been damaged.

Louise Odier
a beautiful, old shrub rose, good in a shrub border.

Silver Jubilee
one of the best large-flowered bush roses for bedding.

American Pillar
an old favourite rambler, but not for walls because of mildew.

Satchmo
a bright and red cluster-flowered bush rose, good for bedding.

Sally Holmes
simple beauty, a good cluster-flowered bush for bedding.

Lilli Marlene
a rich red cluster-flowered bush rose for bedding.

Iceberg
the best white rose of all, for bedding or as a specimen.

Ballerina
masses of small flowers, lovely growing through iron railings.

Arthur Bell
changing shades of yellow, a good cluster-flowered bedding rose.

Roses

Types

●**Bush roses.** These are upright bushes between about 2 feet (60cm) and 6 feet (180cm) in height. Bush roses are grafted on to a vigorous rootstock at ground level, by inserting a bud of the chosen variety. If the graft is made on to a stem 4 feet (120cm) above ground level, the result is a **standard rose.** Bush roses are continuous flowering. They are often classified as either Hybrid Teas or Floribundas. Hybrid Teas are now called Large-flowered bush roses and Floribundas are called Cluster-flowered bushes. The new terms are more accurate, and are easier to understand.

●**Shrub Roses.** These form a shrub, generally between about 4 feet (120cm) and 10 feet (300cm) tall. Their growth habit is generally more vigorous and more 'floppy' than the bush roses, so they are wider. There is great variety in the shrub type. Some are wild species, such as *Rosa rugosa* and *Rosa rubrifolia:* some are Old Roses, such as the Moss Rose and Louise Odier; and some are Modern Shrub Roses, such as 'Nevada' and 'Frühlingsgold'. Many shrub roses flower in a single flush. Some are continuous flowering.

●**Climbing roses.** These roses climb if given support. They generally produce a mass of flowering shoots at the top of one or two main stems, which thicken with age. The stems are generally upright and stiff. Most climbing roses are continuous flowering and carry large flowers. Some are vigorous versions of bush roses.

●**Rambling roses.** These too have a climbing habit but they are more lax, not as woody, and the stems are more flexible. The flowering shoots are carried on many stems from ground level. In fact, ramblers generally produce new shoots at ground level each year, whereas climbers hardly ever do. Ramblers nearly all flower in a single flush of small flowers, mostly in early summer, some in late summer.

●**Miniature roses.** These are dwarf types — smaller than bush roses but very similar in all other respects. They range in height from 6 inches to 18 inches (15 - 45cm).

Using roses

●**Bush roses.** These are mainly used in beds for which their stiffly formal habit is ideal. The large-flowered bushes are best for formal rosebeds near the house, and for cutting. Cluster-flowered bushes are ideal for beds of showy colour and could also be planted in groups at the front of a shrub border, or even singly. Cluster-flowered bushes are better suited to poor conditions, especially wet areas, because their flowers withstand rain better.

●**Standard roses.** These are used in the middle, or at the back of large rose beds, to add a dimension of height. They have long been used as specimens on their own, but less so nowadays. They could also be used in groups, or singly, in a shrub border behind low, non-competitive plants to give summer colour.

●**Shrub roses.** Being true shrubs, these roses are best placed among other flowering and non-flowering shrubs. They too bring summer colour to a shrub border. The shrub roses may also be planted as specimens on their own and some of them make good informal, and secure, hedges.

●**Climbing and Rambling roses.** Their climbing habit of growth makes them ideal for covering walls and unsightly large objects. They may also be grown on flowering garden trees to give double value. An old tree stump, pillar or pergola covered with climbing roses is hard to beat.

Blessings
lovely in bud, a good large-flowered bush rose for bedding.

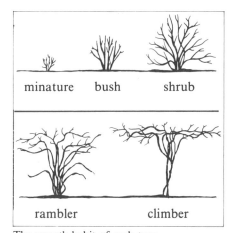
The growth habit of each type determines the shape that develops.

Rose Gaujard
a handsome bud, a good vigorous large-flowered bush rose.

●**Miniature roses.** These have become very popular recently for patio and container growing. They may also be used on rockeries, and as houseplants.

Choosing bush roses

This, like choosing wallpaper or carpets, is a matter of personal taste, but there are some do's and don'ts. Choose either large-flowered bushes or cluster-flowered bushes. Do not mix them — it does not look right. *(See Using Roses above).* Neither should varieties of large-flowered bushes be mixed in the same bed because mixed colours take from the effect of formal elegance.

The more showy cluster-flowered bushes may be mixed, but stick to two or three varieties. Avoid the 'fruit-salad' effect. Try to match the varieties for height, (or at least use the taller ones to the back, or the middle, if it is an island bed) and choose complementary colours. Try to see the variety in life, because books and catalogues can be misleading — visit St. Anne's Rose Garden, Clontarf, Dublin, or a rose nursery during the flowering season.

Site

Roses love sunshine. They grow best, flower most, and suffer least from diseases if placed in a sunny position. The ancestors of today's roses came from warm climates in Europe and Asia. They need all the sun the Irish climate can offer.

Roses do not like windy conditions. Provide shelter if the site is exposed, particularly in the west of Ireland, because the combination of wind and rain will destroy the blooms. But do not over-shelter since movement of air keeps the foliage dry and less vulnerable to disease. Roses do not compete well with tree or hedge roots. Planted in an unfavourable situation, they invariably disappoint.

Soil

Roses need deep, rich soil which drains well in winter but does not dry out in summer. It is worthwhile removing poor soil from the site for roses and replacing it from the vegetable garden or elsewhere.

Work in plenty of organic material such as rotted manure or compost, or a 3 inch (7.5cm) layer of peat. This improves drainage, retains moisture in summer, and promotes deep rooting. The soil should be completely free of perennial weeds. *(See Ground Preparation in Garden Skills. Page 71).*

Planting

Roses are easy to establish but good planting will improve results. November is the best month, but in areas of high rainfall and heavy soil, plant in March. Bare-root plants may be planted from October to March. Container-grown plants may be planted at any time, even mid-summer.

Select a site and prepare the soil as outlined earlier. Dig holes 12 inches (30cm) deep, 15 inches (37.5cm) wide and 2 feet (60cm) to 2½ feet (75cm) apart. The rows of holes may be staggered, to create a fuller flower effect.

Make up a planting mix of moist peat with a fistful of general fertiliser added per bucket. Mix a 2 inch (5cm) layer of this into the soil at the bottom of each hole.

Set up a line to get the rows of bushes straight and parallel to the edge of the bed. Soak the roots in water before planting. Place the bush in the hole and spread the roots. Scatter some soil over the roots, and shake the plant slightly to settle it in. Plant to the depth of the graft union, where the shoots meet the root.

Firm the soil and fill the hole in two or three stages, firming each layer gently. Water each bush after planting and watch for signs of drought later on.

The same planting technique applies to all types. Shrub roses are spaced informally, at 5 or 6 feet (150 - 180cm) apart. Keep them about 5 feet (150cm) away from competing shrubs or trees. Climbers are normally planted about a foot from a wall. Usually planted singly, they may be spaced 8 to 10 feet (240 -

Kerryman
a good cluster-flowered bedding rose, note the two shades of pink.

Pink Parfait
a prolific, peachy-pink, cluster-flowered bush for bedding.

Tip Top
a low-growing, cluster-flowered bush rose, ideal for bedding.

List of Twenty Bush Roses

Name	Type	Colour	Scent	Height	Disease resistance	Remarks
Silver Jubilee	l-f	peachy pink	some	75cm	good resistance	vigorous, bushy
Whiskey Mac	l-f	amber yellow	good	75cm	prone to mildew	needs good cultivation
Trumpeter	c-f	bright scarlet	some	45cm	good resistance	vigorous, bushy
Arthur Bell	c-f	gold/yellow	good	90cm	good resistance	vigorous, upright
Mullard Jubilee	l-f	deep pink	good	90cm	some resistance	vigorous, bushy
City of Belfast	c-f	scarlet	slight	60cm	good resistance	medium vigour, bushy
Satchmo	c-f	scarlet	none	75cm	good resistance	vigorous, bushy
Pink Parfait	c-f	creamy pink	none	75cm	good resistance	vigorous, prolific
City of Leeds	c-f	salmon pink	slight	90cm	some resistance	vigorous, prolific
Blessings	l-f	soft pink	good	75cm	good resistance	medium vigour, bushy
Kerryman	c-f	pink/deep pink	none	75cm	some resistance	vigorous, spreading
Tip Top	c-f	pink	some	45cm	prone to blackspot	vigorous, spreading
Topsi	c-f	bright scarlet	none	45cm	prone to blackspot	medium vigour, bushy
Lilli Marlene	c-f	scarlet red	slight	75cm	prone to mildew	vigorous, reliable
Iceberg	c-f	white	slight	90cm	prone to diseases	vigorous, prolific
Korresia	c-f	yellow	some	75cm	good resistance	bushy, prolific
Sally Holmes	c-f	creamy white	slight	60cm	some resistance	vigorous, spreading
Rose Gaujard	l-f	pink/silver	slight	90cm	good resistance	vigorous, reliable
Josephine Bruce	l-f	deep crimson	good	60cm	prone to mildew	vigorous, spreading
Pink Favourite	l-f	pink	slight	90cm	good resistance	vigorous, upright

'l-f'= large-flowered bush, 'c-f'= cluster-flowered bush.

List of Twenty Other Roses

Name	Type	Flower	Flowers	Height	Spread	Remarks
Pink Perpetue	c	large, double, pink	July/Sept.	3m	2.5m	good pillar rose
Dublin Bay	c	large, double, red	all season	2.5m	1.5m	not vigorous
Schoolgirl	c	large, double, apricot	all season	3m	2.5m	vigorous, healthy
Maigold	c	large, double, yellow	May	3m	2.5m	thorny, healthy
Golden Showers	c	large, double, yellow	June-Oct.	2.5m	1.5m	pillar rose, blackspot
Zepherine Drouhin	c	large, double, pink	June-Oct.	3m	2m	thornless, mildew
Albertine	r	large, double, pink	June-July	4.5m	3m	vigorous, mildew
American pillar	r	single, pink	July	6m	4m	vigorous, mildew
Kiftsgate	c	small, single, white	July	12m	12m	very vigorous
Nevada	s	large, single, ivory	June-Sept.	2.5m	2.5m	vigorous, arching
Fruhlingsgold	s	large, double, gold	June	2m	2m	vigorous, arching
Canarybird	s	medium, single, yellow	May	2m	2m	good informal hedge
Rosa rubrifolia	s	small, single, pink	June	2m	2m	purple foliage, red hips
Rosa rugosa	s	medium, single, pink	June-Oct.	1.5m	1.5m	bushy, red hips
Rosa varsicolor	s	large, double, striped	July	1.2m	1.2m	bushy, mildew
Louise Odier	s	large, double, pink	summer	1.5m	1.2m	vigorous, compact
Ballerina	s	small, single, pink	July-Oct.	1.2m	1.2m	bushy, reliable
Nozomi	m	small, single, pink	July	0.6m	1.5m	good for containers
Rosa rouletti	m	small, double, pink	June-Oct.	0.3m	0.3m	prone to mildew
Starina	m	small, double, red	June-Oct.	0.3m	0.3m	prone to mildew

'c'= climber, 'r'= rambler, 's'= shrub, 'm'= miniature.

300cm) apart from each other, or from other wall climbers. Tie the shoots of climbers into a horizontal position before they get tall. They generally do not flower for two or three years after planting.

If an old rose bed is to be replanted with roses, the soil must be removed to a depth of 15 or 18 inches (45cm). Soak the pit with Jeyes Fluid solution or Clean-up. Refill with new soil which has not grown roses before. This procedure is necessary to avoid a problem called 'rose replant disease' which causes stunting and poor growth.

Old rose bushes can be transplanted quite easily. November is the best month.

Pruning

How and when to prune depends on the type of rose.

● **Bush roses.** February is a good month to prune them. Earlier pruning may invite frost damage in cold areas. Late pruning means delayed flowering.

First, remove all dead, damaged and diseased shoots. Then remove any weak, spindly shoots. Typically, between three and ten shoots will be left. Remove one in three of these from among the oldest, dark coloured shoots. Shorten the remainder to between 6 and 12 inches (15 - 30cm). Large-flowered bushes should have their shoots pruned closer to 6 inches than 12. Cluster-flowered bushes should be left closer to 12 inches than 6. Prune cleanly just above an outward pointing bud.

The 'head' of a **standard rose** is pruned in the same way.

● **Climbers.** Note the difference first of all between a climber and a rambler. *(See Rose Types. Page 33).* Climbers are never pruned at ground level. Only the top framework is thinned out and the shoots which carried flowers pruned back to 4 inches (10cm). Weaker climbing varieties should not be pruned quite so much. Climbers are pruned in February or March.

● **Ramblers.** Depending on variety, all ramblers throw some new shoots at ground level each year. Whatever number of new shoots is produced, remove this number of old shoots, choosing the oldest to go. For ramblers which produce very few new shoots at ground level, but produce some further up on the older shoots, prune the older shoots back to one of these young shoots. Then, just shorten back the remaining shoots which have flowered. Ramblers are pruned in summer or autumn, whenever flowering finishes.

Tie in both climbers and ramblers after pruning. Completely overgrown climbers or ramblers may be cut back hard and re-trained. No pruning, other than light trimming, is needed for miniature roses.

Other points

Some other points on the culture of roses are worth noting.

● **Suckers.** Bush roses, standards and some shrubs and climbers are grafted. Suckers from the root-stock may appear and will take over, if not removed. Dig down below soil level and locate the source of the sucker. Cut it off. Replace the soil and firm it well to discourage further suckering. Suckers are easily recognised because they have more leaflets per leaf, carry more thorns, and grow vigorously.

● **Dead-heading.** Removing the faded flower heads from bush and standard roses, and from continuous flowering climbers, is worthwhile. It increases and prolongs flowering.

● **Wind-rocking.** Pruning the tops off tall varieties in windy situations in November avoids the possibility of root damage. Elsewhere it leaves rose beds tidier over the winter.

● **Cuttings.** Nearly all roses grow well from cuttings. Miniatures are taken in July/August, others in October/November as hardwood cuttings. *(See Propagation in the Section on Garden Skills. Page 72).*

Trumpeter
a very bright red cluster-flowered bush rose for bedding.

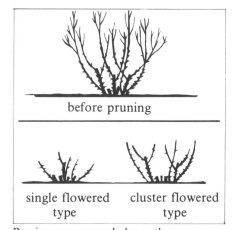
before pruning

single flowered type | cluster flowered type

Pruning roses properly keeps them vigorous and healthy with good displays of blooms.

Nevada
a beautiful shrub rose for early summer colour in a border.

Feeding

In March each year, bush roses should get 2 ounces per square yard ($70g/m^2$) of general fertiliser, or rose fertiliser such as Goulding's Rose Food, Rose Plus, Special Rose Fertiliser or Toprose. Climbers, ramblers and shrub roses should get the same — especially in the early years after planting, and following periods of poor growth, or disease attack. Vigorous types may not need any fertiliser. A dressing of rotted manure, compost, shredded bark or peat, in April/May encourages good growth and conserves vital moisture. Bush roses may be given a further ounce of fertiliser (35g) per bush, in early July, to encourage late flowering.

Weeds

Always keep rose beds free of weeds. A formal feature must be kept tidy. Straighten and trim lawn edges in March. Remove all existing weeds and apply Simazine for lasting weed control. Do not let Simazine get onto the lawn.

Pests

Greenfly are the only major pests of roses. They may be expected every year, from May onwards. Control will more than likely be necessary, especially in dry, warm summers.

Caterpillars and **beetles** may eat a few holes, but damage is generally slight and occasional. Well-fed roses will not suffer. No control is necessary. *(See the Section on Pests. Page 112).*

Diseases

Rose blackspot is inevitable under Irish conditions and is worst in areas of high rainfall, and in wet seasons. It causes black spots on the leaves which then fall off. Some varieties are more susceptible than others. *(See the List of Varieties. Page 35).* A spray of Benlate, Tumbleblite, Multirose, Roseclear, or Supercarb, as the buds break in April, is essential. Spray again in May and June, and more often in a wet season, or a wet locality.

Rose mildew is generally only serious on ramblers. White chalk-like fungus grows on the leaves and stems. With susceptible varieties, spraying with Benlate, Supercarb, Nimrod, Roseclear, or Multirose will be necessary, starting in April. Mulching helps. Plant climbers instead of ramblers on walls.

Rose rust is an occasional problem but serious in some areas when it does occur. Rusty spots appear on the underside of the leaves. Spray with Dithane or Liquid Copper when the disease is first seen. *(See Section on Diseases. Page 117).*

Albertine
very popular, easy to grow rambler, lovely shades of pink.

Dublin Bay
one of the best red climbers, large flowers all summer.

Kiftsgate
the most vigorous climbing rose, ideal for old trees, needs space.

Compassion
a large-flowered climber, not tall, flowers all summer.

Maigold
masses of bronze-yellow in May, can be used as a climber, or a shrub.

List of Vegetables sown outside

Name	Crop	Harvest	Sow	Transplant	Spacing Plants	Rows	Pests and diseases
Cabbage	summer/autumn	July-Sept.	3-4	5-6	40cm	60cm	
	winter	Oct.-March	4-5	6-7	45cm	60cm	flea beetle
	spring	March-June	7	9	30cm	45cm	cabbage root fly
Cauliflower	autumn	Sept.-Nov.	3-4	5-6	45cm	60cm	caterpillars
	spring	March-May	5	7	60cm	60cm	cabbage greenfly
Brussels sprouts	autumn	Sept.-Nov.	3	6	60cm	60cm	snails
	winter	Nov.-March	4-5	6-7	60cm	75cm	pigeons
Broccoli	summer/autumn	July-Oct.	4-6	thin	30cm	60cm	
	spring	March-May	3-4	6-7	60cm	75cm	clubroot
White turnips	summer	June-Aug.	3-6	thin	15cm	40cm	white blister
	autumn	Sept.-Oct.	7-8	thin	15cm	40cm	leaf spot
Swede turnips	autumn/winter	Oct.-March	4-5	thin	30cm	45cm	powdery mildew
Radish	summer	May-Sept.	3-8	thin	3cm	30cm	
Carrots	summer	July-Sept.	3-4	thin	5cm	30cm	carrot root fly
	autumn/winter	Oct.-March	5	thin	5cm	30cm	greenfly
Parsnips	autumn/winter	Sept.-April	3-4	thin	15cm	45cm	
Onions	sets/shallots	July-March	3-4	—	15cm	30cm	onion bulb fly
	seed	Oct.-May	2-4	thin	8cm	30cm	eelworm
	Japanese type	June-Sept.	7-8	thin	8cm	30cm	white rot
Scallions	summer	June-Sept.	3-7	—	1cm	30cm	neck rot
Leeks	winter/spring	Nov.-April	3-5	6-7	20cm	40cm	rust
Peas	early summer	June	2-3	(double rows	5cm	60cm	pea and bean weevil
	summer	July-Aug.	4-6	15cm apart)	5cm	60cm	greenfly/blackfly
Broad beans	early summer	June	10 or 2	(double rows	8cm	60cm	birds
	summer	July-Aug.	4-5	15cm apart)	8cm	60cm	millipedes
French beans	summer/autumn	July-Oct.	4-7	—	10cm	45cm	*see list below*
Beetroot	summer/autumn	July-Oct.	4-7	thin	8cm	40cm	leafspot
Lettuce	summer/autumn	July-Oct.	3-7	thin	15cm	40cm	*see list below*
Potatoes	early	June-Sept.	3	—	40cm	60cm	greenfly, slugs, eelworm
	maincrop	Oct.-May	4	—	40cm	75cm	blight, virus

List of Vegetables sown inside and planted out

Name	Harvest	Sow	Prick-out	Plant out	Spacing Plants	Rows	Pests and diseases
Cabbage	June	1-2	2-3	3-4	45cm	45cm	*see list above*
Cauliflower	June-July	10 or 1	2-3	3-4	45cm	45cm	*see list above*
Brussels sprouts	July-Aug.	1-2	2-3	3-4	45cm	60cm	*see list above*
Lettuce	May-June	2	3	3-4	15cm	40cm	greenfly, grey mould
Onions	Aug.-Sept.	1-2	2-3	4	30cm	45cm	*see list above*
Celery	Aug.-Nov.	3-4	4	5-6	25cm	25cm	celery fly, leaf spot
Tomato	Aug.-Oct.	3	4	5-6	45cm	60cm	potato blight
Sweet corn	Aug.-Oct.	4 (in 8cm pots)	—	5-6	45cm	45cm	slugs, snails
Courgettes	July-Sept.	4 (in 8cm pots)	—	5-6	60cm	90cm	mosaic virus
Runner beans	July-Oct.	4 (in 8cm pots)	—	5-6	15cm	45cm	blackfly, root rots
French beans	June-July	3 (in 8cm pots)	—	4-5	10cm	45cm	blackfly, root rots
Peppers	Aug.-Sept.	3	4	5-6	40cm	60cm	red spider mite

Note: the numbers under Sow, Prick-out, Transplant and Plant out refer to the month of the year.

Vegetables

Healthy vegetables, nicely spaced and weed-free.

Types

Various parts of plants — leaves, stems and roots — are eaten as vegetables. Some 'vegetables' are, in fact, fruits, seeds or flowers. Tomatoes, peppers and courgettes are fruits; sweet corn, peas and beans are seeds; and cauliflower, broccoli and globe artichokes are flowers.

Most of the vegetables grown belong to just a few plant families. The Cabbage family *(Brassica)*, includes cabbage, cauliflower, brussels sprouts, broccoli, turnips, swedes, kale, seakale, kohlrabi and radish. The Carrot family includes carrots, parsnips, parsley, celery and florence fennel. The Onion family includes onions, shallots, leeks, scallions and garlic. The Beet family includes beetroot, spinach beet and seakale beet. The Pea family includes peas, beans, french beans and runner beans. The Potato family includes potatoes, tomatoes, peppers and aubergines.

Vegetables are either grown outdoors in the open soil, or under the protection of glass or polythene. Only the vegetables grown outdoors are dealt with in this section. *(For Protected Crops see the Section on Greenhouse Growing. Page 57).* Outdoor vegetables can be divided into three groups. One group is sown outdoors, the second group is sown indoors and planted out, and the third group is the perennial vegetables, including most of the herbs. *(See the Section on Labour-Intensive Garden Features. Page 84).*

Site

Quick grown vegetables have the best flavour, and to encourage quick growth they should have full sunshine. Vegetables must not be shaded or they will not develop properly. Some low shelter is a big help because it increases air and soil temperatures and so improves growth. A slight south, or south-west, slope is ideal, because it warms up early in the year and stays warm later. Hedges and tree-roots can starve vegetables of moisture and nutrients.

A full range of vegetables in early August, all well within the scope of the home gardener.

Soil

Good fertile soil is essential for vegetables. Quick growers must not have to struggle. Drainage should be good because wet soil delays the start of growth in spring and brings it to an early stop in autumn. However, the soil must be capable of retaining enough moisture to support strong growth in summer. Light, sandy soil is ideal for carrots, onions and early vegetables. Heavier limy soil is good for the Cabbage family. A medium soil, well supplied with organic material, is ideal for most vegetables. It is open, easily worked, warms up quickly and retains moisture in summer. The ground must be completely free of perennial weeds. *(See Ground Preparation in the Section on Garden Skills. Page 71).*

Soil fertility

A high level of soil fertility must be maintained and good soil structure encouraged. To maintain soil structure organic material, such as well-rotted manure, or compost or peat, should be dug in to part of the vegetable area each year. Lime also improves soil structure and should be added to acid soils in the south, south-east and west of Ireland, at 12 ounces of ground limestone, or hydrated lime per square yard (350g/m^2), every three or four years. Vegetables are hungry feeders and they remove large quantities of nutrients from the soil. Manure and compost add back some of these nutrients, but it will also be

Hard to beat a few nice early potatoes, freshly dug. The variety is Sharpe's Express.

necessary to apply general fertiliser, such as 7:6:17, or 10:10:20 at about 3 or 4 ounces per square yard (100g/m²) before sowing or planting each year. *(See also the Section on Soils, Nutrients and Fertilisers. Page 66).*

Crop rotation

Vegetables belonging to the same family tend to be affected by the same pests and diseases — which may build up if the same crops are grown in the same piece of ground for several years. Therefore, it makes sense to rotate the various families around the vegetable plot each year. However, it is very difficult to maintain a strict rotation in a small garden because of the different sized areas for each crop. There may be several crops of a particular vegetable, for example, cabbage, in a single year and this adds to the difficulty of finding a 'new' site each time. Besides, tools and boots are efficient spreaders of pests and diseases, and certain weeds often provide a 'bridge' for harmful organisms when suitable crop plants are not available. Because of the wide variety of crops grown and the restrictions on space in a small garden, only short rotations are possible and these are of limited value. Even so, it is worth trying to avoid following a crop with another of the same family. The illustration gives a basic four-year rotation.

Rotation offers the opportunity to add organic material and lime to the soil in such a way as to be an advantage to particular crops. Organic material is very beneficial for potatoes, celery, courgettes and sweet corn, while it tends to make Cabbage family plants too leafy. So, it should be added before potatoes, etc., and the Cabbage family should be kept away for a while. Adding organic material before potatoes, each year in a four-year rotation, means that a different quarter of the vegetable area gets it every year and the entire site will be covered by the fourth year. If slugs in potatoes have been a problem, apply the organic matter before the Pea and Onion families instead.

If the soil is acid, and lime is to be applied, apply it before the Cabbage family and keep it away from the Potato family. It prevents clubroot disease of the Cabbage family but encourages potato scab disease. If lime is applied before the Cabbage family, in a four-year rotation, then the whole vegetable area will be covered in four years — which is about right on an acid soil.

Seed sowing

Most vegetables are raised from seed each year. Vegetable seed may be sown indoors in trays, or outside in the open soil. Some vegetables are perennial— they do not need to be sown each year. In fact, these are usually purchased as small plants. *(See Seed sowing in the Section on Garden Skills. Page 71).*

●**Outdoor sowing.** Most of the ordinary vegetables are grown in this way: cabbage, cauliflower, sprouts, broccoli, turnips, swedes, radish, carrots, parsnips, onions, scallions, leeks, peas, broad beans, french beans, beetroot, lettuce and potatoes. Starting in March or April, these crops are sown into well-tilled, fine soil. Little drills are marked out with a stick drawn along a line. The depth of the drill and the distance between drills varies. The seed packets give good guidelines. *(See also the List of Vegetables sown Outside. Page 38).*

Vegetable seed has high germination ability but should not be sown into cold, wet or lumpy soil. Do not save seed from one season to the next, as it may deteriorate. Use a seed dressing, such as Murphy's Seed Dressing, for early-sown seeds.

●**Indoor sowing.** Some vegetables are subject to damage by frost and cannot be grown outdoors until the danger of late frost is past — about mid to late May. However, sowing outdoors at that late stage would leave too short a growing season, so these crops should be sown indoors and planted out at the end of May. They include tomatoes, sweet corn, runner beans, celery and peppers. The same trick for extending the season forward can be used on some of the ordinary vegetables such as cabbage, cauliflower, sprouts, lettuce and onions, to get early crops. Indoors, seeds are sown in trays of seed compost, kept moist and warm

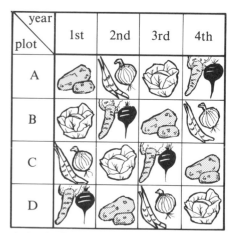

A simple, four-year rotation. For a three-year rotation, just amalgamate the carrot and onion groups.

Fresh herbs have special flavour. Every garden has enough room, they can be quite ornamental too.

Courgettes are easy to grow, even in a cool summer, and are very prolific.

Name	Harvest	Sow	Plant	Spacing Plants	Rows	Pests and Diseases
List of Perennial Vegetables and Herbs						
Perennial vegetables						
Asparagus	May-June	March	April	45cm	90cm	slugs, snails
Globe artichokes	June-July	March	March	75cm	75cm	grey mould
Rhubarb	March-June	—	winter	90cm	90cm	gummosis, leaf spots
Perennial herbs						
Chives	summer	March	March	1 clump		white rot
Thyme	all year	April	March	3 bushes		greenfly
Sage	summer	April	March	2 bushes		leafhopper
Pot marjoram	summer	April	March	2 bushes		greenfly
Mint	summer	—	March	1 plant		greenfly
Fennel	summer	April	March	1 plant		—
Horseradish	October	—	March	30cm	60cm	leaf spot
Tarragon	summer	—	March	1 plant		—
Rosemary	summer	—	March	1 plant		—
Other herbs (annuals, sown each year)						
Parsley	all year	4-7	—	1 row		greenfly
Chervil	all year	4-8	—	1 row		greenfly
Basil	summer	inside	June	15cm	30cm	greenfly
Garlic	Aug.-Sept.	—	10 or 2	15cm	30cm	white rot

until germination occurs. The seedlings are then pricked out into other seed trays, at about 2 inches (5cm) apart each way, or into small individual pots. The larger seeds may be placed directly in twos into small pots, the better seedling being retained. *(For sowing dates and other information see the List of Vegetables Sown inside and Planted out. Page 38).*

● **Perennial vegetables.** Although these may be raised from seed sown indoors, or outdoors, they are often purchased as small plants. Since they are perennial, there is no need to sow each year. These vegetables usually occupy the same piece of ground for several years. Many herbs fall into the perennial category, but a few need to be sown each year. *(See the list of Perennial Vegetables and Herbs).*

Spacing vegetables

Vegetables need enough space for each plant to develop to a usable size. The amount of space varies for each vegetable and may even vary between varieties of a particular vegetable. The seed packets give suggested spacings for each variety. Some vegetables, such as peas, beans, scallions, radishes, potatoes and onion sets, are sown at their final spacing and need no further adjustment. Others, however, do and there are two ways of achieving that final spacing.

● **Transplanting.** Sow the seed in a seedbed and, when the seedlings have six or seven leaves, lift and transplant them to their final spacing. Water the young plants afterwards, to help them to recover. This procedure is used for cabbage, cauliflower, sprouts, leeks and lettuce. Transplanting saves seed, and space, because the plants are usually five to eight weeks old when moved and the ground they are moved into may have been cropping in the meantime. Crops sown indoors are, of course, transplanted outside.

● **Thinning.** Many crops cannot be transplanted. The root crops — carrots, parsnips, turnips, swedes and beetroot — would form a useless forked root if transplanted because of the damage caused by lifting. These must be thinned to their final spacing. Sow thinly, but even so, deliberately sow too much seed. Too many seedlings then emerge and the surplus is simply pulled out, choosing the strongest to grow to maturity. It is a good idea to thin in two stages. If the final spacing is made when the plants are still young and vulnerable, gaps will be left if some die, or are damaged. Leaving the thinning until later may, however, weaken the plants by competition. A preliminary thinning, to half the final spacing, will provide substitutes if there are casualties.

Nicely spaced cabbage and cauliflower.

Onion white-rot disease.

Continuity

Because most seed sowing takes place in March and April, there is often a glut in July and August. Try to avoid sowing a lot of vegetables at about the same time. Sow early varieties in early spring, indoors if possible, to provide supplies in early to mid-summer; sow maincrop varieties in late spring for use from mid-summer to autumn, and for storage; sow early varieties of quick-maturing types in mid-summer for late autumn supplies of tender vegetables. Make several sowings of the quick-maturing salad crops — lettuce, radish, beetroot, scallions — and of white turnips, peas, french beans and carrots. Pay special attention to sowing varieties of cabbage, cauliflower, sprouts, spring broccoli and leeks for use in the period after Christmas and up to June.

Weed control

If ground preparation was good, there should be no perennial weeds. If there are, dig them out, or spot treat them. *(See the Section on Weeds. Page 110)*. Vegetables cannot compete with weeds. Begin with weed-free ground and aim to keep it clean.

Control weed seedlings as soon as they appear. Light hoeing between rows gets rid of the majority. Hand-weed the actual rows of vegetables. Chemical weed control is not a possibility in the vegetable garden. Usually there is only one big flush of weeds and, if this is controlled early on, very little follow-up is required.

As soon as crops go over, remove remaining plants and weeds, and dig the ground. This prevents seeding, discourages pests, and leaves the ground ready for the next crop. Timeliness is all important.

Pests

Quite a range of pests attacks vegetables. Very many of these are occasional or unusual and are not worth taking precautions against. Some, however, may be relied upon to make an appearance. They include greenfly, cabbage root fly, carrot root fly, cabbage caterpillars, slugs and snails and pigeons. *(The Lists of Vegetables, Page 38, give the main pests of each crop. These and their control are described in the Section on Pests. Page 112)*.

Diseases

Not many diseases cause problems in the vegetable garden — those that do are mainly soil borne. Among them are onion white rot and clubroot of the Cabbage family. Blight on potatoes will almost certainly appear, but other diseases are occasional rather than certain. *(The Lists of Vegetables, Page 38, give the main diseases. They are described, together with their control, in the Section on Diseases. Page 117)*.

Harvesting and storage

Begin using vegetables as soon as they are big enough, while still immature. Carrots, beetroot, peas, celery, turnips, scallions, lettuce, french beans, courgettes, cabbage, cauliflower and broccoli may be used before they attain full size. These are very tasty at an immature stage and using them early helps both to extend the period of use, and avoid gluts. Only pick as much as is needed at a time. Harvest vegetables in the cool of morning.

●**Freezing.** Many vegetables keep for only a short time after harvesting. Freezing is a possibility with some types — peas, beans, sprouts, broccoli, cauliflower, carrots, sweet corn, courgettes and tomatoes pulped. Herbs may be frozen in ice cubes.

●**Pits.** Root vegetables store well in pits outdoors, protected by straw and soil. This is successful with carrots, swedes, turnips, parsnips, beetroot, potatoes and even hard round-headed cabbage. Guard against rats and mice.

●**Drying.** Onions store well when properly dried after harvest. Peas and french beans may be allowed to mature for drying too. Herbs dried slowly store well.

Cabbage root fly damage, typical symptoms — the plant is seriously stunted.

Carrot root fly damage, even slight tunnelling like this is off-putting.

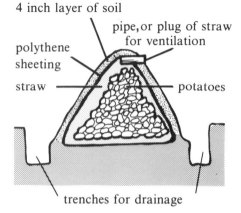

4 inch layer of soil

pipe, or plug of straw for ventilation

polythene sheeting

straw

potatoes

trenches for drainage

Pit storage — a simple and effective method for root vegetables.

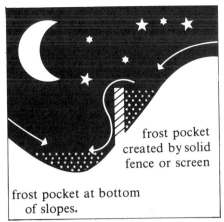

frost pocket at bottom
of slopes.

Cold, frosty air, being heavy, flows
downhill like water, note how it
gathers.

Soft fruit varieties

Strawberries

Cambridge Favourite	July, medium flavour
Elsanta	July, good flavour
Aromel	summer & autumn
Baron Solemacher	summer, alpine type

Raspberries

Leo	August, heavy cropper
Malling Jewel	July, good flavour
Autumn Bliss	autumn fruiting type

Gooseberries

May Duke	June, red variety
Careless	June-July, yellow
Leveller	July, green variety

Currants

Ben Lomond	mid-July, blackcurrant
Baldwin	late July, blackcurrant
Laxton's No. 1	July, red currant
White Versailles	July, white currant

Blackberries & hybrids

Oregon Thornless	August (blackberry)
Thornless Loganberry	July & August
Tayberry	July & August

Note
Refer to the calendars
on pages 121–124

Soft Fruit

Site

The soft fruits like sunshine and shelter. Strawberries must have full sun and an open position. Raspberries, blackcurrants and gooseberries prefer full sun but can tolerate a little shade. None of the soft fruits tolerate exposure to wind very well, so provide shelter. Strawberries, being low-growing, would be the least damaged by some wind exposure.

Frost is a danger for all, but especially blackcurrants, which flower early. These are likely to be disappointing at elevations over 600 feet (200m) above sea level. Although gooseberries flower early too, they are less vulnerable and therefore less likely to lose a whole crop. Strawberries and raspberries flower a few weeks later and are not likely to be damaged — a few early flowers may be caught. Avoid planting any soft fruit at the base of a slope where cold air might collect, creating a frost pocket.

Soil

Good, fertile, well-drained but moisture-retentive, slightly acid soil is the ideal for soft fruit. 'Well-drained' is the key characteristic as the plants will suffer winter root damage in water-logged soils. Poor soil may be made fertile by adding organic manures and fertiliser. Limy soil is fine, as long as it is well-drained. Blackcurrants do not mind a medium-heavy soil. The ground should be completely free of perennial weeds before planting.

Strawberries

● **Planting.** Strawberries planted in September or October give fruit the following July. Planted in March or April, they will not yield much until fifteen months later.

Plant strawberry runners which are Department of Agriculture certified free from disease and pests. Only such runners are reliable. Space the plants about 15 or 18 inches (37.5 - 45cm) apart, in rows about 30 inches (75cm) apart. Plant them so that the crown — where the roots and leaves meet — is at soil surface level.

● **Care after planting.** Strawberries must be kept free of weeds, with which they just cannot compete. Hand weed around the plants and hoe the alleyways for the first year. After that, an overall spray of Simazine, applied to weed-free soil in spring, is easy and effective. Do not apply Simazine to newly-planted runners because it damages them. Planting through a layer of black polythene prevents weeds very effectively, and keeps the fruit clean.

Pick the fruit when it is ripe — not before. It will not ripen further off the plant. After picking is finished, cut away all the leaves and unwanted runners. Remove any weeds that are present. At full cropping, each plant may give up to one pound (450g) of fruit.

Every spring apply 2 ounces of general fertiliser per square yard (70g/m²). On heavy, limy soils, replace this with an ounce of sulphate of potash per square yard (35g/m²), to prevent excessive leafiness.

Replanting should be carried out every second or third year. If the plants are left any longer, the fruit size gets smaller, and there is a likelihood of pest or disease build-up. *(For early crops grown under protection see the Section on Greenhouse Growing. Page 57).*

● **Pests.** Quite a few pests attack strawberries.
Greenfly usually appear in April or May and build up quickly. Apart from weakening the crop, they bring virus diseases which render the plants useless. Control will be necessary.

Slugs and **snails** eat the ripe fruit and may destroy a big proportion of the crop in a wet year. Take precautions.

Birds, in particular blackbirds and thrushes, eat the ripe fruit. Netting is the only answer.

Mites, especially red spider mites, may stunt the crop. Control is not easy and it is best to destroy affected plants.

Eelworms get into the crowns and leaves and may cause stunting. There is no cure, destroy affected plants.

Vine weevil grubs may bore into the crowns below soil level and cause reddening of leaves, poor growth and death of plants. Remove and burn plants affected by eelworms or vine weevils. *(See the Section on Pests for more on control. Page 112).*

● **Diseases.** There are two serious diseases.

Grey mould is the descriptive name of the fungal disease which causes the fruit to rot. Spraying as the first flowers open is essential for control.

Viruses of several kinds result in unfruitful plants. They are spread mainly by greenfly. Destroy virus-affected plants and prevent spread. *(See the Section on Diseases for more on control. Page 117).*

A strawberry plant stunted by virus disease. Too weak to bear fruit, it is now useless.

Raspberries

● **Planting.** November to March is the best time to plant raspberry canes. Plant only Department of Agriculture certified canes.

Dig a trench about 12 inches (30cm) deep, and 15 inches (37.5cm) wide. Put in 2 inches (5cm) of manure, compost or peat, and mix it with the soil. Add back about 2 inches (5cm) of loose soil, and firm lightly. Then, plant the canes about 15 or 18 inches (37.5 - 45cm) apart. If more than one row is being planted, space the rows 5 feet (150cm) apart. In a dry year, water the young canes to get them established.

● **Training.** Raspberry canes should be supported by posts and wire. Use 8 feet (240cm) posts, driven 18 inches to 2 feet (45 - 60cm) into the ground. Space them 20 feet (6m) apart. Fix three wires to the posts, at 2 feet (60cm), 3½ feet (105cm) and 5 feet (150cm). The canes are tied to these wires with soft string.

● **Care after planting.** Well cared for raspberry plants will last twenty years or more. Weeds, especially perennials, must be controlled. Simazine used each spring on weed-free soil will give good control.

A nice crop of ripe raspberries, the variety is Glen Clova.

Feed raspberry canes in March, with one ounce of general fertiliser per yard of row (35g/m). Apply a mulch of well-rotted manure, compost or peat, in May, every year, or every two years. If cane growth is poor because of bad soil, apply an ounce of sulphate of ammonia to each 4 yards of row (10g/m), in May.

Pick the fruit when ripe. Over-ripe fruit falls off the plant. Most varieties are summer-fruiting. Some varieties fruit in September/October. Each foot (30cm) of row will give one pound of fruit (450g). There will be some fruit in the second year after planting and full cropping is reached after five years.

● **Pruning.** After fruiting, untie the canes which have fruited and cut them out at ground level. Also remove the weaker of the new canes. Aim to have three or four good canes per 12 inches (30cm) of row. Autumn fruiting types should be pruned in February. Tie in the new canes to the wires.

● **Pests.** The main pests are greenfly and raspberry beetle.

Greenfly attack the leaves and shoots, reducing yield and spreading virus disease. Control may be necessary.

Raspberry beetle grubs hatch from eggs laid on the young fruit and bore into the berries from the stem end. Control may be necessary. *(See the Section on Pests for more on control. Page 112).*

● **Diseases.** Although there is quite a list, raspberries are not very disease-prone.

Grey-mould *(Botrytis)* is the most serious, causing the ripening fruit to rot. Control is usually necessary, especially in wet seasons and high rainfall areas.

Virus diseases cause mottling of foliage, stunting, and poor cropping — rubbishy small fruit, and blind fruit. Remove affected plants and burn them.

Raspberry fruit with grey mould disease, very common, especially in wet summers.

Cane blight, spur blight and cane spot cause canes or parts of canes to wither and die. Die-back of canes without signs of disease may be due to unfavourable growing conditions.

Raspberry rust causes orange spots on the undersides of the leaves. It does not do much harm. *(See Section on Diseases for more on control. Page 117).*

●Loganberries, blackberries, tayberries. These tolerate poor soil and tough growing conditions quite well—even a north facing wall.

Blackberries are too vigorous for a small garden and they tend to carry fruit into September and October when it may be spoiled by rain.

Training, pruning and feeding, and pests and diseases, are the same as for raspberries.

To prune raspberries, simply cut out the old shoots which have just borne fruit.

Blackcurrants

●Planting. It is best to buy Department of Agriculture certified bushes, but blackcurrants are not so prone to virus diseases and can be raised easily from cuttings. Use young shoots 12 inches (30cm) long, taken from healthy cropping bushes, in November. Place the bottom 6 inches (15cm) in a shallow trench, outdoors, with some sand in the bottom. Firm well. The cuttings will be ready for planting out the following November. *(See Propagation in the Section on Garden Skills. Page 73).*

Plant blackcurrant bushes between November and March, at 6 feet (180cm) apart. If more than one row is being planted, space the rows 6 feet (180cm) apart. Dig in manure, compost or peat before planting. Cut down all shoots to about 2 inches (5cm) at planting.

●Care after planting. Keep the ground free of weeds by hoeing for the first year, and then using Simazine in March each year. Simazine is especially suitable for blackcurrants because they dislike the soil disturbance which is inevitable with hoeing.

Feed blackcurrants well. Each spring, they should get 8 ounces of general fertiliser per bush (70g/m²). This should be followed by a heavy dressing of well-rotted manure or compost, which helps to keep weeds down and conserves moisture in summer.

Consider watering the bushes if the summer is very dry, especially in the early years. The first fruit is produced in the second season after planting, and full cropping is reached after five years. At this stage, each bush will produce between 6 and 10 pounds (3-5 kilos) of fruit.

Blackcurrants ready for picking, the variety is Baldwin.

●Pruning. Blackcurrants carry most of their fruit on young shoots. The shoots pushed out one season flower and fruit in the next. Pruning aims to provide a good supply of young shoots by removing a proportion of the older shoots each year. It may be done after fruiting, but usually it is done in winter, being made easier by the absence of leaves. Each year, prune out one quarter to one third of the number of shoots in the bush. Choose the older, darker-barked shoots to go. Prune them out as low down as possible, avoiding cutting out a lot of young shoots as well. Annual pruning keeps the bushes to a reasonable size.

●Pests. The most serious are big bud mite and greenfly.

Big bud mite causes the buds to swell and take on a round shape. The mites feed inside the buds, which are usually 'blind'. Virus disease is carried by the mites. Pick off and burn any swollen buds.

Greenfly cause curling and discolouration of leaves and reduced growth. They also spread the big bud mites from bush to bush. Control them if there is a bad attack.

Bullfinches eat the buds in winter and may cause serious damage. Use bits of polythene as scares; otherwise, use netting *(See the Section on Pests. Page 112).*

●Diseases. The major diseases are leaf spot and reversion.

Leaf spot is a fungal disease causing small brown spots on the leaves which, after a bad attack, fall off. It is worst in wet years, and in wet localities. Though not as

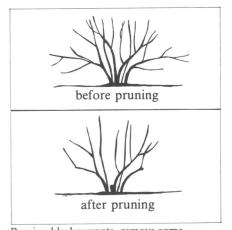

before pruning

after pruning

Pruning blackcurrants, remove some old shoots in winter.

common as it was, control will be necessary, if it appears.
Reversion is a serious virus disease which ends cropping. The leaf edges of affected plants become less toothed. Dig up and burn these plants.
Gooseberry mildew attacks the young leaves and shoot tips of blackcurrants, but not the fruit. Prune out affected shoots when noticed. *(See the Section on Diseases. Page 117).*

Gooseberries

●**Planting.** Plant the bushes in November, about 5 feet (150cm) apart. Gooseberries root easily from cuttings, as described for blackcurrants, except to remove the buds from the bottom two-thirds of the shoot. Gooseberry bushes are best grown on a single stem clear of the ground for 10 inches (25cm) or so, hence the need to disbud the lower part of the cutting.

●**Training.** Maintain the single stem clear of side-shoots for 10 inches (25cm). Allow the side-shoots to develop above this. Select four, five or six strong shoots well separated from each other. Allow these to grow out like the spokes of a wheel, keeping the centre open to prevent disease. These branches form the permanent branch framework. Following this training system makes picking, pruning and spraying a lot easier.

●**Care after planting.** Control weeds by hoeing for the first year and then using Simazine in March each year.

Apply 4 ounces (110g) of general fertiliser per bush in February/March each year. If growth has been very vigorous, apply 2 ounces (55g) of sulphate of potash instead, especially on limy soils.

Water newly-planted bushes if there is a dry spell. Some fruit will be produced two years after planting and full cropping is reached after five years. At that stage, each bush will yield between 8 and 16 pounds (4-8 kilos) of fruit.

●**Pruning.** Gooseberries carry most of their fruit on short spurs on older wood. The same spurs flower and fruit year after year. Pruning of gooseberries means setting up this pattern, and allowing it to continue. Having trained the bushes on a 'leg' with about five main branches, pruning simply involves removing about half of the young side shoots each year, and shortening the rest to within 3 inches (7.5cm) of the main branches. Prune away any low-hanging shoots. This pruning is done in winter. If the growth of young shoots is very vigorous, remove some of them and shorten the others, during June. This summer pruning helps to counteract vigorous growth.

●**Pests.** The most serious pests are bullfinches and caterpillars. **Bullfinches** eat the buds and may seriously reduce the crop. Watch out for damage in winter, and use nets if necessary. **Caterpillars** of **gooseberry sawfly** may eat all the leaves off the bushes. New leaves will appear, and the damage will not be too severe if it occurs just once every few years. Losing the leaves every year weakens the bushes, and control will be necessary in this case. **Greenfly** may attack in large numbers and need to be controlled. *(See the Section on Pests for control measures. Page 112).*

●**Diseases.** The only serious disease is gooseberry mildew.
Gooseberry mildew attacks the leaves, shoots and fruit. The fruit becomes covered with a whiteish or brownish fungus, but it may be used if wiped clean.
Gooseberry cluster cup disease causes little orange spots on the leaves and fruit. It is not usually worth spraying for. Spray with Dithane before the flowers open.
Grey mould disease *(Botrytis)* occasionally attacks a few berries, and may cause branches to die off. Affected branches should be pruned out. *(See Section on Diseases. Page 117).*

●**Red and white currants.** Plant, train, feed and prune them as for gooseberries; they get the same pests and diseases as blackcurrants.

Gooseberries may be used before they reach this size, the variety is Careless.

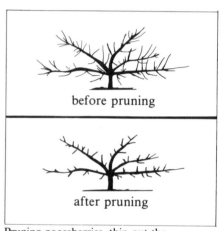
Pruning gooseberries, thin out the young shoots, shorten back those remaining.

Gooseberry mildew on the foliage of blackcurrant, which it frequently attacks.

Tree Fruit

Apples in late summer ripening nicely, the variety is Ellison's Orange.

APPLES

●**Site.** Apples will not succeed on exposed sites, near the sea, or over 600 feet (200m) above sea level. Do not plant on north-facing slopes, or at the bottom of any slope where frost might gather. Choose a warm, sheltered spot, not shaded in any way — especially by large trees that would rob the apple trees of food, water and light. Too much shelter, on the other hand, increases the risk of disease attack, because the foliage stays damp longer.

●**Soil.** The ideal is a deep, fertile, well-drained but moisture-retentive, slightly acid soil, but apple trees grow well on most soils, as long as they are well-drained. They may suffer potash deficiency on dry limy soils and tend to be over-vigorous, and prone to disease, on heavy, limy soils. Peaty soils are too wet and infertile. Replace poor soil, if necessary, to a depth of about 12 inches (30cm).

●**Varieties.** Apples will not form unless the flowers are fertilised by pollen from a tree of another variety. This means that two or more apple varieties must be planted, unless there is an apple tree, even a Flowering crab apple, already growing within about 100 feet (30m). The list of apple varieties gives a selection ripening at different periods. The varieties Bramley's Seedling, Jonagold and Crispin produce sterile pollen and are useless for pollination purposes. Three or more varieties must, therefore, be grown if these varieties are included.

●**Tree shapes.** Tree shape should be chosen to suit the garden. If space is very limited, the restricted tree shapes — cordon, fan and espalier — are ideal. The illustration shows the basic outline of these. Cordons are grown on wires between posts. Use four wires, each one foot (30cm) apart, the first at 18 inches above ground level. Support the wires on strong wooden or steel posts, about 15 feet (5m) apart. Fans and espaliers may also be grown on wires, or on walls or fences. The restricted tree shapes are flat — only about 18 inches (45cm) deep — and about 6 feet (180cm) high. They are suitable only for dessert varieties.

Where there is a little more space, free-standing spindle-bush trees may be grown. These are supported only by a strong 6 feet (180cm) stake. Spindle bush trees are kept to about 7 feet (210cm) high and about 5 feet (150cm) wide. Both spindle-bush trees and restricted trees must have dwarfing rootstocks to keep them small.

If there is more space again, open-centre bush trees may be grown. These are kept to about 8 feet (2.4m) high and about 10 feet (3m) in spread. These trees should have semi-dwarfing rootstocks. Larger trees, up to 25 feet (8m) high, used to be grown on vigorous rootstocks but these are impossible to prune, spray or pick, and are no longer planted.

●**Planting.** November is the best month but apple trees may be planted up to the end of March. Decide first on the planting site, tree shape and varieties. Then remove, or spray, existing weeds and dig the soil. Dig in a couple of buckets of well-rotted manure, compost or peat at the site for each tree.

Buy the trees and soak the roots before planting. Dig holes 18 inches (45cm) wide and a foot (30cm) deep. Mix some peat into the soil at the bottom of the hole. Drive a stake in each hole to support the young trees. Trim any damaged roots. Test the tree in the hole for depth, and plant at the same depth as the soil mark on the stem. Fill in and firm gently. Tie each tree to its stake.

Space cordon trees about 5 feet (150cm) apart; fans, espaliers and spindle bushes about 8 feet (240cm) apart; and open-centre bushes about 12 feet (360cm) apart. The quickest to bear fruit are cordons and spindle bushes — often in the

Apple varieties

Discovery	(8-9)	dessert
Worcester Pearmain (WN)	(9-10)	dessert
James Grieve	(9-10)	dessert
Katja	(9-10)	dessert
Laxton's Superb (WN)	(10-12)	dessert
Lord Lambourne (WN)	(9-11)	dessert
Queen Cox (WN)	(10-2)	dessert
Jonagold	(10-2)	dessert
Idared	(11-4)	dessert
Golden Delicious	(11-3)	dessert
Greensleeves	(10-12)	dessert
Crispin (WN)	(11-3)	dessert
Grenadier	(8-9)	cooker
Howgate Wonder	(9-11)	cooker
Bramley's Seedling (WN)	(11-3)	cooker

(WN) means suitable for the West and North. The figures in brackets denote the months when they may be used.

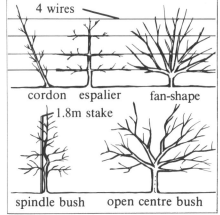

The popular shapes for garden fruit trees.

season after planting. The more vigorous cooking varieties, trained as open-centre bushes, may take up to ten years — especially on heavy soil.

● **Training.** The procedure used will depend on which tree shape is the aim. Restricted trees — cordons, espaliers and fans — are often bought with the initial training begun. Simply tie the shoots into position to hold the shape. Surplus shoots, and those which are badly placed and cannot be tied into position, should be removed.

To train trees from scratch, they should be no more than two years old. The wood is still pliable and the young shoots may be tied into position as they grow. Bare-root trees are usually only two years old, but container-grown trees may be several years old and may already have bad shape that is difficult to correct.

For spindle bush trees, tie-in the main leader to the stake. Allow both the leader and the side shoots to develop. In July, tie the side-shoots down into a horizontal position to induce early cropping. In the winter after planting, release the ties and shorten the first year's growth by about one-third — both leader and side-shoots. Repeat this procedure in subsequent years until the spindle bush shape develops. Maintain the central stem from which the horizontal side branches arise. Do not allow rival leaders to develop.

Pruning spindle bush trees, the central leader is the main feature.

For open centre bush trees, shorten the main shoot to about 30 inches (75cm) above ground level. Select four or five of the side shoots that develop. Shorten these to half their length each year, allowing them to become the main framework branches. Do not allow a central main leader to develop. Remove branches which tend to grow towards the centre of the tree. This is kept open to let in light and air.

This training is all the pruning the trees need for their first five or six years.

● **Pruning.** When the young apple trees have been given their initial training, annual pruning will be necessary to maintain the desired shape, and to promote the production of good quality fruit. Apple trees carry their largest, sweetest fruit on branches between two and five years old. To maintain a fair proportion of branches of this age, some of the oldest branches in the tree are pruned out each year, and younger ones allowed to take their place. The idea of replacement is the key to pruning apple trees.

There are two periods for pruning — December/January and July/August. Winter pruning encourages growth of new shoots. Summer pruning discourages growth.

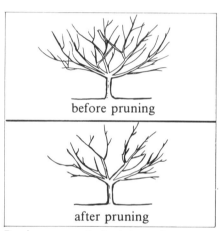
Pruning open-centre bush trees, the centre is kept open to let in light and air.

● **Winter pruning.** This is the main pruning period for the free-standing, open-centre bush and spindle-bush trees. Start by removing all dead, damaged or diseased branches. Next, select two or three fairly sizeable branches from among the oldest on the tree. Make the choice by reference to their position, bearing in mind the correct shape of the tree and the existence of a younger replacement branch. Usually the choice is easy, because an old branch may be crowding a younger one.

Having removed some old wood, next remove, or shorten, all weak, spindly shoots. The remaining strong, young shoots will eventually make good fruiting wood. Shorten these by about one-third of their length. These general guidelines suit all types of bush trees.

For the restricted trees, such as cordons, espaliers or fans, less winter pruning is practised. Too much would only encourage them to grow away from their restricted shapes. In winter, just prune out a few old branches and weak, spindly shoots. Most of their pruning is done in summer.

● **Summer pruning.** Restricted trees produce some young shoots each summer. About mid-July, begin shortening back the stronger shoots to four or five leaves, at the rate of a few each week or so, until September. Do not bother shortening weak shoots — these can be removed in winter.

Bush trees that are very vigorous, but unfruitful, should get this summer pruning, and no winter pruning for a few years — until cropping starts.

Well-set fruit and healthy foliage, the two small fruits will fall and two others should be thinned.

●**Feeding.** Apple trees should get 2 ounces of general fertiliser, or Fruit Fertiliser, per square yard (70 g/m²), in February or March each year. The area of the spread of the branches should be used to calculate how much. Even quite small trees will need at least one pound (450g) each on this basis. Fertiliser is essential for good growth and cropping.

If the trees have tended to be too vigorous and not produce much fruit, apply one ounce of sulphate of potash per square yard (35 g/m²) instead, especially on heavy, limy soils.

●**Weeding.** For the first few years after planting, keep the ground around the trees free of weeds. Simazine may be used for this purpose, applied to clean ground, in March. As the trees get bigger, grass may be grown underneath, but it should be kept short.

●**Restoring neglected trees.** Old, over-grown trees may be brought back into production by pruning, feeding and spraying. Prune out some of the old wood and thin out the branches. Feed and spray as normal. Old trees which have deteriorated too much, or are of a bad variety, may be grafted with a new variety.

Codling moth damage, the grub has bored into and fed inside the fruit.

●**Grafting.** In December or January, collect young shoots of the new variety. These should be about 12 inches (30cm) long. Tie them into a bundle and place it in a cool corner of the garden with the bottom 3 inches (7.5cm) in the soil. In mid-April, cut down the main branches of the old trees, leaving them about 3 feet (90cm) long. Remove any small branches.

Make a sloping cut on one of the young shoots above the soil mark. Trim the top end to leave the piece about 6 inches (15cm) long. Make a slit in the side of a branch of the old tree. Insert the prepared shoot, making sure the cut surface is in good contact with the wood beneath the bark of the old branch. Tie the grafted shoot tightly in place and seal all the cut surfaces with grafting wax, such as Tenax. Cut the ties as soon as the buds break. Train the new shoots to replace those removed. The first fruit will be produced two years later.

●**Unfruitful trees.** Apple trees can be unfruitful for a variety of reasons, usually the site is wrong, the soil is poor, or there is no cross-pollination. If these reasons are eliminated and the trees have grown very strongly, producing wood and leaves but few flowers or fruit, the problem is over-vigorous growth. This may have been caused by too-severe winter pruning, or by wrong feeding. However, some varieties, planted in heavy, fertile soils, have this tendency.

Bark-ringing is a possible remedy. This involves removing a half inch (1cm) strip of bark from around the stem at blossom time. Seal the cut surface with tape or pruning paint. The restriction in the flow of sap encourages the production of flower buds, and fruit eventually.

Successful grafting onto an old tree. One of the shoots is removed later.

●**Thinning.** Established apple trees often produce too many fruits which are usually small and of poor flavour because the tree has not the vigour to swell them all. A certain amount of natural thinning takes place. Only those apples with several seeds actually develop to maturity. Many just drop off after initial development. This usually happens in early July, although it is called the 'June drop'.

Wait until mid-July when the 'June drop' is past. If surplus fruit remains, thin it out to leave one apple for every 4 inches (10cm) of branch length. The apples may not be spaced evenly along the branch, but use this ratio as a guide to numbers.

●**Picking.** Apples ripen on the tree and should not be allowed to fall. Pick them when the fruit stalk parts easily. Some varieties must be used quickly — James Grieve, Worcester Pearmain. Others keep for a while — Laxton's Superb, Jonathan. Some varieties keep well up to March/April — Golden Delicious, Bramley's Seedling, Crispin, Idared, Queen Cox.

The keeping varieties may be stored in polythene bags with the top left untied and with a few small holes in the bag to allow air exchange. Store only clean, unbruised fruit. It is a waste of time storing varieties which do not keep.

Greenfly symptoms on an apple shoot— curling and discolouration of the leaves.

●**Pests.** The main pests are codling moth and greenfly.

Codling moth grubs hatch from eggs laid on the young fruit and bore in through the 'eye'. Feeding and growing inside, they eventually eat their way out. Affected apples ripen prematurely and fall off. The pest is very common in town gardens and precautions are usually necessary.

Greenfly cause stunting of shoots and fruit. A version of greenfly — **woolly aphid** — produces woolly masses on the branches, and severely weakens the tree. Control is necessary.

Caterpillars may attack the leaves, but damage is usually slight.

Red spider mite may attack in warm summers, causing the leaves to go bronze. If damage is severe, control will be necessary.

Bullfinches may attack buds. Netting may be necessary in rural areas. *(See the Section on Pests for more on control. Page 112).*

●**Diseases.** The most common is apple scab.

Apple scab disease attacks leaves, young shoots and fruit — causing black or brown scabs on the latter which sometimes crack. Spraying will be necessary, especially in wet years and wet localities.

Apple canker is a serious disease causing sunken cankers on branches and trunk. Branches may die. Avoid injury and control apple scab which creates an entry for canker on young shoots. Prune out affected branches. Paint all wounds with pruning paint.

Powdery mildew causes whitish discolouration of young leaves and shoots. A bad attack weakens the tree. Prune out affected shoots when noticed in May and June. *(For more on control, see the Section on Diseases. Page 117).*

PEARS

●**Site.** Pears need a good site to succeed. They flower earlier than apples and so they are more vulnerable to frost. Fruit quality, too, is better in a warm situation. Pears will not be a success if there is any exposure. Not being as prone to diseases as apples, the concern about too much shelter is not as great. The best results are got by growing them on a wall facing south, or west, to provide shelter and extra warmth.

●**Soil.** Ideally, this should be deep, free-draining, moisture-retentive and fertile. Pears tolerate heavy soil better than apples, and dislike dry conditions at the roots. For wall trees, it is worthwhile removing the top 2 feet (60cm) of soil and replacing it with good soil mixed with well-rotted manure, compost or peat.

●**Varieties.** The best variety is Conference — it is the most reliable. It needs a pollinator and two good possibilities are William's Bon Chretien and Doyenne du Comice.

●**Planting.** Plant pear trees as described for apples, but be more careful as pears do not take root as easily as apple trees. November to March is the planting period and November is the best month.

●**Training.** The restricted shapes suit pear trees well. They may be trained as cordons on wires, or as espaliers or fans on a wall or fence. Train them as for restricted apples, tying in the young shoots to the desired shape and removing surplus.

　As free-standing bushes, pears quite naturally take on the pyramidal shape described for spindle bushes in apples. The same training procedure is followed except not to tie down the young shoots. They take about five years to begin fruiting. The open-centre bush shape is not suitable for pears.

●**Pruning.** Pear trees carry most of their fruit on short spurs on older branches. There is, therefore, no need to replace old wood. Once pears settle down to fruiting they need very little pruning ; just remove dead, damaged or diseased branches, and an old branch here and there if there is crowding. Remove some of the old fruiting spurs on restricted trees. Summer prune as for apples, if growth is over-vigorous on restricted trees.

Apple mildew disease, the affected shoots should be pruned out and burned.

Apple scab disease, spraying is essential, especially in a wet year.

A young fan-trained pear tree on a south-facing wall carrying a nice crop.

Mature pears ready for picking and ripening off the tree, the variety is Conference.

Summer pruning, shortening back the young shoots in late summer restricts vigorous growth.

The best plum variety, Victoria, but be careful it does not break its branches.

●**Feeding.** Pear trees should be given 2 ounces of general fertiliser per square yard (70 g/m^2) in March. A mulch of rotted compost every few years is beneficial by conserving moisture in summer.

●**Weeding.** Keep the ground free of weeds by hoeing, or using Simazine each March. The mulch will help to keep down weeds. Pear trees are better not grown in grass, even when established.

●**Neglected trees.** Pear trees do not suffer as much as apples if neglected. Removal of dead and damaged branches and some branch thinning is all that is needed in pruning. Feed and mulch, and spray if considered necessary. Over-vigorous young trees may be bark-ringed, as described for apple trees.

●**Thinning.** This is not usually necessary. Sometimes, the variety Conference produces too many fruits. Reduce the fruit to one per spur, or two if many of the spurs have no fruit. Early July is the time to thin.

●**Picking.** Pears do not ripen on the tree. They fall off and ripen on the ground. Pick them when they look mature, and put them in a cool place, indoors. They will soften for eating within a few days or a few weeks, depending on variety, but do not continue to store them once they have softened.

●**Pests.** Pears are not much troubled by pests.
Greenfly may attack, and may need to be controlled.
Pear midge is a little fly whose maggots bore within the fruit, hollowing it out and causing it to fall early. Though· not very common, this pest may be troublesome. Destroy all the early fallen pears.
Birds may attack both fruit and buds. *(See the Section on Pests for control measures. Page 112).*

●**Diseases.** Pear scab is the most common disease.
Pear scab causes black spots on the fruit, which often cracks. Though it is not as widespread as apple scab, precautions may be necessary in wet seasons and in wet, cool localities. Cracking may also be caused by sudden changes in the weather or by drought. *(See the Section on Diseases for control. Page 117).*

PLUMS and CHERRIES

These are closely related, have similar requirements — and similar problems.

●**Site.** Both plums and cherries flower early, plums a bit before cherries. This means they must have a warm site. Do not plant where cold winds might damage the blossoms, or where cold, frosty air might collect. Plums and sour cherries may be grown on a west, south or north-facing wall.

●**Soil.** Both plums and cherries like heavy, limy soil, but it must be well drained. Acid soils should have lime applied before planting these fruits.

●**Varieties.** The best and most reliable plum variety is Victoria. Czar is a small black plum, and Denniston's Superb is a greenish-yellow gage of good flavour. All three are self-fertile, needing no pollinator. Victoria and Czar may be grown as free-standing trees or as fans on a south, west or north wall. Denniston's Superb is best grown on a south or west wall.

The best sour cherry variety is Morello which can be grown as a tree or a wall-trained fan. The only variety of sweet cherry suitable for gardens is Stella, a recent introduction. Other sweet cherries are too large, and need pollinators. Both Morello and Stella may be grown on their own.

●**Training.** Plums and cherries may be grown as trees or wall-trained fans. Of the restricted shapes only the fan is suitable for the growth habit of plums and cherries. Train wall trees into a fan shape by tying in the young shoots as they grow and pruning out badly-placed shoots. Victoria is too vigorous as a wall tree, unless there is a lot of space. Train plums and cherries as free-standing trees by shortening the young shoots by about one-third of their length, each April for the first few years, letting the trees take their own shape.

●**Pruning.** Never prune plums or cherries in winter because there is a good chance of diseases getting in through the wounds. Prune plums in spring in the early years and, once established, prune after fruiting. Plums fruit on wood of all ages, and so, some thinning, and the removal of dead, damaged and diseased wood is all that is necessary.

Sour cherries fruit on the previous year's wood so, each year, some old shoots should be removed in late spring, to encourage new growth.

Sweet cherries fruit on spurs on old wood. Little or no pruning of free-standing trees is necessary. Wall trees should have new shoots shortened to 4 inches (10cm) in July, once the branch framework is established.

●**Feeding.** If the trees are growing vigorously and failing to crop, do not feed for a year or two. Then only give one ounce of sulphate of potash per square yard (35 g/m²) in March. If the trees have cropped heavily or growth is not good, give 2 ounces of general fertiliser per square yard (70 g/m²). Well-rotted compost or manure could be used in this case too. On distinctly acid soils, apply some lime every three or four years.

●**Weeding.** Use Weedol to burn off weeds under plums and cherries. Hoeing, or Simazine, may damage the surface roots. Established plum trees and sweet cherries grow happily in grass.

●**Thinning.** Plum trees, especially Victoria, often set too many fruits — even to the point of breaking branches. If too much fruit is allowed to develop, it tends to be small and of poor quality. Thin out plums to about 2 inches (5cm) apart in late June. Wait until the natural fall is complete. No thinning is needed for cherries.

●**Picking.** Pick plums and cherries ripe off the tree and use them within a few days, they keep for only a short time. Remove all the fruit from plum trees, as the old, dried fruit can be a source of disease the following year.

●**Pests.** The main pests of plums and cherries are greenfly and birds.
Greenfly usually attack plums, and blackfly attack cherries, each year. Keep a close watch and spray if numbers begin to build up.
Plum sawfly grubs bore into the fruit making them fall early. Treatment is as for codling moth on apples.
Bullfinches often strip out the flower buds on plums and cherries in rural areas. The crop may be badly affected. Netting may be necessary.
Blackbirds and **starlings** may attack ripe cherries. Again, netting may be considered. *(See the Section on Pests for more on control. Page 112).*

●**Diseases.** Plums and cherries suffer three main diseases — silver leaf, bacterial canker and brown rot.
Silver leaf causes a silvering of the leaves, and a dark stain in the wood of affected twigs. If the stain is not present, feeding usually restores the tree. If it is present, remove the affected branches completely as soon as they are noticed, as the disease is a killer.
Bacterial canker affects the trunk and main branches, causing off-colour, leaf spotting, wilting and death of the tree, often during winter. A lot of gum usually oozes from an infected tree. There is no cure. Both silver leaf and bacterial canker attack through wounds and unpainted pruning cuts. Do not prune in winter and paint all wounds. Apply Liquid Copper, Dithane or Bordeaux Mixture at leaf-fall as a precaution — especially in wet localities.
Brown rot attacks plums and, occasionally, cherries. The fruit turns brown, with white spots. Do not leave any old fruit on the trees over winter as it will be a source of infection the following year. *(See the Section on Diseases. Page 117).*

Denniston's Superb, a good variety for a warm wall, not as vigorous as Victoria.

Morello Cherry, really a cooking variety, it may be eaten fresh when very ripe.

Silver leaf disease, a major problem of plums and cherries.

Morning glory
Ipomoea 'Heavenly Blue'
one of the most beautiful blue flowers.

Jasmine nightshade
Solanum jasminoides
will grow outside in mild areas.

Forest cactus
Epiphyllum ackermannii
light shade and needs frost protection.

Greenhouse Growing

Protective structures

●**Greenhouses.** Greenhouses may be free-standing, or 'lean-to' against a solid wall. If this wall is part of the house itself, the greenhouse becomes a 'conservatory'. A free-standing greenhouse is usually cheaper, and traps more light, but it is more difficult to heat — if this is intended.

●**Frames.** A garden frame is just a large, low, bottomless box with a translucent lid. The sides of the box may be made of wood, concrete, galvanised iron or any other building material — very often scrap will do. The frame may be any length but should not be wider than 4 feet (120cm) for comfort and safety. It should be about 10 inches (25cm) high in front, and about 20 inches (50cm) high at the back. The 'lid' is a number of 'lights', each consisting of a wooden frame with glass or plastic — on it. Each 'light' matches the width of the garden frame in its own length and should be about 30 inches (75cm) wide.

●**Cloches.** French for a bell, a cloche originally was a bell-shaped glass jar placed individually over tender plants. The term was extended to include continuous structures of glass sheets supported by iron brackets. These were about 18 inches (45cm) high, and are nowadays unusual, because plastic tunnels have taken over.

●**Walk-in tunnels.** The 'walk-in' tunnel substitutes for a glasshouse. Being cheaper to put up, it is possible to cover a larger area for similar, or less, expense. They may be made any length — simply use a greater number of the tubular steel supporting hoops. They are generally sold as kits and the standard widths commercially available are 14 feet (4.2m) and 17 feet (5.1m). Walk-in tunnels can be difficult to ventilate properly, and the plastic has to be replaced every two or three years.

●**Low tunnels.** These are simply a row of wire hoops, 18 inches (45cm) high, 30 inches (75cm) wide, supporting a 6 feet (1.8m) wide film of polythene. Again, length is not fixed. At each end of the low tunnel the film is tied firmly to a short stake. The hoops are 6 feet (1.8m) lengths of strong wire with an 'eye' twisted into them 9 inches (22.5cm) from each end. Strings tied into each 'eye' and stretched across the polythene hold the tunnel in place.

Although both garden frames and low tunnels are limited in use by their size, they are very successful for low crops such as early and late vegetables, early strawberries, and cuttings.

Glazing materials

●**Glass.** Once the only available material, glass is still the best, letting in light and retaining heat better than any alternative. It is more expensive and not as safe as plastics, but it lasts much longer. Safety glass is available, however, and though it is more expensive again than ordinary glass, it might be considered for a conservatory.

●**Rigid plastics.** Not as dear as glass, and safer, but they do not let in as much light; nor do they look as well, except for perspex, but this is expensive, too.

●**Plastic film.** This is usually polythene which is cheap and safe and lets in light but does not last so well. PVC and Ultra-violet inhibited films are more expensive than polythene but last longer.

Heating

A 'cold' greenhouse means that there is no artificial heat. A 'cool' greenhouse has a heating system which will provide some artificial heat — usually just enough to protect against frost. A 'warm' greenhouse has a heating system capable of providing an air temperature of at least 10°C (50°F).

●**Heat conservation.** In an unheated, 'cold' greenhouse it is important to conserve all available heat, but even if a greenhouse is heated, maximum heat conservation will reduce the running cost. Lean-to greenhouses, by having one solid wall, lose less heat because of the lower area of glass. The solid wall acts as a heat reservoir too, heating up by day and releasing this at night. Greenhouses exposed to wind, apart from risking damage, quickly lose heat, especially if there are broken or ill-fitting panes. A layer of polythene inside the greenhouse acts like double glazing to conserve heat but it may not look well. Covering tender plants with newspaper or cloth on frosty nights may be enough to prevent damage.

●**Heating systems.** If basic frost protection is all that is required, there are two options — paraffin or electricity. A simple paraffin heater is relatively cheap to buy, and to run, but needs to be lit and refuelled, and may give off fumes if not set up correctly. An electric fan heater is dearer to buy, but very easy to operate, usually featuring a built-in thermostat. Seek professional advice when installing an electric heater and set it up so that it does not get wet. Running costs for a fan-heater are low, if it is used only for frost protection. A two kilowatt fan-heater will keep a 12 feet (3.6m) by 8 feet (2.4m) greenhouse free of frost on a night when it is minus 8°C (18°F) outside.

Heating a warm greenhouse to about 10°C (50°F) is a more difficult proposition. An extra radiator may be taken off the domestic heating system if the greenhouse is attached, or very close, to the house. Most central heating systems are on a timeswitch which shuts down the system at night — just when the greenhouse needs it most! However, usually enough heat will have built up earlier to protect plants adequately. A thermostat over-riding the timeswitch may be installed to prevent very low temperatures. Electric storage heaters may be used in a conservatory too. These use night-rate electricity and they come on at night, but there must be no danger of them getting wet, for safety reasons. They tend to be bulky too. Free-standing greenhouses are difficult to heat economically beyond basic frost protection. A separate hot-water boiler is ideal, but few people would consider this necessary or affordable.

Ventilation

On a sunny day in summer, greenhouse temperatures could rise above 40°C (104°F). Plants dry out quickly and may be scorched or killed at these temperatures. It will be necessary to allow the hot, dry air to escape. Vents in the roof and sides should be provided. Opening the door helps too. Roof vents are important not only because hot air rises, but also, because it may not be possible to leave side vents or doors open in a conservatory for security reasons.

'Walk-in' plastic tunnels are difficult to ventilate properly, usually relying on leaving the ends open. This is adequate, once the tunnel is not too long.

Siting the greenhouse

To trap as much heat as possible, a greenhouse should be situated in an open, south-facing position without shading from buildings or trees. The ridge of the roof should point east-west. The next best aspect is west because it heats up late in the day, and stays warm longer into the night. An east-facing site goes cool even before sunset and the morning sun can cause damage to plants by too-quick thawing. A north-facing greenhouse, to be of any use, will need artificial heating — even for the usual range of plants. Do not site a greenhouse in a hollow where cold air might seep in, nor in a windy position. Do not forget the strong eddies of wind around a house, though the site may seem sheltered.

Bougainvillea
Bougainvillea glabra
needs room and frost protection.

Fuchsia
Fuchsia 'Swingtime'
beautiful large flowers.

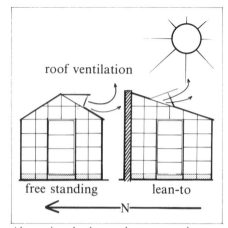
Alternative glasshouse shapes, note the position of the sun, and the roof ventilators.

Skills of greenhouse growing

Plants in a greenhouse need extra care because of the high temperatures and the exclusion of rainfall.

●**Watering.** Watering is a constant demand of greenhouse plants, and in summer, daily watering will often be necessary. Plants in pots need more frequent watering than those growing in the soil. In winter and spring, be careful not to over-water. Wet compost is cold; it stops growth, and may invite root death.

●**Cooling.** Ventilation on hot days is necessary to keep plants cool. About 25°C (77°F) is a maximum for most plants. Beyond that, growth slows down and stops. High temperatures may be reached from late spring onwards. In summer, ventilation alone may not be enough, so shading may be necessary. Apply Coolglass, or Summer Cloud, in June or early July and remove it at the end of August. A simple way of cooling the house on really hot days is to damp down the floor.

Ventilation in winter and spring, on dry, breezy days, dries the greenhouse atmosphere, helping disease control.

●**Feeding.** Greenhouse plants must be fed much more often than plants outdoors. Frequent watering tends to wash the feed from the restricted reserve of a pot. Feed little and often — even as often as once a week for large, quick-growing plants. Liquid feeding is simplest and most effective. Take care not to feed a dry pot, for fear of scorching the roots.

●**Hygiene.** Pest and disease damage is usually more severe in a greenhouse, where conditions are ideal, and predators are absent. Remove old and diseased or pest-ridden plants to break the cycle of infection. Control pests and diseases when they appear. Wash the glass, pots, trays and benches in the winter. Consider soil sterilisation with Basamid, Clean-up or Jeyes Fluid, every few years. Flood the greenhouse soil in early spring to leach out excessive salts left over from frequent feeding.

Greenhouse ornamental plants

A great variety of ornamental plants may be grown in a greenhouse or conservatory. Some of these must have the protection of a greenhouse and some, though they may be grown outdoors, do better inside.

●**Shrubs and climbers.** With the limitations on space, shrubs suitable for greenhouse growing must not be large-size. Climbers are ideal because they may be grown on a wall or trellis out of the way. Suitable shrubs include Hydrangea, Lantana, Abutilon, Oleander, Miniature orange, Camellia, Silk oak and Rose. Some of these, such as Hydrangea and Oleander, should be grown in pots to restrict their size. Good greenhouse climbers include Jasmine, Plumbago, Jasmine nightshade, Lobster claw, Senna, Bougainvillea and, in a heated greenhouse, Stephanotis. Climbers are best planted into the greenhouse soil.

●**Flowers.** A very wide range of herbaceous plants may be grown in the greenhouse. The more usual ones are contained in the List of Twenty Flowering Houseplants (page 65). Some of these are bulbs, corms or tubers such as Gloxinia, Tuberous begonia, Amaryllis and Lily which are potted up in March or April. Freesia, Cyclamen and Anemone may be potted up in August or September. Hyacinth, Tulip, Grape hyacinth, Crocus and Dwarf iris may be potted up in September or October. Most of these plants come into flower about three or four months after potting up.

Many greenhouse flowers may be raised from seed. Cineraria, Primula, Calceolaria and Butterfly flower are sown in June, July or August to flower in March, April or May the following year. Cyclamen is sown in August to flower 15 months later. Quite a few bedding plants, both spring and summer, may be used as flowering pot plants. Petunia, Everflowering begonia, Ageratum, Tobacco flower and French marigolds may be sown in March to flower in

Blackeyed susan
Thunbergia alata
flowers all summer, easy.

Butterfly flower
Schizanthus
good spring/early summer pot plant.

Ageratum
Ageratum houstonianum
makes a good summer houseplant.

summer. Polyanthus and Double daisy are sown in early summer, and Stock in late summer, to flower in spring. Two very valuable greenhouse plants also raised from seed are Morning glory and Blackeyed susan. These are climbers, but they only last one season. Of course, many of the plants on the List of Twenty Foliage Houseplants (page 65) may also be grown in a greenhouse. Shading may be necessary and, in winter, they must have frost protection, or be taken indoors.

●**Alpines.** Demanding little space, alpines make excellent greenhouse plants. They enjoy the dry air, but they must have it cool too, and are best placed near the door or the ventilator. Special alpine houses with a lot of ventilation are sometimes set up by alpine enthusiasts. Just a few of the alpines which enjoy greenhouse conditions are included in the List of Twenty Greenhouse Ornamental Plants, below.

Plumbago flowers all summer and autumn.

List of Twenty Greenhouse Ornamental Plants

Name	Latin Name	Type	Colour	Flowers	Propagation
Jasmine	Jasminum polyanthum	2.5m climber	white	spring	cuttings July
Wax plant	Hoya carnosa	4m climber	white	summer	cuttings July
Plumbago	Plumbago	3.5m climber	blue	April-Nov.	cuttings July
Lobster claw	Clianthus puniceus	3.5m climber	red	late spring	cuttings July
Jasmine nightshade	Solanum jasminoides	4m climber	white	July-Nov.	cuttings July
Senna	Cassia corymbosa	2m climber	yellow	late summer	cuttings July
Morning glory	Ipomoea	2.5m climber	blue	summer	seeds March
Blackeyed susan	Thunbergia	2.5m climber	yellow	summer	seeds March
Hydrangea	Hydrangea paniculatus	.6m shrub	white	early summer	cuttings July
Lantana	Lantana camara	.6m shrub	yellow	all summer	seeds February
Abutilon	Abutilon	1.5m shrub	yellow/red	summer	cuttings July
Oleander	Nerium oleander	2.5m shrub	white/pink	all summer	cuttings July
Mini orange	Citrus mitis	.6m shrub	fruits	all year	seeds March
Silk oak	Grevillea robusta	2.5m shrub	foliage	all year	seeds April
Camellia	Camellia	2m shrub	pink/red	March/April	cuttings July
Roses (large-flowered)	Rosa	1m shrub	various	April/May	potted in November
Rock jasmine	Androsace	10cm alpine	pink	late spring	potted in April
Lewisia	Lewisia	20cm alpine	pink	late spring	potted in June
Gentian	Gentiana	10cm alpine	blue	late summer	potted in March
Rhodohypoxis	Rhodohypoxis	8cm alpine	pink	summer	potted in April

Greenhouse fruit

●**Grapes.** A grapevine may be grown in any size of greenhouse, but the bigger the better. 'Black Hamburg' is the best variety for Irish conditions. Planting is usually done in December with the root outside the greenhouse and the vine taken in through a hole in the lowest wall. This reduces watering needs.

Train the vine to grow up into the roof of the greenhouse. First, train it up to gutter height. Then train a single shoot along the wall at this height. When it reaches the other end, allow side-shoots to grow up the roof on wires, tied into place 12 inches (30cm) apart. From these side-shoots, which form permanent rods, come the flowering shoots. These arise every 12 inches (30cm) or so. Allow only one shoot to develop at each station and pinch out its tip one or two leaves past the flower bunch. Tap the rods each day, during flowering, to ensure pollination. Pinch out subsequent side-shoots at one leaf.

Mulch the root each spring with well rotted manure. Use some general fertiliser as well, if growth is weak or after a heavy crop. Watch for red spider mite. The main diseases are powdery mildew and grey mould. Spraying with Benlate in May and June helps. Prune out the fruit-carrying shoots in autumn when the fruit is picked, leaving the main rod framework.

Bunch of grapes sizing up nicely in July, note the correct training method.

Indoor peaches ripe in July, very reliable once pollination is carried out.

Melons in a frame ripen in August, the variety is Sweetheart, an easy one to grow.

Strawberries in low polythene tunnel in May, Cambridge Vigour is the variety.

●**Peaches.** Closely related to these are nectarines and apricots, and they may all be grown in the greenhouse, as fan-trained trees on a wall. Planted into the soil, train them by tying their branches to wires set 12 inches (30cm) apart. Pollinate the flowers by hand, using a child's paintbrush. If a lot of fruit sets, thin them out to about 6 inches (15cm) apart. When the fruit is picked, prune out the shoots which have carried fruit and tie in the new ones.

In the spring, when the buds break, rub away excess young growth, leaving only enough to replace the fruiting shoots and maintain the branch framework. These trees always produce too many shoots. Never let the roots go completely dry. Use a mulch and water as necessary. Watch out for red spider mite and spray with Sybol, Malathion or Liquid Derris, if necessary.

●**Melons.** Sow seeds singly in little pots in late March or April. Plant them into rich greenhouse soil, pots or growing-bags when they are about 6 inches (15cm) high, in May. Pinch out the growing-point. Side-shoots then develop. Retain the two strongest and train them up strings by twisting them around. Further side-shoots will be produced from the two chosen. These are the fruiting shoots. When the flowers appear and open, take a male flower, peel away its petals and push it gently into the female flower, which may be recognised by the tiny fruit just behind the petals. Pinch out the side-shoot one or two leaves past the young developing fruit. Allow only one melon to develop per fruiting side-shoot. Feed and water well once the fruit starts to swell. 'Ogen' and 'Sweetheart' are good varieties. Melons may be grown on the ground in a frame or low tunnel. Watch out for red spider mite and spray with Liquid Derris on a dull day as soon as it is noticed. Repeat spraying will be necessary.

●**Strawberries.** Easiest of the greenhouse fruits, they are only temporary residents. In August, plant strong runners 12 inches (30cm) apart outdoors in good soil. In October, lift the plants and carefully pot them in 6-inch pots. Leave the pots outdoors until the middle of January and then bring them into the greenhouse, or frame. When the plants begin to grow, check them for greenfly and spray, if necessary. Depending on the heat available they will flower in March/April and fruit in April/May.

Alternatively, the plants may be covered, where they were planted, by a low tunnel to fruit in May/June. Plants 'forced' under glass or plastic may be grown on outdoors, but are not worth forcing again.

Spray against grey mould with Benlate, Fungus Fighter or Murphy's Systemic Fungicide at first flower, and again a fortnight later.

Greenhouse vegetables

●**Tomatoes.** Sow seeds in February for planting in April in a 'cool' greenhouse, a month later for 'cold' greenhouse growing. Suitable varieties are 'Alicante' and 'Moneymaker'. 'Big Boy' is a beef tomato variety. Sow three seeds to a 3-inch (8cm) pot and retain the strongest seedling. When the first flower truss is just showing in the top of the plants, move them to their final position in the greenhouse, planting direct into the soil, pots or growing-bags. If plants are purchased, buy only strong, bushy ones, all at the same stage of growth. Water sparingly until established. Do not feed until the first fruit is the size of a pea. Tap the flowers gently, to encourage pollination.

Feed the plants twice a week and keep the roots just moist. This is especially important for plants in pots or growing-bags, to avoid blossom-end rot which is a hard, brown sunken area at the base of the fruit. If plants growing in the soil continue to wilt despite proper watering, it is a sign of root rot disease. The soil will need to be replaced to a depth of 10 inches (25cm), or sterilised with Basamid, Clean-up or Jeyes Fluid when the crop is removed. This disease is quite common when tomatoes have been grown for a few years, especially bought-in plants.

Train tomato plants up strings by twisting them around the string which is tied at the bottom of the plant. Remove all side-shoots and remove the top of the plant in early August. Keep up the feeding to swell this late fruit. Fruit not ripe at the end of September should be picked and placed in shallow trays in a warm room to ripen. Watch for greenfly, red spider mite and whitefly, and spray as necessary.

●**Cucumbers.** Sow seeds singly in pots in April. Good varieties include 'Pepita' and 'Femspot'. In a 'cold' greenhouse, plant out the young plants in mid-May. One or two plants provide enough cucumbers for most people's needs. Plant into soil enriched with plenty of organic material, or into growing-bags. Be careful when watering, to keep the stem at soil level dry, to prevent stem rot. Watch for red spider mite from the first few weeks and spray with Liquid Derris or Malathion when they are noticed.

Train cucumbers up strings, as described for tomatoes. Remove all side-shoots and flowers from the bottom 2 feet (60cm) of stem, retaining only those that develop over 2 feet (60cm). Allow one fruit to form on each side-shoot before pinching it out at one or two leaves beyond the fruit. When the plant reaches the roof, let it trail back down again. Feed and water regularly.

●**Peppers.** These are closely related to Aubergines (Eggplant) the two being grown in the same way. Sow seeds in early March. Plant the seedlings into good greenhouse soil, pots or growing bags, in May. Support the plants with a cane. No training is needed. Six to eight peppers and four to six aubergines may be expected per plant. Delay feeding until the first fruit has set, and then feed twice a week. Watch for greenfly and red spider mite, and look out in particular for greenfly on the aubergines and red spider mite on the peppers.

●**Sweetcorn.** Only reliable in a warm summer outdoors in Irish conditions, sweetcorn is not worth growing under protection unless where plenty of space is available, as for example, in a 'walk-in' tunnel. Sow seeds in late March, either direct into the greenhouse soil or into small pots, for planting five weeks later at a 15 inch (37.5cm) spacing. 'Earliking' and 'First of All' are good varieties.

When the silky tassels, which are the female flowers, appear, the plants should be shaken gently, each day, to ensure pollination. The cobs are ready for picking when a milky juice can be pressed out of the seeds. There are no major pests — except slugs and snails when the plants are small.

●**Lettuce.** Greenhouse-grown lettuce is of better quality than outdoor crops and it is available from November to May when they are not. Sow the variety 'Kwiek' in late August for winter lettuce, and 'Emerald' and 'Kloek' in September/October for late winter and spring supplies. These varieties tolerate cold weather, but without frost protection at least, there may be some losses and the plants will not 'heart' up. Watch for greenfly. Do not splash water about or grey mould will attack some of the plants at soil level. Lettuce may also be grown in frames or in low tunnels.

Other crops

Early and late season supplies of carrots may be had from the greenhouse, frame or low tunnel. Sow 'Early Nantes' or 'Amsterdam Forcing' in December or January for supplies in late May and June. A late sowing of the same varieties in August gives a December crop.

White turnips, broccoli, radish, scallions and parsley may be grown under protection too. Sowing can start in January in a cold greenhouse or frame, December in a cool greenhouse. Delay sowing until early February under low tunnels but put up the tunnels about three weeks before sowing.

Florence fennel and chinese cabbage are two crops which are difficult to get right outdoors — they both have a tendency to bolt if the weather is not warm and moist. Sow florence fennel in late March and chinese cabbage in May. Keep both well-watered to prevent bolting.

Early and late potatoes may be produced under protection. Planted in December or January they will be ready in May.

Cucumbers developing nicely, note how the plant is twisted up the string.

Carrots in late May from a frame, the variety is Amsterdam Forcing sown in January.

Early potatoes get a boost from a low polythene tunnel, note how the tunnel is set up.

Houseplants

Gloxinia
Sinningia 'Emperor Frederick'
beautiful flowering houseplant.

Types

Houseplants may be grown for their foliage or flowers, or both.

●**Foliage plants**. These are probably the longest lasting houseplants, often surviving very many years. They are grown both for the colour and shape of the foliage, and the overall shape of the plant itself.

●**Flowering plants.** These may be very short-lived — just one step up from cut flowers, or they may be quite long-lived. Some types, such as Cineraria and Primula, are disposed of after flowering finishes; some, such as Begonia and Cyclamen, have a bulb or tuber which is retained to flower again; and others, such as Geranium and Azalea which stay green and leafy after flowering, are grown on as foliage plants until they flower again.

Light

Most indoor situations have some light. This ranges from very little to quite a lot — even within an average-sized room. There are plants to suit any situation where daylight reaches.

●**Low light.** Gloomy hallways and corridors are obvious low-light situations, but the side of a room away from the window, and any part of a north-facing room, are low light situations too. Some plants tolerate, and a few even enjoy, these conditions. Ferns of all types are obvious candidates for these positions, being shade-lovers. Generally, plants with dark green leaves tolerate poor light. The extra chlorophyll is an adaptation enabling them to trap whatever light is going. Aspidistra, Sweetheart vine, Devil's ivy, Creeping fig, Mother-in-law's tongue, Kangaroo vine, Kentia palm and Parlour palm will grow in poor light. *(See also the List of Houseplants. Page 65).*

Flame nettle
Coleus 'Dragon Sunset'
foliage can be colourful.

In really poor light situations, leave the plants in position for only a couple of months at a time, rotating them between good light and dull conditions. Otherwise consider installing artificial lighting of sufficient power to allow plants to grow in shaded corners. The lights should be aimed at the plants, and placed fairly close to them. Use 'cool' lights which will not scorch the leaves.

●**Good light.** The majority of houseplants need good light, such as the window-sill of an east, or west-facing room and near, but not on, the window-sill of a south-facing room.

Flowering houseplants, variegated foliage plants and green foliage plants all need good light — the needs of flowering plants being greatest and those of green foliage plants least. Follow this order of priorities in placing plants in the available good light situations.

●**Bright light.** Many houseplants cannot tolerate the very bright light in south-facing windows and porches. Some plants revel in it though — Geraniums, Cacti, Succulents, Yucca and Bougainvillea.

●**Too little light.** Green foliage plants tend to go pale and variegated foliage plants tend to go green if there is too little light. Flowering plants flower badly, or not at all. Plants become lanky, with smaller leaves on long leaf stalks and with bigger gaps in between, and they turn towards the source of whatever light there is. Danger time is winter and spring.

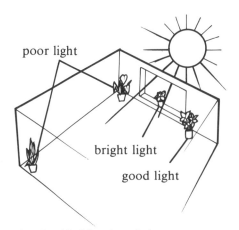

poor light

bright light

good light

Light is critical for plants indoors, match the available light to plant requirements.

● **Too much light.** Fading is the tell-tale sign of too much light. Flowers lose their colour and often dry out at the edges of the petals. Foliage plants often fade to yellowish green, and variegated plants, though they enjoy some sun, may fade to whitish yellow. Ferns go brown from scorching, and other plants may develop brown spots on the leaves too. Danger time is summer.

Heat

Although houseplants need warmth for growth, the main concern is to provide conditions warm enough for healthy survival through winter. Many houseplants come through in such bedraggled condition that they are thrown out. Because indoor temperatures are usually higher than outdoors, most of the plants used as houseplants are native to warm climates. If certain minimum temperatures are not maintained, they suffer.

● **Heated rooms.** The living-room and kitchen are generally maintained at about 16° to 18°C (60° - 64°F) all year round. In summer, temperatures will rarely go above 25°C (77°F), and this is ideal. In winter, these heated rooms are prime locations for the plants which need a reasonably high minimum temperature — Stephanotis, Anthurium, Bird of Paradise flower, African violet, Croton and Finger aralia.

● **Partly heated rooms.** Rooms which are heated for part of the day in winter are suitable for the majority of houseplants. The temperature usually stays above 10° to 12°C (50° - 54°F), and this is adequate for most houseplants. Flowering houseplants stay in flower longer in cool conditions.

● **Unheated rooms.** Rooms which are not heated at all are suitable for only a limited range of houseplants. Temperatures often fall to 5°C (41°F) in such rooms, and even close to freezing on occasion. These are harsh conditions for houseplants and many types will lose condition. Plants which can survive in unheated rooms include Geraniums, Rubber plant, Fatsia, Ivy, Silk oak, Spider plant, Mother of thousands, Cacti and Succulents, Cyclamen, Primula and Cape primrose. Note, that behind the curtains of unheated rooms, plants may be exposed to frost. Freezing conditions often occur in greenhouses and conservatories in winter, and since very few houseplants can survive sub-zero temperatures, greenhouses are not suitable for overwintering houseplants, unless artificially heated.

● **Too much heat.** Excess heat is usually localised — caused by heaters or radiators. Any plant in direct contact with a heat source will be scorched and, even though the heater may be some distance away, brown marks could still appear on the leaves nearest to the source. If the air in the room is generally too warm, brown edges often develop on the leaves over a period of time.

● **Too little heat.** The main symptom of this problem is leaf drop. Plants drop leaves for several reasons — too much water, too little water, root damage, old age — but in winter, if leaves drop off suddenly, it is usually from cold. They are often still green when they fall. Some plants sacrifice part of the leaf, which later goes brown. Many plants can adapt to low temperatures over a period, but even normally hardy plants may suffer if they get a sharp shock. This may be caused by a sudden move from a warm room to a cold one, or by draughts causing low temperatures at floor level. Avoid sudden changes and, if plants are suffering, move them for a while to a warm room to recover. A first sign of trouble, very often, is listless appearance — a slight droopy look — not quite wilting. Plants can tolerate cool conditions better if they are getting good light, and are not over-watered.

Water

Water is a critical need of houseplants for growth, and for keeping cool by transpiration — the plant version of sweating. It follows that more water is needed in the warm months. Water is lost from the compost in the pot, and through the pot itself if it is clay.

Everflowering begonia
Begonia 'Devon Gems'
will grow in an unheated room.

Croton
Codiaeum 'Reidii'
needs a heated room in winter.

Bellflower
Campanula isophylla
thrives in an unheated room.

The 'Touch Rule' is a simple test. Place a finger firmly on the compost in the pot. If it feels dry and hard, the plant may need water; if it feels cool and soft, the plant has enough moisture; if it feels cool and wet and moisture remains on the skin, the plant is over-watered.

●**Summer needs.** In the growing season, from April to September, houseplants should be kept nicely moist, as per the 'Touch Rule'. Large plants need more water than small plants, especially if they are confined to too small a pot. Plants in warm, bright situations need more water than those in cool, dull positions. Certain types of plant need less water — those with thick, waxy, shiny or hairy leaves conserve water better than those with fine, soft foliage. Taking all these factors into account, houseplants generally need watering every day to every seven days during the growing period.

●**Winter needs.** In the October to March period, houseplants need only a fraction of their summer requirements. Using the 'Touch Rule', keep the plants between moist and dry — certainly not wet. Ideally, the compost should be dry on the surface and moist just below. Plants maintained like this resist cold and disease much better.

Watering will be necessary only every seven to thirty days in winter. The winter flowering houseplants make an exception to the general guideline. Cyclamen, Azalea, Poinsettia, Potmums and Christmas cactus should be kept just moist in winter.

●**How to water.** The method of watering has an influence on the frequency. Soaking the pots to half their depth in a basin of water will ensure that a full complement of water is absorbed. Allow to drain afterwards. Plants watered by this method need less frequent watering. Watering from the top of the pot is easier because the plants may be watered in situ. Fill the rim space with water. If it soaks away quickly, fill it again. It can be quite difficult to re-wet dried out pots by this method as much of the water escapes between the compost and the pot. A compromise is to soak-water every third or fourth watering during the growing season. In winter, top-watering is probably best, because a full soak-watering might leave the compost too wet, with less prospect of drying quickly enough.

Always use water at room temperature, as cold water may cause plants to drop their leaves. Use only 'soft' water for Azaleas, Camellias and indoor Heathers. If the water supply is hard — 'fur' in the kettle — use rainwater, or melted water from defrosting the fridge.

●**Misting.** The indoor atmosphere may be quite dry. Many houseplants, being forest floor plants in their native habitats, enjoy some humidity in the air, especially ferns and large-leaved, non-waxy foliage plants. It is most beneficial during the warm months, but plants in dry, central-heated rooms in winter benefit too. Do not mist plants in sunshine, as it may cause scorching.

●**Too much water.** Wet compost is cold, and this slows down or even stops growth. New leaves may be small and weak. In winter, cold, wet compost exhausts the plant's food reserves, leaves turn yellow and fall off, or parts of leaves turn brown — often without drying out. It is very common for entire plants to die if rotting of the roots follows over-watering. A heavy pot is a good indicator of too much water.

●**Too little water.** Wilting is the most dramatic manifestation of water shortage. The plant cells, empty of moisture, deflate like a balloon and rigidity goes from the leaves and soft stems. Following wilting, plants seem to recover upon watering, but later, brown patches often develop. Plants running frequently short of water, even without wilting, suffer considerably, because parts of the root system may die. Growth will be affected — new leaves will be small. Flowering may be hastened but the flowers tend to be small and often shrivel without opening. Plants look 'hard' — often with a blueish or greyish tinge. A light pot is a good indicator of dry compost, even though the surface looks moist.

Cape primrose
Streptocarpus hybridus
will survive in an unheated room.

Two methods of watering pots, each has its advantages.

Living stones
Lithops
a curiosity houseplant.

Feeding

Houseplants depend entirely on whatever nutrients are in the compost, or are added to it subsequently. Potting composts have enough food for about two months. After that, plants must be fed for continued good growth.

●**When to feed.** Since plants only need food when actually growing, they need only be fed during the growing period from April to September. Food in the winter may even be detrimental, causing damage to the roots. Plants which flower in winter are the exception — they should be fed up to, and during, the time they are in flower. Food needs vary greatly. Some of the larger leaved plants need considerably more than Ferns or Cacti, for example. Flowering plants need regular feeding, especially when in bud.

A good rule of thumb for feeding is to put feed in every third or fourth watering. Never feed a dry pot. To avoid this, follow the watering system suggested earlier — soak-water once in three or four waterings and put feed in the next watering after the soaking. This feeding system will give a feed at least every three or four weeks in summer. Do not exceed the recommended dose.

●**Which feeds.** Soluble feeds are easy to use and safe to the plant; solid fertilisers too easily lead to overfeeding. It is best to stick to special houseplant feeds. There are many brands: Phostrogen, Kerigrow, Baby Bio, Hygeia Plant Food, Miracle Gro, Algoflash, KAL, and J. Arthur Bowers. Some brands are high in nitrogen — the first figure in the analysis given on the packet or bottle, for instance 10:2:4. These are suitable for foliage plants. Flowering plants need a more balanced feed, such as 7:7:7 or 5:4:4. Since most houseplants are grown in peat composts, it is an advantage to use a feed which contains trace elements, otherwise plants may run short. Using slow release plant food tablets, or spikes, reduces the frequency of feeding.

●**Too much feed.** In extreme cases, too much feed can cause a plant to wilt and die, especially where applied to a dry pot. Constant over-feeding may cause stunting and brown edges to the leaves. Sometimes, over-feeding causes rapid, dark-green leafy growth, often at the expense of flowering, especially Geraniums. Over-feeding may give rise to a white salt deposit on the compost surface. However, in a 'hard' water area, this simply may be lime.

●**Too little feed.** Plants look sickly. Growth is poor with small, pale leaves. Often, the leaves have yellowish blotches, or markings, between the veins. Flowers sometimes have poor colour, and the flower heads are small. Stems and leaves may take on a purple tinge, especially in peat composts. Older leaves, or young leaves, may go yellow, and fall off or shrivel. Stems are spindly.

Air

Plants need air for the gases it contains — carbon dioxide for growth, oxygen for efficient root action. Air sometimes delivers gases and dust which plants do not need.

●**Carbon dioxide.** This is about the only need of houseplants which is automatically taken care of. In fact, human breathing increases carbon dioxide levels to the benefit of plants. The old notion that plants in the bedroom are unhealthy, is not true. Plants marginally increase the carbon dioxide level at night, having reduced it during the day — another person sleeping in the same room increases the carbon dioxide level many times more.

●**Oxygen.** Plants need oxygen at the roots for the uptake of nutrients. Without oxygen, nutrients leak back out of the roots, causing them to die, and eventually rot. They actually drown. This will not happen if the compost is open enough to let air containing oxygen down to them. Compaction and waterlogging block the passage of air in the compost.

●**Fumes.** The air in a house often carries fumes arising from gas or oil heaters or cookers, or from solvents in cleaning fluids, polishes or aerosols. Some of these fumes are capable of damaging plants, even in very low concentrations.

Poinsettia
Euphorbia pulcherrima
drops its leaves if it gets chilled.

Indoor azalea
Rhododendron indicum
dislikes a very warm room.

Primula
Primula obconica
flowering plant for unheated rooms.

Blushing bromeliad
Neoregelia carolinae tricolor
beautiful foliage plant.

Dumb cane
Dieffenbachia
needs a warm room in winter.

Houseplants need regular feeding, especially flowering types like this **Pendulous begonia**.

Polka-dot plant showing the correct stage for moving to a bigger pot — but not too big.

Symptoms include brown spots, which may appear long after the fumes are gone, and leaves falling suddenly.

●**Dust.** Air-borne dust is another pollutant that affects plants. House air invariably carries a lot of dust from open fires, clothing and furnishings and even smoking. A thick layer of dust not only spoils the look of the plant but it blocks already scarce light. Leaves should be cleaned, from time to time, but especially at the start of the growing season, by spraying with clean water, or sponging large leaves. Leaf shine products, such as Bio Leaf Shine and Kerishine, may be used to enhance the shine of leaves, but only on naturally shiny-leaved plants. Never use household polish, cleaners, oil or milk on houseplants.

Pots and potting

All indoor plants are grown in a pot or container of some sort. The compost in the pot provides a medium for supplying moisture and nutrients, and it also supplies anchorage for the plant. As plants grow, they need to be moved into larger pots.

●**Pots.** Very many different types of pots are available. The traditional clay pot has lost out somewhat to the cheaper, lighter plastic pots. However, clay pots look well and last better than plastic pots, many of which have a tendency to split after a few years use. Plastic pots are available in a range of colours and black and green ones set off certain plants very well. Plants in plastic pots do not dry out as quickly as those in clay pots. This is usually an advantage, but not always — in summer, it helps to avoid damage through water shortage, but in winter, may cause damage through water-logging. Glazed clay pots are expensive, but they are very ornamental, and they also avoid excessive moisture loss.

Pots are available in many shapes. Choose one which matches the growth habit of the plant. If a plant is tall, a tall pot will only accentuate its height. However, a weeping, or trailing plant looks well in a tall pot. Avoid using narrow-bottomed pots, because they have the disadvantage of adding height without adding much by way of extra volume of compost, and they are more inclined to topple over at a touch.

●**Compost.** Ordinary soil is not suitable for houseplants because frequent watering eventually cakes it into a hard mass, which admits neither water nor air. An open compost is necessary for houseplants, and this means peat-based or containing a fair proportion of peat. Peat-based composts include Shamrock Seed and Potting Compost, Erin Potting Compost, Bio Potting Compost and Levington Compost. Use lime-free compost, Brown Gold, for lime-haters.

These purchased composts, besides being convenient, are practically sterile— that is there is little risk of pests, diseases or weeds. It is possible to make excellent, cheap composts from peat, sand and soil. (*See the Section on Garden Skills for details. Page 73*).

●**Potting.** Soak-water the plant before potting. If the new pot is clay, soak it too. If an old pot is used, wash off all traces of old potting compost. Place a piece of broken pot, or a flat stone, over the drainage hole if it is large. Put some moist compost into the pot. Knock the plant out of the old pot and test it for depth in the new one. Set it deep enough to allow $\frac{3}{4}$ to 1 inch (2 - 2.5cm) of rim space for watering, and $\frac{1}{4}$ to $\frac{1}{2}$ inch (1 - 1.5cm) to cover the existing rootball with new compost. The bigger the pot the greater should be the rim space. Fill in around the rootball with new compost and firm gently. Clean the sides of the pot and soak-water it before returning the plant to its position. Keep plants out of direct sunlight for a few days after potting.

March/April is the best time for potting because plants get the full benefit of the growing season. However, potting may continue through the summer until

August. Avoid potting in September or October. There is generally no advantage in potting this late — plants will be fine until the start of the next growing season. Besides, with late season potting, there is a risk of root rots during the winter months.

●**How often?** Plants need to be re-potted when they outgrow their pots, which depends on the vigour of the plant. Every two or three years is enough for most, once they have been fed regularly. The best indication of a need for re-potting is when a plant dries out its pot very quickly after watering. Move gradually up through the pot sizes — do not put small plants in large pots.

Pests

Houseplants are attacked by quite a few pests which appreciate warm, dry air, soft growth and the absence of predators.

Greenfly. The most common houseplant pest, greenfly, may appear on any plant at any time of year. Black, sooty moulds may grow on the greenfly excretions.

Red spider mite. These cause yellowing and curling of leaves and are difficult to control. Busy lizzie is often attacked.

Whitefly. When an affected plant is touched, tiny white flies fly out. Though not as common as the other two, whitefly can cause severe stunting too.

Scale insects. Protected by waxy scales, these sap-suckers can reduce growth and cause leaf-fall.

Among the specific houseplant insecticides are included Derris, Malathion, Tumblebug, Kerispray, Bio Sprayday and Picket. Take the plants outdoors for spraying, and spray all affected plants at the same time to avoid re-infestation. Repeat if necessary. Alternatively, plants may be immersed, pot and all, in a bucket of diluted spray material. Use rubber gloves. Scale insects may be controlled by dabbing with cotton wood dipped in methylated spirits. Avoiding the need to spray, paper spikes containing insecticide, called Plant Pins, are pushed into the compost. The insecticide is taken up by the roots and travels in the sap to the leaves. Always check new plants for pests before purchasing.

Caterpillars and **earwigs** sometimes eat holes in houseplant leaves. Affected plants are usually near an open window. Damage is usually slight and not worth controlling.

Vine weevil. The white grubs of this pest eat the roots of many houseplants, especially Cyclamen and woody plants. The adult weevil crawls into the house and lays eggs in the compost. Sudden wilting, although plants have been watered, and the presence of white grubs in the compost are the usual indicators. Drenching the affected pots with Hexyl, or mixing Murphy's BHC Dust into the compost before potting, gives reasonable control.

Midges. Tiny black flies crawling on the surface of the compost are often taken as pests. They do not harm the plants and are an indication of over-watered compost. (*See the Section on Pests. Page 112*).

Diseases

Root-rot. The most common disease of houseplants, this is usually caused by over-watering, and using unsterilised soil. Affected plants usually die.

Leaf and **Stem-rots.** These are caused by various fungi, but mainly *Botrytis*. Avoid over-watering or misting in the dormant season. Place plants in a warmer, brighter place. If they do not recover, discard them. (*See the Section on Diseases. Page 117*).

Plume flower
Celosia plumosa
a disposable, summer houseplant.

Busy lizzie
Impatiens
new indoor types are remarkable.

Red spider mite symptoms, this is a serious pest of all indoor plants.

List of Twenty Foliage Houseplants

Name	Latin Name	Light requirements	Minimum winter temp.	Size
Grape ivy	*Rhoicissus*	some shade	unheated room	large
Castor oil plant	*Fatsia*	some shade	unheated room	large
Cast iron plant	*Aspidistra*	some shade	unheated room	medium
Prayer plant	*Maranta*	some shade	unheated room	small
Ivy	*Hedera helix*	some shade	unheated room	small
Creeping fig	*Ficus pumila*	some shade	unheated room	small
Devil's ivy	*Scindapsus*	some shade	partly heated	medium
Parlour palm	*Neanthe bella*	some shade	partly heated	medium
Sweetheart vine	*Philodendron*	some shade	partly heated	large
Mother in law's tongue	*Sansevieria*	shade or sun	unheated room	medium
Begonia	*Begonia rex*	good light	partly heated	small
Bromeliads	(Various)	good light	partly heated	small
Ferns	(Various)	good light	unheated room	small
Mother of thousands	*Saxifraga*	good light	unheated room	small
Wandering jew	*Tradescantia*	good light	unheated room	small
Spider plant	*Chlorophytum*	good light	unheated room	small
Croton	*Codiaeum*	good light	heated room	medium
Rubber plant	*Ficus elastica*	bright/sunny	partly heated	large
Weeping fig	*Ficus benjamina*	bright/sunny	partly heated	large
Succulents	(Various inc. *Yucca*)	bright/sunny	unheated room	small

'some shade' means these plants tolerate low light but will grow better in good light.
'good' means bright light but only a little direct sunshine.
'sunny' means a south-facing window.
'heated', 'partly heated', 'unheated' describes the amount of heating in winter.
'size' means the usual plant size.

List of Twenty Flowering Houseplants

Name	Light requirements	Minimum winter temp.	Colours	Aftercare
Cineraria	bright	unheated room	red/blue	discard
Primula	bright	partly heated	pink/mauve	discard
Calceolaria	bright	partly heated	yellow/orange	discard
Schizanthus	bright/sunny	partly heated	mixed	discard
Potmum	bright/sunny	partly heated	mixed	plant outdoors
Hippeastrum	bright	partly heated	pink/red	retain bulb
Begonia	bright	partly heated	pink/red	retain tuber
Gloxinia	bright	heated room	red/purple	retain tuber
Cyclamen	bright	partly heated	pink/red	retain tuber
Hyacinth	bright	partly heated	mixed	plant outdoors
Jasmine	bright/sunny	unheated room	white	grow on
Ageratum	bright/sunny	partly heated	blue	discard
Poinsettia	bright	partly heated	red/white	grow on
Fuchsia	bright	partly heated	red/purple	grow on
Azalea	bright	unheated room	pink/red	grow on
Streptocarpus	bright	unheated room	pink/blue	grow on
Geranium	sunny	unheated room	pink/red	grow on
Busy lizzie	bright/sunny	unheated room	pink/white	grow on
African violet	bright	heated room	pink/blue	grow on
Cacti	sunny	unheated room	red/yellow	grow on

'Light requirements' and 'Minimum winter temperature' as for List of Foliage Houseplants.

'Colours' mean usual colour range.   'Aftercare' means treatment after flowering: 'plant outdoors' means plant in the garden.

Soils, Plant Nutrients and Fertilisers

Soil

●**Composition.** Soil is composed of a complex variety of materials, some of which come from the actions of weather on rock, and some from living sources.

The material which comes from rock includes stones, sand, silt and clay. Stones and sand are fairly obvious contents, silt and clay less so. Silt is made of very fine particles and would compare to the finest powder. Clay is composed of very fine particles too, but it is the result of the chemical decay of rocks as much as their physical breakdown. Clay is chemically active, which means that it can bind strongly to itself, and to other soil constituents. It bonds sand and silt together into tiny soil particles. The presence of a lot of clay causes too much binding, and the soil becomes a hard, lumpy mass.

The material from the decay of once-living organisms — both plant and animal — arises when plants and animals die and the remains are food for bacteria, fungi

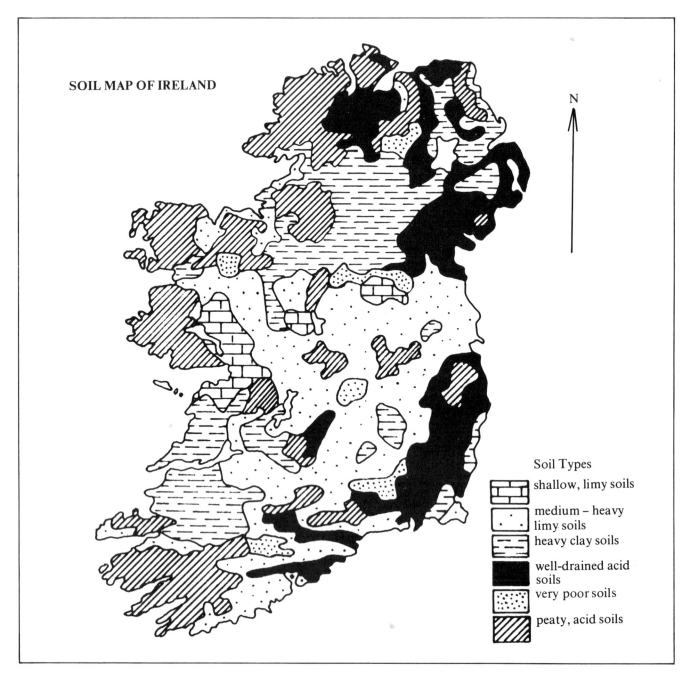

SOIL MAP OF IRELAND

N

Soil Types

shallow, limy soils

medium – heavy limy soils

heavy clay soils

well-drained acid soils

very poor soils

peaty, acid soils

and algae in the soil. These, in turn, die and become food for other tiny organisms. The cycle continues until the original dead plant tissue is broken down into tough, insoluble materials such as waxes, resins and gums. Mixed closely together, those materials, dark-brown in colour, are collectively called 'humus'. Humus, like clay, is chemically active and bonds itself to other soil constituents almost like an adhesive. Apart from stones, sand, silt, clay, dead plant and animal material, living organisms and humus, soil also contains air and water, and plant nutrients released by the decay of rock material and organic material.

●**Soil types.** Soils are described according to their main constituents. Thus, soil with a lot of sand is a sandy soil; soil with a lot of clay is a clay soil; and soil with a lot of organic material is an organic soil. Because this is usually peat, it is generally called peaty soil.

If soil has a good balance of all the important constituents — sand, silt, clay and organic material, but no preponderance of any one of them, it is called a 'loam'. It might tend a little towards sand or clay and this would define it as a 'sandy loam' or 'clay loam'. Sandy loam might also be called a light loam and clay loam might be called heavy loam. The terms are interchangeable. Some soils contain a lot of stones or shale and may be called stony, or shaly loams.

●**Distribution of soil types.** There are peaty soils and other very poor soils associated with them in parts of many counties in the midlands, west, and north particularly in mountainous areas, but most Irish soils are loams. There are well-drained, sandy or shaly loams in parts of Kerry, East Cork, Waterford, Kilkenny, Carlow, Wexford, Wicklow, Dublin, Louth, Armagh, Down, Derry and Antrim. These are easy soils to work, but need plenty of manure and fertiliser. Parts of these counties, and Tipperary, East Limerick, Kildare, East Galway, Laois, Offaly, East Donegal, Longford, Westmeath, Meath, Sligo and Roscommon, have medium-heavy loam soils. These are generally good, fertile soils, not quite as easy to work, but easier to keep fertile. Counties Westmeath, Meath, Dublin, Roscommon, Longford, North Kildare, West Limerick, Clare, Cavan, Sligo, Monaghan, Tyrone, Fermanagh and Armagh, have clay loam soils which are heavy in varying degree. Most of these are derived from glacial boulder clay deposits and can be stony. They are fairly fertile soils, but often difficult to work and need high potash fertilisers. In counties Sligo, Leitrim, Cavan, Monaghan, Clare, Fermanagh, Tyrone and parts of other counties impeded drainage adds to the heavy nature of the soil, making cultivation difficult and limiting growth.

●**Structure.** The bonding action of humus and clay on the other soil constituents causes soil 'crumbs' to form. These are constantly forming, breaking and reforming because the bond, though strong, is not perfect. The crumbs loosely bond to neighbouring crumbs but because they do not fit tightly together, spaces exist in between. These spaces, or pores, vary in size — the smaller ones fill with water, which sticks to the crumbs and provides a reservoir for plant roots. The larger pores initially fill with water too, but this drains

away and is replaced by air.

Good structure is where there is extensive crumb formation, and the crumbs are arranged so that there is plenty of pore space for water and air. Poor structure exists in a soil where the soil constituents have not formed into crumbs, or have formed into very small, tight crumbs. In this case there will be little or no pore space and, though there will probably be plenty of water, there will be very little air. The result is a heavy, wet, hard and lumpy soil.

●**Improving soil structure.** Practically any soil type can have good or bad structure, depending on the presence or absence of crumb formation. Certain soils however can have good structure even without crumbs. In very sandy soils, the sand particles are large and about the same size as soil crumbs. They fill the function of crumbs, creating plenty of pore space. However, these are nearly all large pores, which drain quickly and, because of the absence of small pores, there is no reservoir of water for plants. These soils tend to dry out very quickly. The addition of humus-forming organic material will create small pore space and improve their moisture-holding capacity. Very peaty soils are almost pure organic material. The fibrous nature of the peat creates both large pore space and small pore space, resulting in soil which is well structured and retains adequate moisture.

Heavy soils with poor structure can be improved by adding sand or organic material. Sand is not nearly as efficient as organic material because it works only by taking the place of soil crumbs. This also means that an awful lot of sand must be added to achieve the same structural effect. Organic material — farmyard manure, garden compost, straw, peat — breaking down into humus, is about ten times as efficient a soil improver as sand, on a weight for weight basis.

Good soil structure develops naturally in well-drained soil by the action of roots, and the build-up of humus. Improving the drainage of wet soil is an important step towards better soil structure.

Removing plant material without adding organic matter back leads to progressive deterioration of soil structure. Walking on wet soil, and cultivating it when wet, quickly destroys the soil crumbs.

●**Soil acidity.** The acidity of a soil depends on the parent material — the rock from which it was formed. Soils over limestone in the Midlands and North Munster, are limy.

Over red sandstone, in South Munster, shale, in Southeast Leinster, and granite, in Wicklow, Kerry, Connemara and Ulster, soils tend to be acid, as are peat soils.

Simple kits are available to test soil acidity. Hydrangeas are good indicator plants — acid; blue flowers; lime; pink.

Plant nutrients

Plants get their food from the soil. Rock material and decaying organic matter contain tiny quantities of the nutrients essential for plant growth. As they are released gradually, they become bonded to clay and humus in the soil. These then act as reservoirs of nutrients, slowly letting them back into the soil solution where plant roots can absorb them easily. This is a second important function of humus and clay.

● **Nutrients.** Plants require considerable quantities of the major nutrients but these tend to be scarce in soil.

Nitrogen (N) is the scarcest of plant nutrients but among the most important, being essential for protein production. Dead plant and animal material, and animal waste, are sources of nitrogen as they break down. Bacteria in nodules on the roots of certain plants — particularly the Pea family — are capable of extracting nitrogen from the air which is 80% nitrogen. Lightning is another source, as it 'knocks' nitrogen from the air. Plants that are short of nitrogen turn pale, yellow-green all over, and produce weak spindly growth. This occurs on soils that are light and dry, low on organic material, or constantly wet. Too much nitrogen causes leafy, green growth, and fewer flowers and fruit. Nitrogen is especially important for grass and leafy vegetables.

Phosphorus (P) is involved in root growth, and the development of buds and growing points. Plants short of phosphorus show stunted growth and a purple tinge to stems and leaves. Deficiency occurs most often on acid soils — especially in high rainfall areas, and in peat composts.

Potash (K) is essential for flower and fruit production, and for balancing out the vigorous leafy growth caused by nitrogen. Plants short of potash tend to be leafy, and often have pale, or brown, margins to the leaves. Deficiency occurs most commonly on light sandy soils, and limy soils.

● **Minor nutrients.** The minor nutrients are not needed in as great quantity, nor are they as scarce.

Calcium (Ca) is important in its own right as a nutrient, apart from its effects on soil acidity and the availability of other nutrients. It is involved in the building of plant structures. Shortage can cause browning within the tissue of plants such as tomatoes, apples and brussels sprouts. Deficiency occurs in peaty soil, acid soil and sandy soil. Apply lime as a remedy.

Magnesium (Mg) is part of chlorophyll, and essential for good growth. Shortage causes yellow 'netting' of the leaves. Deficiency occurs on acid soils, or where too much potash has been given. Apply a spray of Epsom salts.

Iron (Fe), too, is part of chlorophyll. Shortage causes yellow leaves at the growing points. Deficiency is common on limy soils and it is the main reason why lime-hating plants suffer in such soils. Apply Sequestrene.

Boron (B) is closely associated with the actions of calcium in building the structure of plants. Similar symptoms of shortage appear — internal browning of brussels sprouts, swedes, cauliflowers and apples. Shortage occurs on limy soils where boron is bound up by calcium. Apply a spray of borax diluted at one ounce in 2 gallons of water (30g/10 litres) to 10 square yards (10m^2).

● **Other nutrients.** There are other nutrients which are important for plant growth such as manganese, copper and molybdenum, but deficiencies rarely appear because most Irish soils contain adequate amounts. The application of organic material, especially farmyard manure, supplies additional quantities of most of them. Organic material also provides plants with other useful food. As it is broken down, a vast range of chemical compounds is formed — bits of protein, sugars, oils, enzymes and growth-promoting substances. Plants can make these themselves, starting from the basic plant nutrients, but they benefit if they can taken them in, part-formed, as a short-cut.

Fertilisers

● **General fertilisers.** These provide the three major nutrients in correct balance and are suitable for general garden use to improve soil fertility. The formulae vary between the various brands: 7:6:17, 5:5:10, 10:10:20, 7:7:7. General fertilisers include Vegyflor, Growmore, John Innes Base Fertiliser, Potato and Vegetable Fertiliser and Potato Fertiliser.

● **Specific fertilisers.** Again, these provide all the major nutrients but some of the minor ones too, and the balance is set so as to suit the specific needs of certain plants, or groups of plants. Lawn fertilisers, such as Goulding's Lawn Feed Special, Lawnsman Spring Feed, Lawnsman Winterizer, Special Lawn Fertilizer, Lawn Food, Toplawn and Autumn Toplawn are specially balanced for grass growth. The spring lawn feeds suit the spring and summer needs of grass. The autumn feeds suit the autumn and winter needs.

Rose fertilisers, such as Goulding's Rose Fertiliser, Toprose, Rose Food, Rose 'Plus', and Special Rose Fertiliser have matching amounts of nitrogen and potash — nitrogen for growth, potash for flowers. Tomato and fruit fertilisers — Liquid Tomorite, Tomato and Fruit Fertiliser — have a balance towards potash.

● **Straight fertilisers.** These fertilisers contain just one major nutrient. Sulphate of Potash contains just potash; Sulphate of Ammonia, Urea and C.A.N. contain just nitrogen; and Superphosphate contains just phosphorus. These can be used on their own where plants really only need one major nutrient. For example, lawns may not need phosphorus or potash, just nitrogen, so Sulphate of Ammonia (or Urea or C.A.N. on large areas) would do. Fruit trees may not need further boosting by nitrogen, being already too vigorous. So, using just Sulphate of Potash would balance vigorous growth, and encourage fruiting. The straight fertilisers may be mixed together to provide general fertiliser, or any specific formula required.

● **Manures.** These have the dual effect of improving soil structure by adding humus, and improving soil fertility by adding both major and minor plant nutrients. Farmyard manure contains the three major nutrients, and a full range of minor nutrients. Garden compost contains a range of nutrients similar to farmyard manure, but in lesser quantity. Mushroom compost is at least as rich as farmyard manure, but contains a lot of lime. Meat-and-bonemeal contains nitrogen and phosphorus, but no potash. Leafmould has some nitrogen and potash. Wood ash has some potash. Seaweed has considerable quantities of minor nutrients. Peat has very little fertiliser value, and is used solely for its fibrous organic matter. None of these manures has enough fertiliser value to improve soil fertility, unless they are used at high rates. An annual application of 8-10 pounds of farmyard manure per square yard (4-5kg/m^2) is the equivalent of the recommended application of general fertiliser. Usually, fertiliser is used in conjunction with manures. But they should not be mixed. Scorching of plant roots may result.

Tools and Equipment

●**Spade.** The basic gardening tool, it is used for digging, planting, hoeing, shovelling, cutting lawn edges — and even banging in small stakes. Long-handled spades have more leverage when digging, but the short-handled spade encourages the user to grip the handle lower down — more under the load, and to use the leg muscles more. The T-piece, or D-piece on the short-handle type, gives some twisting leverage — a help when turning over spadefuls of soil during digging. Use whatever feels comfortable; for example, tall people do not usually like short-handled spades.

●**Rake.** A rake may be used to make a fine seedbed, to open and close seed-drills, to remove lawn clippings and leaves, to tear out moss and dead grass, and to freshen up gravelled areas and flower beds. Long, even strokes of a rake are best, so a long handle is essential. The head should not be very wide or narrow. The teeth should be straight, or only slightly curved, and set not too far apart.

●**Hoe.** There are basically two types of hoe: push hoe and draw hoe. With a push hoe, the user moves backwards on to the un-hoed ground, and thus avoids walking on the newly-hoed weeds. With a draw hoe, the user moves forward towards the un-hoed ground and walks on the newly-hoed area. However, a draw hoe is easier to use because the pulling action involved is much easier than the pushing action of push hoes. A draw hoe may also be used in a standing position with a sweeping brush action. A good hoe of either type should be of solid material and have a long handle. It is the main weapon in the fight against weeds.

●**Trowel.** A planting trowel is essential for planting bedding and vegetable plants. The handle should be fairly short, and broad and smooth at the end for comfort in the palm of the hand. The blade should come up close to the end of the handle. Ideally, it should be slightly curved — making it easier to take out a planting hole quickly, but not so curved as to have moist soil stick to it. The trowel may also be used to assist hand-weeding. Little hand-forks are useful for this, too.

●**Secateurs.** The secateurs, or pruners, is the basic pruning tool. Essential for roses or fruit trees, it will be needed for flowering shrubs on occasion, too. Secateurs are ideal for dead-heading, and for cutting flowers and foliage for indoor use. The type with curved blades cause less damage to the bark of the pruned stem. Buy a good quality secateurs because, being better designed, they are easier to use, and last longer. A comfortable hand-grip is important.

●**Hedge-clippers.** Essential if there is a hedge to be trimmed, they may also be used to keep lawn edges neat. Hedge-clippers should not be used on shrubs, except in certain cases, such as Heather, Broom and Lavander where there are a lot of shoots close together. It is also useful for trimming rockery perennials after flowering. A big range of

sizes and designs is available. Choose one with a lock-nut assembly, which allows it to be tightened properly.

●**Watering can.** This piece of equipment has a vital role in ensuring the establishment of young plants, especially shrubs. It may also be used for applying weedkillers to paths and lawns. It may be used as a substitute for a sprayer to apply insecticides, but can be a little wasteful of spray chemical. Most watering cans are sold in a 2 gallon (10 litre) size, which is ideal — not too heavy when full. Buy a watering can rose of a fine droplet size, as this is suitable for a wider range of uses, including watering seedlings and applying weedkillers. If the can is used frequently for weed-killing, it might be advisable to have a separate can for that purpose to avoid mishaps.

●**Sprayer.** An essential piece of equipment, particularly if roses or fruit trees are grown. Mainly used for applying insecticides and fungicides, it can also be used for weedkillers, and the application of foliar feeds.

In a small garden, or for houseplants, a small hand-sprayer, or mister, is adequate. For most gardens, a one-gallon (5 litre) sprayer is ideal. Pressurised first and then carried around, it is easy to use and very effective. If the garden is large, with more than a couple of dozen rose

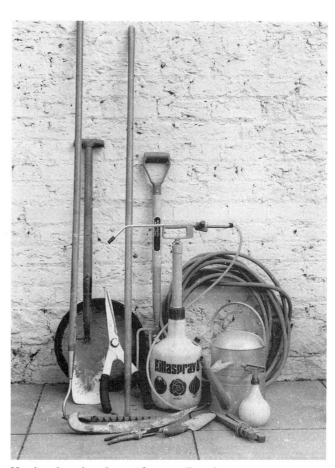

Hand tools and equipment for a small garden.

bushes, half a dozen fruit trees, or a lot of potatoes, a knapsack sprayer would be appropriate. It would hold $3\frac{1}{2}$ to $4\frac{1}{2}$ gallons (15 - 20 litres) and is carried on the back. The spray is pressurised in the course of delivery. Modern knapsack sprayers nearly all have plastic tanks which makes them lighter, and cheaper. Check before buying that a full range of spare parts is available.

●**Garden line.** A simple piece of equipment for getting lines of vegetables, bedding, roses and hedging straight. A good line can be made from coloured nylon builder's line, tied to and wound around two pieces of metal rod or hardwood, about 12 inches (30cm) long.

●**Lawn mower.** This is the most expensive piece of garden equipment — a 'must' in all Irish gardens. For small lawns, up to about 100 square yards (100m²), a push-mower is adequate. Between 100 and 200 square yards (100 - 200m²), an electric mower is ideal. These are cheap and easy to operate. They give a neat finish but should be used regularly because they cannot cope with tall, rough grass. For lawn areas over 200 square yards (200m²), there are large electric rotary mowers which are suitable and cheaper than petrol motor mowers. For large lawns, and lawns with a lot of trees or beds, the cable for electric mowers is inconvenient, and petrol mowers come into their own. Of course, petrol mowers may be used on lawns of any size, even small areas — there is the cost factor but this may be outweighed by speed. In any case, always choose a mower which will do the job comfortably — the lawn is more likely to be cut as often as it should be, and the mower itself will last longer by not being forced beyond its capacity.

'Cylinder' mowers have a cylinder of curved blades which cut the grass by pinching it against a fixed blade. 'Rotary' mowers have a single blade that spins at high speed cutting the grass in the process. Cylinder mowers cut the grass more evenly, leaving a smoother finish, but rotary mowers can take rougher conditions, longer grass and wetter grass. Rotary mowers are not as safe as cylinder mowers, although modern designs have better safety features. The rotary type puts the cut grass more efficiently into a grass-bag — an important point. Grass-bags made of porous material are more efficient at filling.

●**Garden fork.** A garden fork may be used for digging, but is not essential. It is useful for picking up debris such as prunings. For compost-making, it is a tool without which it is difficult to keep the heap tidy.

●**Hose and sprinkler.** Essential in a large garden with a lot of watering to be done, or a garden on dry soil. Very handy attachments such as reels are available.

●**Lopping shears.** Useful if a lot of roses, or fruit bushes are grown. It will deal with branches too large for the secateurs, because it gives the user more leverage.

●**Edging shears.** Useful if there is a lot of lawn edging to be cut around flower beds and pathways. Their long handles make this job easier on the back.

●**Riddle.** Necessary if garden soil must be sieved for home-made composts, it is very useful for sieving moss peat which can be a bit coarse.

●**Wheelbarrow.** While a strong plastic bucket will do in small gardens, a wheelbarrow would be necessary in medium and large gardens. It is essential if a garden is being started from scratch.

●**Pruning saw.** A very useful tool in an established garden with trees and shrubs, it is essential if large branches have to be removed. A bow-saw type may be used to cut up firewood as well.

●**Strimmer.** A modern replacement for the scythe, the strimmer is far more versatile at cutting rough grass and weeds. Being electrically operated, it is very easy to use. Be sure to wear eye protection.

●**Powered hedge cutter.** Essential for large hedges, they take the hardship out of hedge cutting. Both electric and petrol-motor models are available.

●**Powered edging tool.** Useful for gardens with a lot of lawn edging and for less able-bodied gardeners. A range of types is available.

●**Rotavator.** Useful if a lot of vegetables are grown in a large garden but, otherwise, finds only occasional use. It can be hired for a special job by the hour, or the day. The other power tools mentioned can be hired too — as can certain hand tools which might be needed occasionally, such as sledgehammer, pick axe, axe or crowbar.

Maintenance

Buy good quality tools — well made of strong materials, not necessarily luxury bracket models. Avoid gimmicky tools — they are usually more expensive and not as serviceable. Never leave tools outdoors. Clean them after use and keep them in a dry place. Otherwise, they will rust and become difficult to use. Put some oil on tools not in use during winter. Oil moving parts regularly. Keep cutting edges sharp — this makes the equipment much easier to use.

Have motor mowers serviced each winter when there is no last minute rush. The engine will last longer and be much easier to start if looked after properly. Get the blades of push mowers sharpened — it makes them easier to use and gives a better finish. Always wash out sprayers after use and empty out metal watering cans. Never store equipment which has plastic or rubber components in direct sunlight since it will cause them to split and crack.

Garden Skills

Any site can be tamed, using chemicals to kill rough vegetation.

Ground preparation

Clear the site of stones, bits of timber or any other rubbish. Cut down tall weeds and grass, with a strimmer. Spray the area with Tumbleweed, or Roundup — which is the same chemical but more economical on a large area. If weeds such as bindweed, docks or nettles re-appear, spray the area with Nettlex Brushwood Killer. If bracken is a problem, use Asulox — available from agricultural merchants. Do not waste effort cultivating the ground until all vegetation is dead; only then should it be dug, or ploughed and rotavated, if the area is large. Large trees may require expert attention.

Drainage

Drainage is necessary if there are springs in the garden; if water flows down from higher ground; or if, in winter, water lies in pools for more than one day after rain stops.

If there are springs, or water flowing from higher ground, a drain will be necessary to intercept the surplus.

The pipes, which may be plastic, or clay drainage tiles, should be laid to give a fall of about one foot (30cm) in 100 feet (30m). Make sure there is an outfall such as an existing ditch to drain the water into.

When water lies on a flat surface for long periods after rain, the problem is often compaction. The passage of heavy machinery during building may compact the soil so much that water cannot escape to the subsoil. Use a crowbar to make small holes through the compacted layer as deeply as possible. Fill the holes to nearly the surface with stone chippings. These holes should be about 2 feet (60cm) apart.

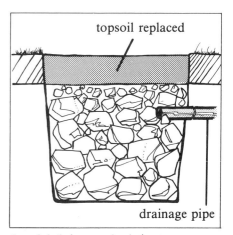

A soak-hole is a good solution to a small drainage problem.

If this does not solve the problem, and the wet spot is too small to warrant a pipe drain, or there is no outfall, put in a soak-hole. This may be made any size or depth, but to be effective it should be at least 2 feet (60cm) square and 2½ feet (75cm) deep. Short pipe drains can be run into the soak-hole to extend its drainage area. Remember that wet spots may be used to grow bog plants.

Digging

Digging with a spade is the main method of cultivating garden soil. The idea is to break the hard surface of the top-soil, mix the upper and lower layers and bury dead plant material, weeds or manure. Digging to the depth of a garden spade is adequate for most purposes. Take manageable spadefuls, and make sure to turn the spadeful upside down. Break up lumps with the back of the spade. Dig a piece of ground in stages. Ease into it, doing very little the first day.

Carry out as much digging as possible before the year ends to allow winter frosts to break down lumps, making the soil easier to get ready for seed-sowing, and to expose hibernating pests and diseases to predators and to harsh weather.

Dig in organic material, such as rotted manure, compost, straw or peat if ground is being prepared for permanent planting. Each year, part of the vegetable area should have organic material applied to maintain soil structure.

Seed sowing

●**Conditions.** Seeds need warm, moist conditions for germination. They must have air too, or they may rot without sprouting. Seeds are sown outdoors only when the soil is warm and moist enough, but since conditions may be controlled indoors, seed sowing is possible all year round. Some seeds have built-in

Digging — just turning over the soil with a spade, burying debris at the same time.

dormancy. This is usually a hard seed coat, or chemical, that prevents seeds germinating before the winter. Dormancy is usually broken by a period of exposure to cold, leaving the seeds ready to germinate right at the start of the growing season. Seed packets usually carry instructions about breaking dormancy, if this is a factor for a particular type of seed.

●**Sowing seed outdoors.** Vegetables, many flowers, trees and shrubs may be raised from seed sown outdoors. Dig the soil well in advance of sowing. Break down all lumps and rake the soil until it is fine. The soil should neither be too wet nor too dry. A useful test is to squeeze a handful of soil into a ball; if it does not fall apart at a touch, it is too wet; if it does not even form a ball, it is too dry. Rake in a dressing of general fertiliser at 2 ounces per square yard (70 g/m²), before sowing. Using a garden line to keep the row straight, draw a little drill in the fine soil with a stick. Sow the seed at the depth and spacing suggested on the seed packet, cover lightly, and mark the row with a label. The packets also give suggestions on sowing dates. These usually cover between eight and ten weeks, to allow for British conditions. For Ireland, as a general rule, take the middle four weeks, leaning towards the first two in the south and east, and the second two in the midlands and north.

When the young plants are large enough, thin them to their final spacing, or lift and transplant them to their final spacing. Thin by selecting strong plants at the required intervals and removing the rest.

●**Sowing seed indoors.** Indoor sowing allows for the provision of warm, moist conditions, making it possible to germinate more difficult seeds. Seeds are sown in trays or pots of seed compost. Make sure that the trays are clean, and use only good quality seed compost — for example, Shamrock Seed and Potting Compost, Bio Seed and Cutting Compost, Fison's Levington Compost. Water the trays before sowing, but not too much or the seeds may rot. Sow the seeds evenly and thinly, and cover lightly with fine compost shaken from a sieve. Cover the tray with a sheet of glass and a sheet of paper. Place in an appropriate temperature — a warm room, propagator or greenhouse for most types of seed, the hot press for the few that like a high temperature. Watch carefully for germination. Remove the paper when the first seedlings emerge, and the glass a few days later. When the seedlings are large enough to handle, which is after ten days, prick them out into trays of fresh compost, at 2 by 2 inches (5 by 5 cm), or into small individual pots. Ease them gently from the compost, holding them by the seed leaves to avoid damage to the stem. Water lightly with a fine spray, after transferral.

Vegetative propagation

There are several ways of raising new plants which do not involve seed sowing. They include division, cuttings, layering and grafting, and have the advantage of exactly reproducing the parent, since the new plant is raised from a part of the parent.

●**Division.** Very many plants produce runners, bulbils, offsets or just additional crowns. These may be used as new plants as soon as they have produced a few roots of their own, and sometimes even before. Simply separate them from the parent, cutting runners, breaking away bulbils and offsets, and dividing or cutting away groups of healthy crowns. Division is the main method of raising new plants of perennial flowers, many houseplants and quite a few rockery plants.

●**Indoor cuttings.** Semi-hardwood cuttings are rooted indoors — or at least under protection of some sort. 'Semi-hardwood' describes the stage of growth of the shoot from which the cutting is made. In July, August and September, the young shoots have almost fully extended, and they begin to go woody at the base as part of the ripening process before winter. These young shoots are full of growth and vigour, and root relatively easily.

Prepare cuttings between 2 and 5 inches (5-12.5cm) long depending on the

Sowing seeds outdoors, French beans here. Do not forget to mark the rows— the empty seed packet is ideal.

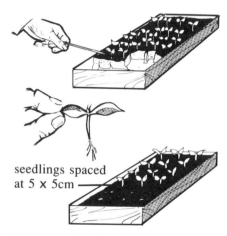

seedlings spaced at 5 x 5cm

Pricking-out should be done as soon as the plants are big enough to handle.

Division is a good way of getting more houseplants, here Boston fern is divided.

type of plant. Trim the base with a sharp blade, just below a leaf or pair of leaves. Remove the leaves from the bottom half of the cutting and dip it in rooting powder, such as Keriroot, Murphy Rooting Powder, Bio Roota, Strike or Seradix. Insert the cuttings into trays or pots of 50:50 peat/sand mix, at about 2 by 2 inches (5 by 5 cm) apart. Use only clean horticultural sand. Firm the cuttings and water them lightly.

Tie a white polythene sheet or bag over the pot or tray, piercing a few small holes to let air in. Place the tray in a shaded part of a greenhouse, or in a bright, but sunless, window in the house. Semi-hardwood cuttings may also be placed in a shaded garden frame in trays, or, if a lot of cuttings are to be rooted, inserted directly into the same peat/sand mixture in the frame itself. Taking semi-hardwood cuttings is a suitable way of propagating a wide range of shrubs. The same technique is used, without polythene, for alpines and some houseplants such as Campanula, Fuchsia, Geraniums, Ivy, Busy lizzie, and Succulents

When the cuttings begin to produce new leaves, remove the polythene, and water as necessary until roots appear at the drainage holes. This may only take six weeks with fast growers. At this stage, the cuttings should be potted singly, in 3 inch (8cm) pots of good potting compost, and grown on — unless it is getting into late autumn. In that case, leave the potting-up until March or April. The young plants may be potted into larger pots, or planted out into nursery beds, to put on some size before planting into their permanent positions.

● **Outdoor cuttings.** Although not suitable for such a wide range of trees and shrubs, this method is both simple and effective. In late autumn, at the end of the growing season, the young shoots will have gone quite woody and hard — hence 'hardwood' cuttings. Take 10 or 12 inch (25-30cm) pieces of the young shoots. Leaves may or may not be gone. Trim the shoot below a bud and take off any lower leaves. Insert the cuttings in 6 inch (15cm) deep trenches, with some clean sand at the bottom, in a sheltered part of the garden. Fill back the top-soil and firm well. Space the cuttings 6 to 12 inches (15-30cm) apart. Trees and shrubs for which this technique is suitable include Poplar, Willow, Blackcurrant, Gooseberry, Griselinia, Escallonia, Forsythia, Roses, Bay laurel, Dogwood, Tamarisk and Flowering currant. Leave the cuttings in position for a year, keeping them free of weeds. The following autumn, plant them in nursery rows, or in their final position.

● **Layering.** For shrubs that are difficult to root, such as Rhododendron and Clematis, or when only one or two new plants are required, layering is a useful technique. Select a branch that is young and bends to ground level fairly easily. Remove leaves if they are in the way. Make a 2 inch (5cm) sloping cut in the branch, cutting halfway through. Insert a match stick to keep the wound open, and dust with rooting powder. Make a shallow depression in the soil; fill it with good compost and a little sand mixed in; press the branch gently down onto this; and pin it in place with a strong piece of bent wire. Heap on some more compost. Place a heavy stone, or sod, on top, to keep the whole arrangement steady. Layering is done in June or July and the new plant is cut away when it has clearly rooted, usually eighteen months later.

Compost-making

● **Garden compost.** Good hygiene — clearing away old crops and weeds — is an important preventative measure against pests, diseases and weeds. In addition, there is always a lot of grass clippings, and foliage from hedge-trimming and pruning — not to mention fallen leaves! The best way of disposing of this material, turning it into a valuable asset — garden compost — is to set up a compost heap.

Simply stack up a 10 inch (25cm) layer of plant waste in an out-of-the-way corner. Scatter a handful of general fertiliser over it and put on a 2 inch (5cm) layer of soil. Start another layer of plant material and repeat the procedure until the heap is about 3 feet (90cm) high, and 5 feet (150cm) square. Timber or galvanised sheeting may be used to retain the sides of the heap. Turning the heap

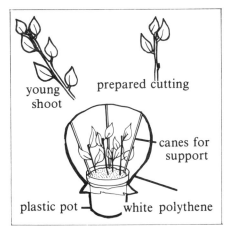

Cuttings indoors — a suitable technique for a very wide range of plants.

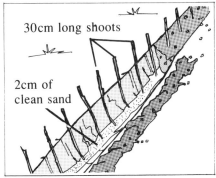

Hardwood cuttings — a very cheap and easy way of getting new plants.

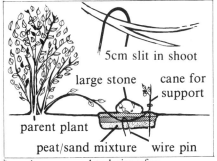

Layering — a good technique for difficult shrubs.

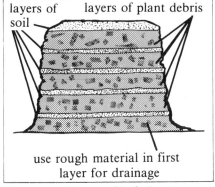

Compost-making gets rid of all waste plant material.

speeds up the process. The compost is best left for a year or so, but may be used after six months if sufficiently decomposed.

●**Potting compost.** Home-made potting composts can be quite satisfactory. They are made from soil, peat and sand in the ratio 7:3:2 by volume. The soil should be good quality garden soil, sieved to remove big stones and sterilised by cooking in an old saucepan, or such like, for about half an hour. The steam generated kills pests, diseases and weeds. Allow the soil to cool and then mix it with the new peat and sand. The latter should be clean horticultural sand, and if not, sterilise it too. Do not use sea sand. Into the mix, put John Innes Base Fertiliser at the rate specified on the pack. This varies depending on how rich a compost is to be prepared. Compost for seedlings and small plants need not be rich — older plants, though, need more food. Lime will need to be added if the soil used is acidic.

Planting

●**Preparation.** Dig the ground, break up lumps and remove large stones to make it easy for the plant's roots to grow out into the soil. The addition of organic material, especially peat, encourages quick rooting. Fertiliser should always be applied before planting, because the plant will need ready access to food. About two ounces per square yard (70 g/m^2) of general fertiliser such as 7:6:17, 10:10:20, John Innes Base, Growmore, or General Purpose Fertiliser should be used.

●**Planting.** When the ground is ready, take out a hole wide enough to allow the roots to be fully spread out, and deep enough to allow the plant to be at the same depth as before lifting. Place it in the hole, making sure it is upright, spread out the roots, and lightly cover them with good, fine soil. Firm gently. Then fill the hole and firm well, with hands or feet — depending on the size of the plant. Firming makes sure the roots are in contact with the soil, but do not over-firm.

●**Watering.** Always water immediately after planting, especially if the weather is dry or windy. Apart from helping the roots to settle in, watering establishes the capillary rise of moisture up through the soil — like priming a pump. Avoid planting where water-logging may occur. The roots actually drown for lack of oxygen, and rot, often causing the death of the plant itself.

●**Support.** The plant's root system anchors it to the soil. When a plant is moved, losing some of its roots, it may no longer be adequately anchored. Trees and tall shrubs especially need to be staked. The stake should be driven after the hole is dug, but before planting. Temporary shelter, by means of a screen of sacking, is useful for conifers, which tend to blow over and get dried out by the wind.

●**Timing.** The correct planting times for the various types of plants are given in the previous sections. In general, plants suffer least set-back when moved during dormancy — they have less foliage and the weather is moist and cool. As a result, they do not come under stress so quickly. When plants are moved while in full growth — bedding plants and vegetable transplants — make the move as quickly as possible, and water before and after. Container and pot-grown plants suffer no damage to their root system, and so may be safely planted at any time — though they should be watered until well established.

Spraying

The aim in spraying is to apply a chemical substance accurately and safely. The chemical may be a weed-killer, insecticide, fungicide, or foliar feed. Some of these are harmful to plants, animals, the environment and the user when not properly used.

●**Is it necessary?** Chemical sprays should only be used when necessary, and there are very few situations in the garden where a routine spray is justified. Blackspot of roses, apple scab, grey mould on strawberries, and potato blight are four diseases which may be depended upon to appear under Irish conditions, and which may be routinely sprayed against. Special caution should be exercised

A simple set-up for sterilising small quantities of soil for use in home-made seed and potting composts.

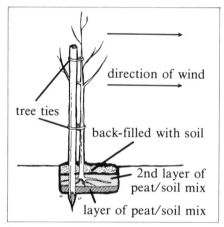

Bare-root planting — the traditional way, care at this stage pays off later.

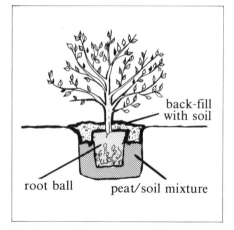

Planting container-grown stock, more plants are offered in this form now.

when using insecticides; the particular pest involved, the amount of damage it may cause, and the numbers of the pest present are important considerations. There may be ways other than spraying of dealing with a problem *(See the Sections on Pests, Diseases and Weeds for more on this)*. If you decide to spray, apply it correctly.

● **Correct application.** First, make sure that the chemical is capable of doing the job required. Next, ensure that both the crop and the pest, disease or weed are at the right stage for it to work. Too early, or too late, may be a waste of time. Make sure the weather conditions are right. Do not spray on windy days, because the chemical may get on to the wrong plants. Do not spray on hot, sunny days, for fear of scorching the plant foliage. Do not spray while foliage is wet, or when rain threatens, unless the chemical is rain-fast. The cool, calm of evening is often a good time for spraying. Mix the correct amount of material in the appropriate quantity of water, and make sure it is thoroughly dissolved. Do not use extra spray chemical "for good measure". Not only is this wasteful and potentially dangerous, but may even give a poorer result than the correct amount.

Apply sprays under fairly high pressure, and thoroughly wet all foliage, top and undersides of leaves, and the centre of the plant. Apply enough liquid to give 'run-off', when the first drops drip from the leaves. A single correct application will be more effective than repeated bad spraying, besides causing less damage to the environment.

● **Spraying precautions.** General safety precautions include the following: reading the label on the bottle or packet and any other supplied leaflets; keeping the chemical, in its original pack along with the instructions, in a safe place; staying out of the spray mist and wearing rubber gloves and protective gear, if necessary. Chemicals may not be poisonous, but they can cause irritations and allergic reactions. Dispose of empty bottles and packets by placing them in the rubbish bin — do not burn them or wash them out. Rinse the sprayer, at least twice, immediately after spraying, and throw the rinse water onto soil in a waste corner — not down the drain.

Spreading

Scattering out powders or granules by hand is quite a difficult skill that can only be acquired by practice. Start by measuring the area of ground over which the substance is to be scattered. Simply pace out the length and width, and calculate the area. Multiply the area by the application rate per square yard, or square metre, and then measure out, or buy, enough of the substance for the area. Divide the quantity evenly into two buckets.

Aim to spread the material in parallel strips about 2 steps wide. Put a stick one step in from the edge at one end. From the opposite end, walk directly towards the stick, spreading as you go — as evenly as possible. When you reach the stick, move it over two steps, and do another strip. If there are only six strips, half the quantity in the bucket should be gone after three. Adjust the rate of application accordingly. Spread from the second bucket, in strips at right angles to the first strips. This helps to even out the application.

When spreading fertilisers around trees or shrubs, measure, by pacing, the extent of the spread of the branches. That is the extent of the root system too. Measure it in two directions, and multiply the two figures. For example, take an apple tree two paces wide in one direction and four paces wide in the other. The area under the tree would then be roughly 8 square yards ($6.6m^2$). This method is an over-estimate of about 25 percent, but then the paces are likely to be less than a yard anyhow.

Watering

Watering is obviously necessary indoors. The Sections on Greenhouse Growing and Houseplants go into some detail. Outdoors, watering may be necessary if rainfall has been inadequate, or if a plant's root system is not

'Run-off' stage — the leaves will be thoroughly wetted when this occurs. Do not forget the undersides.

For use only as an agricultural/horticultural insecticide

TOXIC | IF SWALLOWED

HARMFUL | IN CONTACT WITH SKIN

TOXIC

Caution
This substance is poisonous. The inhalation of its vapour, or spray mist may have harmful consequences. It may also be dangerous to let it come into contact with the skin or clothing.

Read all labels and literature carefully and wear protective gear if this is advised.

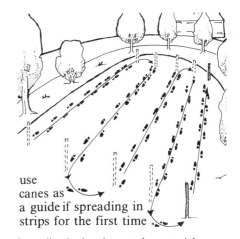

use canes as a guide if spreading in strips for the first time

Spreading by hand — get the material out as evenly and as accurately as possible.

properly established. Seedlings, young plants — especially vegetables — and plants growing in shallow or dry soil, are principally at risk.

● **Requirements.** Normal summer rainfall is at least 2 inches (50mm) per month. This just matches plant requirements. One inch (25mm) of rain is equivalent to almost 5 gallons of water per square yard (25 litres/m²). If there has been no rain for a week, plants need about 2½ gallons per square yard (12.5 1/m²) — maybe even more if it has been very hot. Established plants with deep roots can keep going but young plants, and small ones, will be under stress.

● **Application.** Apply water to vegetables, lawns, flower beds and borders and rockeries with a hose and sprinkler. Allow enough time for an adequate amount to be delivered, letting it soak down where it will be effective. Heavy, short bursts are no good — the water just runs off. When watering larger plants, make a little dyke around them and fill it with water. Re-fill it, if the water disappears quickly. Shallow rooting shrubs such as Rhododendron often need this attention. Wall shrubs, too, are very drought-prone.

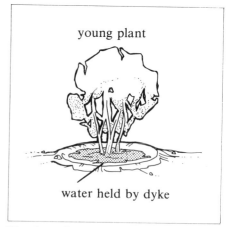

Watering — be sure to deliver enough, let it soak away and then give the plant more.

Training

The aim is to improve plant performance: better fruit or vegetables, better shape, better flowers or foliage. Very often, training is just a matter of facilitating what the plant itself wants to do. Training should always be done in time. Do not delay until the plant has got on with the job, on its own, and then try to change it. Since a lot of tying and staking is involved in training, make sure that the ties or stakes themselves do not cause any damage. Use soft ties which break, or expand. Never tie a plant with wire, or plastic twines that do not rot. Un-do ties before they get too tight, and check for loose ties before winter, to avoid damage. Details on training are given where appropriate in the earlier Sections.

Pruning

Pruning is the removal of part of a plant. At its simplest, the fingers may be used to pinch out the soft growing point. It puts a stop to extension growth and encourages side-shoots to grow. Dis-budding is the rubbing out of surplus shoots or flower buds and is sometimes used to increase the size of the remaining flowers. Dead-heading means removing flowers that have dropped their petals, preventing seed production which has a tendency to weaken plants and reduce flowering in the following year.

These are types of pruning, but what is generally taken to mean pruning is the removal of branches, or parts of branches. There is a balance in any plant between root and top. Pruning away part of the top creates an imbalance since the remainder has more root serving it and, as a result, grows more rapidly. The part removed will be replaced by young growth, thus pruning both re-juvenates a plant and changes its shape. Skillful and careful pruning can actually improve shape, but bad pruning destroys it. Any pruning means injury to the plant and if the cuts are large, pruning paint should be applied. Information on pruning specific plants is given as appropriate in the earlier Sections.

Not the way to prune a tree, apart from looking bad, this tree died because fungi got in through the pruning cuts.

Construction

A garden must have boundaries and pathways; and it can be made more attractive by the addition of paved areas, low walls, terraces or a pool. The non-living "hard" part of the garden is as important as the plants — the "soft" part. The hard part fills the important functions of division and access, but a secondary role as a foil to set off the soft part is no less important — though often forgotten.

● **Paths and paving.** Laying tarmac and concrete accurately is skilled work, best left to a professional. But gravel and paving slabs may be attempted. For paths, choose the obvious route. If there is no obvious route, create one by using obstacles or barriers. Put paved areas in a position of full sun, as far as possible. They will be used more often, and stay cleaner. A paved area must be situated so

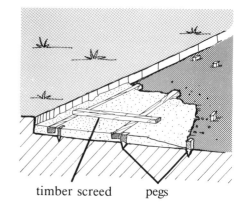

timber screed   pegs

A screed is very useful in getting a proper level. Uneven paving looks bad and may even be dangerous.

that it is private, or can be made private by screening. Otherwise, there will always be a feeling of discomfort.

To lay gravel paths or paving, start by removing the top 4 inches (10cm) of soil, or more if the ground is soft. As the site for paving must not be boggy, drainage may be necessary first. Pack the remaining soil well. Put in 2 inches (5 cm) of hardcore for gravel; 2 inches (5cm) of sand for paving slabs. Gravel laid on hardcore lasts longer than if laid on soft soil where it tends to sink. Firm the foundation well, and for gravel, there is no need to get an accurate level.

However, this is essential for paving slabs, especially for areas wider than a few feet. To achieve it, a screed should be set up. First, drive in short pegs to set the level of the foundation. Allowing for the thickness of the slab to come on top, use a long, straight piece of timber with a spirit level, to get the tops of the pegs at the correct height. A slight slope, to throw off water, should be built in at this stage — one inch in 10 feet (1 cm/m) is enough.

Lay two straight pieces of 5 x 5cm timber beside the pegs and level with their tops. Fill in the sand accurately and firm it well, levelling all the time with a third 'straight edge' laid across the two pieces of timber. When the sand is level and evenly firm, lay the slabs in position, leaving a very small gap to allow for manœuvre. Level and lay the slabs by degrees. Some cement — 1 part dry cement to 8 or 10 parts sand — may be used to give a firmer base. The cement sets in time.

If a kerb is to be used to retain the sides of paved or gravel areas, especially paths, it should be put in place before laying foundations. Stand the kerbing on a bed of sand and cement (3:1) and let it set. It will need to be laid level. Rough kerbing may be put in place without fixing in concrete. A useful kind of kerb is a mowing strip of bricks laid level with the soil of the lawn. It reduces edge cutting and may be continued around the lawn edge — not just at pathways. The mowing strip need not be set in concrete.

● **Walls.** High walls of concrete blocks or bricks are a difficult task without some expertise — and badly built walls are always an eyesore! However, low walls are well within the ability of most people. A low wall, 12 inches to 2 feet (30-60cm) high is a useful divider of space in a garden, and plants look well, set against the level uniformity of the wall.

Lay a foundation first, by digging out the soil to a depth of 6 inches (15cm) — enough to support a couple of courses of blocks. Dig deeper if the wall is to be higher. Fill the trench with concrete made of 4 parts gravel, 1 part sand and 1 part cement.

Give the foundation a few days to set, then make up mortar, of 3 parts sand and one part cement. Lay the first block at one end, on a half-inch (1cm) bed of mortar, and level it, using a spirit level. Lay a second block at the other end, stretch builder's string between the two, to give a straight line, and then lay the rest, making each one level. The second course goes on top, in the same way, but 'staggered' to give strength. Block walls will need capping and the simplest way is to buy capping, and lay it on top. 'Screen', or open, blocks are made to a variety of patterns, and they make very attractive boundaries without the 'closed-in' feeling of a solid wall.

● **Fencing.** Wooden fences are more easily put up than walls, but they are not as permanent. Posts must be put in the ground firmly, to hold the wooden fencing panels. Measure out accurately where the posts should go, marking each spot with pegs. Dig holes about one foot square (30cm) and 12-15 inches (30-37.5cm) deep. Drive the first post about one foot (30cm) into the bottom of the hole. Measure off the next post accurately and drive it firmly into position. Continue until all the posts are in place, and straight — test them with a spirit level. Some good-sized stones may be used to part fill the hole and help to retain the posts in position; otherwise, three-quarters fill the holes with concrete made of 4 parts gravel, one part sand and one part cement. The posts should be of pressure-treated timber — not just painted. The panels may then be nailed into position, with constant checking that they are straight and in line.

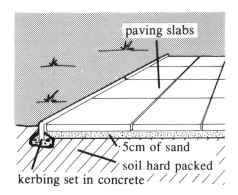

Do not be in a hurry to lay the slabs. Get the foundation right first.

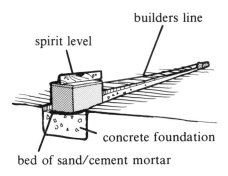

Simple set-up for laying blocks, low walls are no problem.

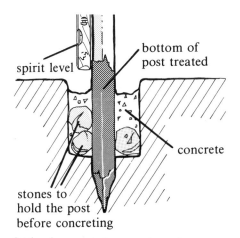

Setting fence posts in concrete, make sure they are properly treated, and set straight.

Rustic fencing can be tackled in the same way, except that forest poles are used instead of panels. The base of the poles in the ground should be treated, but the rest need not.

●**Dry stone wall.** This type of wall is used as a retaining wall, where a sloping piece of ground is terraced into two pieces of level ground. It is an attractive ornamental feature in itself.

First, set about moving soil to change the levels. If the slope is steep, several terraces will be needed. Having no mortar, a dry stone wall is not stable at a height greater than about 3 feet (90cm). Move soil down the slope to fill the lower level. When this is done, a face, or bank, of soil is left half way up the slope. Begin building the wall about two feet out from this bank. Use the bigger stones at this stage, as they are easier to manoeuvre on the ground. Fill in behind the first course of stones with soil and pack it tight. Then lay another course of stones, with more soil and firming. When the height of the bank is reached, soil may be brought down the slope to fill in, raising the wall until the upper area is levelled. Place the stones with the broad end out and the pointed end into the soil, and put a slight, backwards tilt on the wall to give it stability. Plants may be put in the gaps between the stones. This type of wall is a lot of work, but worth the effort — a garden on a number of levels is always more interesting.

●**Garden pools.** Water is restful and reinforces a garden's air of calm and tranquillity. A pool of some sort may be chosen to suit most gardens. Concrete pools are difficult to build and often crack. Ready-formed fibreglass is quick and easy to install, but unless well disguised, it tends to look artificial. Pool liners of polythene, PVC or butyl rubber are cheap, easy to put in, and can be made to any size or shape — except formal.

Dig a hole to the size and shape required. The depth should be 18 inches (45cm) for a small pool, 2-2½ feet (60-75cm) for a large one. A 'shelf' to one side, about 8 inches (20cm) deep, is ideal for marginal water plants. The sheet to fit the hole should be the maximum length plus twice the maximum depth, and the maximum width plus twice the maximum depth. Line the hole with a layer of sand; spread the liner; weigh down the edges with bricks or stones, and fill the pool with water.

Around the edges of the pool, the polythene, or PVC, must be hidden from sunlight or it will break down and crack. Usually a pool is associated with a paved area and the paving could be laid to overhang the liner.

Water lilies need deep water, and remember to get some oxygenating plants, such as Canadian pondweed or Water milfoil. As these compete with algae for nutrients, they prevent it from clouding the water. Plenty of oxygenators are needed in a new pool.

A cascade fed by a submerged circulating pump can be a great addition and is simple to install. Make a concrete course for it to flow down, or else use stones. Strips of pool liner could be used too, but they look a little obvious.

●**Rockery.** Most rockery plants are sun-lovers — do not place a rockery in the shade of buildings or trees. Next choose suitable stone; make sure of having enough; and do not mix different types. Start by clearing the site of all existing vegetation, especially perennial weeds. Build the rockery in stages — do not just heap up the soil and then dot it with stones. Lay a tier of stones with the big ends outwards and a slight backward tilt to trap rainwater. Fill in behind with soil and firm it well. Mix some broken bricks, small stones or rubble into this fill-in material. Lay another tier of stones in the same way and fill in behind — repeating the procedure until all the rocks and soil are used up. Remember to hold onto some nice stone for the top of the rockery.

Before planting, it is a good idea to make a special planting mixture for the top 2 inches (5 cm) into which the plants will go. Even if some soil has to be moved to make room for this layer, it is worthwhile doing so. A mixture of 3 parts soil (2 parts, if the soil is heavy), 1 part coarse sand and 1 part peat is ideal. It might be a good idea to sterilise this before spreading, with Basamid, to get rid of weed seeds. Use a one inch (2.5 cm) layer of shingle or stone chippings over the soil as a mulch to prevent weed germination.

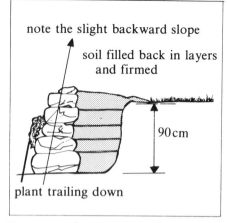

note the slight backward slope
soil filled back in layers and firmed
90cm
plant trailing down

Dry stone wall — an attractive feature in its own right, properly done, it lasts forever.

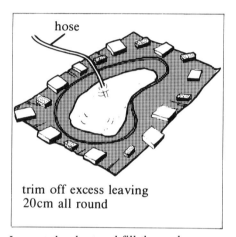

hose
trim off excess leaving 20cm all round

Lay out the sheet and fill the pool with water, leave a 20cm strip at the edges.

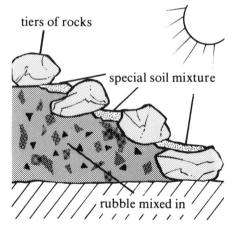

tiers of rocks
special soil mixture
rubble mixed in

Build a rockery in stages, note the position of the sun.

Principles of Labour Saving

Although some people have plenty of time to spend in their gardens, most of us find that time is a problem. It is possible to greatly reduce the amount of time spent in the garden by choosing plants and features carefully, and by adopting some simple ideas.

Living Plants

It may seem rather obvious to state that plants are living things. However, from that simple statement, important conclusions can be drawn. Plants are alive; they have the quality of life. Unlike non-living machines that eventually break down, plants have the capacity to reproduce and repair themselves, and go on living. We can turn this to our advantage.

●**Suitable conditions.** If plants have the capacity for life, that means they will succeed if conditions are right. Since we gardeners are the providers of conditions for plants, it is our job to see that they are provided with suitable conditions.

●**Competition.** Not only do plants have the capacity for life, but they are fiercely competitive about staying alive. They compete vigorously with each other for space and light above the soil, and for nutrients and water below soil level.

●**Defences.** In the face of attacks by other organisms that would seek to live off them, plants are far from helpless. They have very good defence mechanisms against both pests and diseases.

Suitable Conditions

The growth of plants is affected by climatic conditions as well as local conditions of site and soil. Since they emerged from the sea millions of years ago, plants have evolved so as to be able to grow in almost every corner of the Earth's land surface, from freezing mountain slopes to steamy jungles.

It can be taken for granted that whatever set of conditions exist in a garden, there are plants suited. Usually, gardens do not present very extreme conditions, but the amount of variation of local climate and soils can be very significant, none the less.

●**Winter cold.** The nearer the garden is to the coast, and the further south, the longer the growing season and the less likely there will be severe winter frost. There are many plants that will survive light frost down to –5°C(23°F). The chances of going below this temperature increase dramatically inland and further north.

Try to find out exactly how frosty the area is by looking at other gardens. Plants like Cordyline, Hebe, Fuchsia and Pittosporum are good indicators of the relative mildness of the area. If they have grown to good size, the winters must be fairly consistently mild. If they are completely absent, the locality is prone to severe frost. Because of the ameliorating effect of the sea, it is possible to grow plants in coastal gardens that would not survive inland, although wind damage near the sea is generally more severe.

The damage caused by winter cold is influenced by other factors. Warm sunny summers encourage the development of tough woody growth and high sugar content in plant cells. Freezing will not occur until lower temperature levels are reached. Plants growing in free-draining soil will have a longer growing season and complete their preparation for winter earlier than those on heavy soil. Plants growing on south-facing slopes suffer less because the extra warmth encourages better development of tissue.

●**Soil type.** Soil type can greatly affect the growth of plants. Acid-loving plants suffer from iron deficiency on limy soils; the youngest leaves turn yellow. Some lime-loving plants such as Flowering cherries lack sufficient calcium on acidic soils. A simple test can be carried out using kits that are available in any garden shop. Alternatively, look at local gardens to see whether Rhododendrons are

Ivy
struggles up through a hedge.

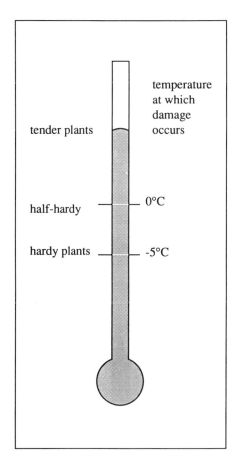

The point at which the damage is done determines whether a plant is 'hardy', 'half-hardy' or 'tender'.

79

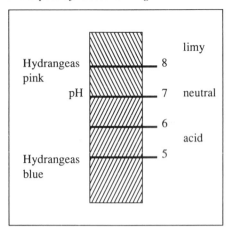

pH 7 is neutral, neither acidic nor limy.

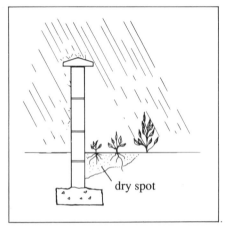

A 'rain shadow' at the base of a wall.

Anemone blanda
likes the shade of trees.

growing in the open soil, and also the colour of Hydrangeas. On limy soil, Rhododendrons eventually fade out. Hydrangeas will be pink or red on limy soil; on acid soil, they will be blue, and if they are purplish, the soil is likely to be neutral.

●**Soil moisture.** All plants are adapted to a preferred level of soil moisture. Some need moist, even wet, soil; others like free-draining, even dry, ground. Very many garden plants like it in-between the two, neither too moist nor tending to dryness. Most garden soils fit into this middle category.

However, it is important to realise that parts of the garden might vary from the average. Dry spots can occur near walls where the rain cannot reach. Wet spots may result from poor drainage or compaction. It is important to choose plants that like the conditions available to them. Very often, plants that like dry soil languish in a damp spot, while on the other side of the garden, a soft plant with large leaves may be struggling in dry soil.

The plants themselves will provide a clue as to their preferences. Those with silver, hairy, leathery, very small, rolled or very waxy leaves are adapted to deal with moisture shortage. Those with broad, lush leaves and soft juicy stems are used to moist soil. (*See the Lists of Plants for Dry and Moist Soil. Page 101–2*).

●**Shade.** All plants need light but some have adapted to coping with less than full sunshine. These are mainly woodland plants which must make do with whatever light reaches the woodland floor. They have evolved strategies to cope with reduced light.

Climbers have developed the ability to climb up host trees to reach the light. Understorey plants like Holly, Laurel and Rhododendron have often got darker foliage with greater amounts of green chlorophyll to make best use of the light that reaches them. Very often these are evergreen, which allows them to make growth early in the year before the leaves come on the deciduous trees overhead.

Some woodland floor plants have bulbous roots which allow them to grow very quickly early in the year, flower and produce seed before mid-summer. Many of the spring bulbs fit into this category. Some woodland plants have broad thin leaves to present as much surface area as possible to the light above. At the same time, this flimsy foliage is protected from weather damage by the trees. For example, ferns are natural shade-lovers that generally open their fronds at the same time as the trees unfurl their protective leaves. (*See the List of Plants for Shade. Page 99–100*).

However, many plants have also adapted to growing in the full glare of the sun. Without it, they will not flower well and may even die after a while. Many of these plants are natives of open grassland or scrub areas where there are no large trees to cast shade.

Very often, plants which like full sunshine also like dry soil, but not always. Equally, the ones that like shade do not always like moist soil. In fact, many woodland plants are adapted to withstand drought caused by the competition of the tree roots — another excellent reason for getting all the growing done in the early part of the year and dying back to a bulbous root during the dry summer months!

●**Wind.** Wind can have drastic effects on the growth of plants. This occurs in a number of ways. Wind lowers the temperature of the air around plants and reduces their rate of growth. It causes moisture loss from the leaves during dry weather and increases the damaging effects of frost during cold spells. Apart from these effects, wind can cause direct physical damage to leaves and stems. Young leaves are very soft and easily damaged during their expansion in springtime.

Plants which are adapted to withstand the effects of wind usually have small, often narrow waxy leaves. Heathers and needle-leaved conifers are wind-resistant, for example. Many grasses and other non-woody plants have flexible stems that bend and twist away from the wind. Trees which leaf up late in the spring like Ash and Sycamore are relatively wind-resistant.

Near the coast, the wind problem is more severe because of greater wind speed off the sea. Added to that is the salt spray carried by strong gales, and sometimes even sand. Some plants are well adapted to salt spray in their native habitats.

They can be used near the seaside as ornamental plants in their own right, and also to protect less resistant plants. (*See the List of Seaside Plants. Page 103–5*).

● **Space.** The amount of space available to any plant has a major influence on its success. Each plant species has a normal height and spread. It seems obvious that plants should have enough space available to them. However, it is very common to see gardens where plants have not got enough space and never had the prospect of having enough space for their proper development.

Plants are competitive for space and they tend to grow into each other in the attempt to reach the light. The faster growers will usually squeeze out the smaller plants, but plants of even vigour just end up spoiling each other — becoming one-sided, or very lanky, for example.

It is very important to find out the likely eventual size of any plant before planting. When a plant gets too big for the space available to it, it must be pruned drastically, or removed. The original planting and the subsequent pruning, or removal, all involve wasted time and effort as well as the destruction or complete waste of a good plant.

The problem is most acute with the largest plants, namely trees. However, it can occur with shrubs as well and even with non-woody flowers when over-rampageous kinds are put in the wrong place.

However, it is important to point out that achieving the correct spacing for plants is not as easy as all that. Waiting for the plants to reach mature size, and fill their allotted space, takes too long and there will be ugly gaps in the mean-time. On the other hand, although close planting fills up the space more quickly, the plants soon become too crowded. Guidelines about spacing trees and shrubs are given on page 6. The other classes of plants — perennial and annual flowers — can be used to fill some space in the early years.

Wind-battered **Arbutus**.

Competition

Because plants cannot move position to a more suitable place, they are forced to compete where they are. Competition for light and space takes place overground; for water and nutrients, the struggle ensues below soil level.

● **Competitors.** Every plant competes for light, water and nutrients. Some are much better at the struggle than others. Trees, for example, are the top competitors, which explains how they managed to cover the Earth with dense forests. (They would again, given the chance!)

The trunk of the tree holds the canopy of leaves higher than competing plants. In a mature broadleaf forest, the massive array of foliage traps eighty per cent of the sunlight and about the same proportion of rain. Down below, the smaller plants must get by with the remainder.

By way of complete contrast, tiny alpine plants are adapted for survival on the cold windswept slopes of mountains where, despite plenty of other difficulties, they have no competition. Their success depends on the ability to tolerate condi-tions that would kill other plants. When they are planted in lowland gardens without the harsh conditions to which they are adapted, they are easily swamped by bigger plants, even relatively small weeds such as annual meadow grass.

● **Ground-cover.** All garden plants compete vigorously for space and resources. Trees, especially the large forest trees like Oak, Ash, Beech, Elm, Lime, Pine, Horse chestnut, Spruce and Sweet chestnut, are very dominant, smaller trees less so but still capable of dominating in the absence of larger trees. Shrubs are gen-erally fast-growing and stake a claim to their space quickly. Perennial flowers do a lot of their competing below ground level by means of extensive roots. Annual flowers grow quickly to fill their allotted space.

We can use the competitive nature of plants to our advantage. If we fill the space with plants that we want, then the ones we do not want are less likely to succeed. The principle is that of ground cover. It is important to realise that every plant, from the largest tree to small annual flowers, has the potential for

Over-crowded plants may need to be moved.

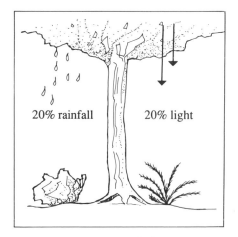

20% rainfall   20% light

The tree canopy is very efficient.

Hypericum calycinum
— an aggressive competitor.

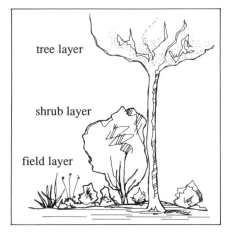

tree layer

shrub layer

field layer

The layers of vegetation.

Wild plants quickly cover the soil; bare soil is an invitation to weeds.

ground-covering. Very often, the term is applied only to low-growing, ground-hugging shrubs and perennial flowers. These are certainly good for the task, but it must be realised that all plants have this ability.

●**Layers.** Because plants have worked out their own hierarchy of size — large forest trees, smaller trees, shrubs, climbers, perennial flowers, annual flowers — they arrange themselves naturally in several layers of vegetation.

In natural woodland, the top layer is the forest canopy of large trees. The understorey layer contains the smaller trees like Holly, Yew, and Hazel together with the trees of woodland clearings like Cherry, Hawthorn, Crabapple, and Birch. Lower again are the shrubs and climbers. Then, the perennial flowers and grasses that colonise the soil below ground with their extensive root systems, or bulbous roots. The last layer of all is the moss layer, usually ignored for garden purposes but it can be important. This consists of mosses, liverworts, lichens sometimes and small ferns. These compete for resources and can interfere with the germination of seeds of bigger plants.

Each layer catches some sunlight for itself and thereby makes life more difficult for the plants below. We can use this feature of the competitive nature of plants to our advantage. Instead of setting up one layer of ground-cover plants to shade out weeds, why not have two or more layers?

The various layers of vegetation can easily be set up in garden woodland planting because it approximates to a natural woodland. Large gardens of two thousand square metres, or more, can easily accommodate some woodland planting. In any size of garden, mixed borders of trees, shrubs and perennial flowers compare to natural woodland edge, with shade-tolerant plants meeting those that enjoy full sunshine. It is possible to use the shade-tolerant kinds to underplant trees and shrubs, and to use the sun-lovers in front of the taller woody plants.

●**Bare soil.** In a natural setting, there is rarely any bare soil to be seen. Even land slips, and river banks stripped of vegetation by floodwaters, are quickly reclaimed. Any piece of bare ground is colonised by plants, especially the great opportunists of the plant world — the common weeds. To clear the soil of weeds, and leave it bare, is to offer a further invitation which will be gratefully accepted. As a general principle, the less bare soil in the garden, the less work of weeding. Bare soil can be covered up with desirable plants and mulches, or in some cases, it can be treated with chemical weedkillers.

Defences

Although plants appear fairly helpless in defending themselves, this is not the case. They have a formidable range of defences against both pests and diseases.

●**Pests.** The most obvious defence against pests are the various kinds of thorns, spines and stings. These prevent animals from grazing the stems and leaves of plants. Some have irritant hairs which are very unpleasant. A few plants, such as the Giant hogweed, contain chemicals in their sap which render the skin sensitive to the ultra-violet rays of the sun.

Many plants have hairy or sticky stems and leaves. These aim to slow down the movement of greenfly and other small pests. Another very effective trick of plants against sap-sucking insects is the natural pressure of the plant sap. Sucking insects like to use the pressure of the sap to feed themselves but when the plant is growing actively, the pressure may be too great for comfort. When the plant is short of moisture, the sap will be thick with sugars and released at a slower rate after the cells are punctured by the insect's feeding tube.

Some plants have distasteful substances, even poisons, in the sap. Foxglove contains poisonous digitoxin; rhubarb has poisonous oxalic acid in the leaves. Yew trees contain poisons called taxines. The seeds of Spurges contain powerful laxatives. Oak leaves, indeed many plants, contain tannins which are very bitter and dissuade many animals that would like to eat them. Even so, Oak is an important food source for hundreds of animal species that have adapted to the bitter taste.

Despite the effectiveness of physical and chemical defences against the majority of potential pests, most plants are attacked successfully by a variety of animals, especially insects. However, the pests of any one species are usually relatively few in number. Some plants have no pests at all, some are attacked occasionally, a few are prone to more frequent attack. It is important to realise that while an insect, or other pest, might cause light damage to plants on occasion, it cannot be considered a significant pest.

In fact, the number of really significant pests of ornamental plants — that is, those which cause severe damage to plants — is very few. They include slugs and snails, and greenfly, occasionally rabbits are a serious problem in country gardens. Vegetables and fruit are prey to a few others like caterpillars and root flies that frequently cause problems, and can be considered serious pests.

Plants have another solution to the problem of pest attack; they simply outgrow it. Strong-growing healthy plants quickly outgrow the damage caused by pests. A few holes in leaves, even though the plant may look bad, is not significant to a healthy plant. It is constantly producing new leaves that replace any losses.

Remember, too, that plants are not on their own in this struggle because the pests themselves are prone to the attacks of parasites and predators. There is a long list of these: ladybirds, lacewings, hoverflies, groundbeetles, wasps, chalcid wasps, capsids, anthocorids, spiders, ichneumon wasps, frogs, hedgehogs and birds. In fact, every insect or other animal seen in the garden that is not identifiably a pest is a beneficial predator or parasite.

●**Diseases.** Although the plant defence mechanisms against pests are perhaps more obvious, the defences against fungi are no less effective. Defences against fungi are mainly barriers of one kind or another.

Leaves are usually coated with wax which prevents the germination of disease spores. Within the sap, there are substances which reduce the growth of fungi, including the tannin mentioned above. The bark of trees and the thick skin of stems, like the waxy coating of leaves, act as a barrier against fungi.

Plants that are attacked by fungi sometimes react by allowing a section of the leaf around the affected area to die. This causes a leaf spot and, occasionally, the plant may react to a disease by dropping all of its leaves, producing a new crop when the worst of the disease attack is over.

As is the case with pests, strong-growing healthy plants are better able to resist diseases. For example, during dry weather with growth reduced, plants are less able to withstand mildew. On the other hand, if plants are growing very rapidly in over-rich soil, their tissues will become soft and watery; they are likely to suffer cankers, grey mould and leaf spot diseases.

●**Knowledge.** The main principle of labour saving in the garden is to suit the plants. When the plants are given the right conditions, they will do most of the work themselves. They will grow properly, not needing cosseting and coaxing, feeding, spraying or watering. They will compete vigorously with weeds, and they will be able to withstand the attacks of pests and diseases on most occasions.

However, to suit the plants means to know what conditions they require. This means finding out their needs and supplying them, if possible. First of all, know what the garden can supply in terms of local climate, soil, size and situation. Then before buying, much less planting any plant, find out what it needs. If the garden cannot provide it, forget about growing that particular plant. There are lots of others; equally beautiful, equally interesting!

Gardening is not an exact science. In approaching any garden job, there are a number of possible approaches. While all of these may be equally correct, some are easier than others. If you choose to take the easier path, the time and effort involved is reduced. In the same way, some garden features require more time and effort than others. By eliminating, or reducing, the labour-intensive garden features and replacing them with labour-saving features, time and effort can be saved, without any reduction in the beauty or interest of the garden. In fact, it can very often be increased.

Nettles
have a very effective defence mechanism.

Nasturtium leaves
have a thick protective coating of wax.

Too much farmyard manure leads to apple scab disease.

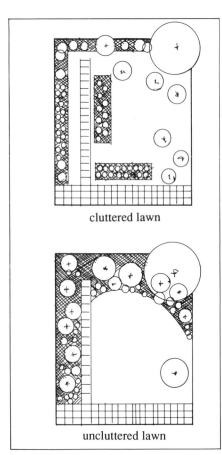

cluttered lawn

uncluttered lawn

A lawn with obstacles is more difficult to mow.
An uncluttered lawn is not only easier to mow, but looks bigger.

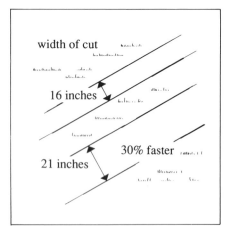

width of cut

16 inches

21 inches   30% faster

Wider mowers reduce mowing time.

Labour-Intensive Garden Features

Even though some garden features are labour intensive, it is hard to visualize most gardens without them, for example, lawns and containers. However, the amount of time and effort spent on them can be lessened by reducing the area of garden given over to them, and by adopting easier methods.

Lawns

●**Size.** Despite the seeming ease of maintaining a lawn, there is no more time-consuming garden feature. It may only take half an hour to an hour to mow the grass, and that does not seem long. However, when the accumulated hours of a whole season's mowing are added together, it becomes obvious that no other garden feature takes as much time.

It is estimated that 10 sq. feet (1m²) of lawn takes three minutes to mow each season. 1200 sq. yards (1000m²) takes about fifty hours in a season. The amount of time depends on the frequency of cutting, the lawn layout and the mower used. The first solution to consider is to reduce the area of lawn. Every fifteen per cent cut in the space given to the lawn means a fifteen per cent reduction in time spent mowing every week and every season!

A reduction in lawn area is easily achieved by widening existing borders, or creating borders where there were none. It is quite amazing how much space can be taken out of a lawn by adding even quite a narrow border. Although reduced in area, the impression of size will be little affected. In fact, a small lawn backed by an ornamental border can look much bigger than a larger lawn that is not well bounded. This occurs because the space is defined by the new boundary.

●**Obstacles.** A lawn with sharp corners and awkward angles takes much longer to mow. Little strips of grass between flower beds or shrubs present further difficulty. Flower beds, shrubs and trees dotted about the lawn turn it into an obstacle course for mowing. Each one has to be circled, pushing the mower under the low-hanging branches. The removal of some, or all, of these obstacles by lifting and relocating shrubs or young trees, or removing a flower bed or two, makes mowing much easier.

●**Mowing.** The most important aspect of achieving a good lawn is regular, correct mowing. Although this sounds like more effort, it is in fact compatible with reduced work. Mowing frequently — at least every fortnight in the spring and every week during good growing weather — is easier because there is but a small amount to remove each time. Irregular, infrequent mowing makes the job much slower and more difficult when it is tackled.

Mow to a height of an inch (2–3cm), no tighter. Grass at this height retains enough foliage to be able to compete; mowing too tight encourages weeds and moss. Over-close mowing tends to shave little humps, making the job more difficult and the result less satisfactory.

The kind of mower used, and its size, make a big difference. Rotary mowers with a single blade are more robust. They are better at mowing grass when it is slightly damp. They are also faster than cylinder mowers although the latter give a more even cut and a better finish.

The bigger the mower, the less time spent mowing. A 21 inch mower will cut a given area in thirty per cent less time than the 16 inch mower. There are other advantages to using a large mower. The chances are that, because it takes less time to mow, the mowing will be done more regularly. The work is easier and the lawn will be of better quality as a result. A powerful mower is less likely to break down than a small mower which is forced to struggle. Although the initial cost is higher, a large powerful mower may cost less per year of mowing, apart at all from the mowing time saved.

●**Edges.** A lawn poses problems around its edges. Usually lawns are delimited by beds, borders, walls, paths and driveways. In each case, there is a low maintenance way to fit the lawn to its boundary.

Where beds and borders join a lawn area, the usual thing is to have an edge cut down into the soil of the border. The lawn is trimmed to where it protrudes over the edge. Usually these edges are made too deep, making it difficult to run the mower over them. It is best to have edges no more than 2 inches (5cm) deep. The wheels on one side of the mower can be let down into the bed or border, cutting the edge easily.

A mowing strip of bricks or paving slabs can be set down in the soil of the bed or border to make a level run for the mower's wheels. The mowing strip should be set about 1 inch (2cm) below the level of the soil. A rotary mower has advantages when it comes to cutting lawn edges. The spinning blade creates a suction effect which lifts the grass into the path of the blade. Cylinder mowers have no lifting effect.

Mowers can only cut horizontally and even with the lifting effect of a rotary mower, the grass still grows out horizontally over the edges. Edges still have to be trimmed occasionally — less frequently if a rotary mower is used. Mowing strips facilitate the lifting/cutting action of rotary mowers and they also make it easier to trim the grass that the mower does not reach.

Where the lawn meets a wall, the narrow strip of grass next to the wall is impossible to mow because the wheels of the mower are in the way. The solution to this problem is to remove the sod and lay a mowing strip along the wall base.

Where a lawn meets a path or driveway, the level of the lawn should be slightly higher than the path or drive. If the path has a kerb, it will be higher than the path but just below the level of the soil of the lawn. In this way, the path or driveway acts as a mowing strip along its length. Where the lawn level is below that of the path or drive, the situation is the same as that beside a wall. The same solution can be adopted, if it is not possible to simply bring the level of the lawn up to the kerb height.

Reducing the number of lawn edges is the best way to reduce the work of edging. Beds can be filled in. Borders can butt onto paths, rather than have a strip of lawn between a border and a path making two extra lawn edges to trim. Edging can be greatly speeded up by using a powered edger or strimmer. The latter is fast but not as neat.

Fruit and vegetables

●**Size.** The size of the area laid out to fruit and vegetables is obviously going to have a large influence on the amount of work involved. Many people make the decision to have no fruit or vegetable area and this is a big time saving. However, it is quite easy to maintain a small vegetable area, and fruit trees can be grown in the ornamental part of the garden.

●**Fruit.** Fruit trees like apples, pears and plums are very ornamental apart from providing fruit. They all have lovely blossom and, sometimes, good autumn colour as well, especially pear trees. Fruit trees can be grown in a mixed border of trees, shrubs and perennial flowers, or they could even be grown as specimen trees within a lawn area.

Neighbouring gardens usually contain fruit trees that act as pollinators, so there is no need, in this situation, to have more than one or two trees. Most fruit trees are now available on dwarfing rootstocks which keep them from growing too large. These smaller trees are much easier to manage. Fruit trees can also be grown as trained trees on walls, making good use of space and providing wall cover. However, they will require more pruning and training than free-standing trees.

Other fruits like raspberries, blackcurrants and strawberries are a mixed lot. Raspberries are easy to grow but they must be pruned and tied up each year. Strawberries need no work once they are planted. Blackcurrants are a nuisance to pick; the fruit is not versatile in kitchen use, and there is pruning as well.

●**Vegetables.** Many people no longer bother with vegetables at all. Growing bulky vegetables in an ordinary garden is more or less a waste of time. Potatoes, cabbage, cauliflower, carrots and onions can be bought more cheaply, and as

A mowing strip at a pathway.

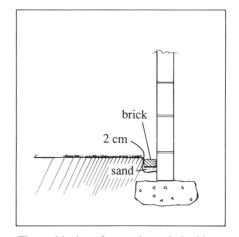

The positioning of a mowing strip beside a wall.

Fruit and vegetables are labour intensive.

French beans require very little effort.

A small herb garden is well worthwhile.

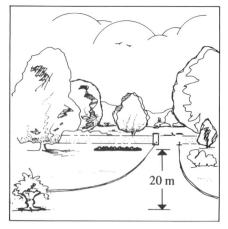

A flowerbed in the distance is completely lost.

good quality, as they can be grown in a home garden. Some first early potatoes that will not need spraying are nice to have, and some early fingerling carrots too perhaps, but maincrop are not worth the effort.

The vegetables which are best fresh from the garden are worth growing — lettuce, radish, salad onions. These are easy to grow, and the easiest vegetable of all is french beans. Also very easy are white turnips, swiss chard, mangetout peas and leeks. All of these are crops which can be sown where they are to grow to maturity; they do not need transplanting.

Weed control is the main time-consumer in vegetable growing, although sowing, thinning and transplanting take up time too. The secret of weed control with vegetables is to make sure the plot is weed-free to start with. Then, never let the weeds go to seed. Regular light hoeing is the easiest way to keep on top of weeds. It is remarkable how large an area can be kept free by hoeing for an hour about every two weeks during the growing season.

●**Herbs.** If a decision is made not to bother with vegetables at all, it is still worth growing some herbs. Fresh herbs are hard to buy. Most kitchen herbs are perennials that come up each year. Apart from an annual tidy-up, and an occasional run-over with the hoe during the summer, a small herb plot needs no work.

Herbs that are easy to grow include Sage, Thyme, Mint, French tarragon, Chives, and Marjoram. Fennel gets big and could be included as an ornamental plant in a mixed border. Horseradish can be grown in some rough corner. Rosemary is a pretty shrub for the border too. Parsley is awkward because it must be sown each year; try it in April and July. Basil is a very nice herb but must be grown indoors in a greenhouse, or on a windowsill. Three or four plants are very little trouble and will give plenty of leaves for freezing.

Flower beds

●**Reasons.** Formal flower beds, usually containing roses or bedding plants, require quite considerable maintenance in terms of edging, weed control and plant care. Formal flower beds comprise large areas of bare soil that invite colonisation by weeds. Very often, there is no good reason for flower beds as they are seen in gardens. Sometimes, it is a case of having too many flower beds, or they may be too distant from the house to be worthwhile. Quite frequently, they are placed beside paths and driveways to alleviate their functional ugliness, but invariably, they only serve to draw further attention.

Almost without exception, formal flower beds should only be considered at the base of the house walls, or internal garden walls, flanking paved areas, or decorating grass terraces. Flower beds near the house can be smaller, but more effective, than a flower bed some distance away. It is often possible to remove inappropriate, or surplus, flower beds.

●**Formal rosebeds.** Bedding Roses are the most common kind of garden Roses, generally grown in a formal rosebed of rectangular, semi-circular, or some other geometric shape. These have all the drawbacks, in terms of effort, mentioned above. Yet, because bedding Roses are formal plants, a formal rosebed still provides the ideal setting. By keeping the number and size of rosebeds small, it is possible to greatly reduce the amount of edging, pruning, weeding and spraying.

Rose beds can be treated with the weedkiller, Simazine, to prevent weed germination. The ground must be completely free of existing weeds, especially perennial weeds. Simazine is best applied in spring to moist soil. Bark mulch is sometimes used on rosebeds but tends to be messy and is not really suitable.

●**Informal roses.** For those who like Roses but not the attendant bother, it is possible to grow them at the front of a mixed border. In this situation, they can be planted a bit less formally — more randomly spaced in a group of five or nine bushes, for example. The edging job will be largely dispensed with.

The ground at their base could be planted with Alchemilla, Sedum roseum, smaller Campanulas, even Catmint or Centranthus for the taller Rose varieties.

When the ground cover is established, there will be little bother with weeding. Tulips could be placed in clumps to brighten the scene in spring while the Rose leaves are still expanding. This kind of planting extends the season of interest for an area of ground informally planted with Roses, but would be inappropriate and messy in a formal rosebed.

●**Formal flower beds.** Formal beds of half-hardy annual flowers are very popular, but labour intensive. The flowers must be replaced twice each year to give a separate spring and summer display. This means digging the flower bed twice a year, apart from edging and weed control. In the case of flower beds, there is no possibility of chemical weed control. The only possibility is hoeing and considerable handweeding. In addition, watering will usually be necessary to get the young plants established.

Keep the area planted with bedding plants to a minimum, and like formal rosebeds, keep them near the house itelf. A common mistake is to have a big formal bed of bedding plants away at the bottom of a large lawn where, if it can be seen at all from the house, the bed looks no more than a splodge of bright colour.

●**Informal bedding.** Bedding plants can be used informally to great effect, and little effort, at the front of a mixed border. Especially in new gardens, where there are more gaps at the front of new borders, six or ten bedding plants in a group can provide a spot of colour to brighten the rest of the display. The size of the groups should not be the same; they should not be spaced an equal distance apart, nor should there be too many of them. Another mistake is to use more than one or two complementary colours.

With informal planting, edging is largely avoided and weed control is not as much of a burden. Much better value is got from a smaller number of plants. Nor is it essential to use both spring and summer bedding; gaps at the front of a border will not look as empty as a formal flower bed when the summer bedding has been cleared.

Rockery

●**Siting.** As a garden feature, rockeries are probably most sinned against. Very often, any problem slope or awkward corner seems to invite a rockery as the solution — usually the worst possible choice. Far from being easy, it is very difficult to succeed with rockeries. They need to be sited, ideally, on a gentle slope in full sunshine. Very few rock plants like shade. Try to position the rockery so that it fits into the slope and rises naturally out of it. It should not back onto a boundary wall, or worse still a fence. There is quite a bit of work in building a rockery, especially if it is done properly.

●**Weeds.** Far from being the labour-saving solution to a steep bank, a rockery is quite a labour-intensive garden feature. Small rockery plants are not adapted for competition with weeds. Weeding is usually a major job, made more difficult by the niches between rocks that make weeds hard to dislodge. Weedkillers cannot be used.

Before planting a rockery, make sure that the soil is completely weed-free. It is worth waiting a few months and controlling weeds properly. When the plants are in place, or beforehand if preferred, cover the soil with at least 2 inches (5 cm) of gravel or broken stone. Make sure that the colour of the gravel matches the stone of the rockery. The layer of gravel will reduce weeding dramatically, as long as weeds are never allowed a foothold. Besides, the gravel helps to make a rockery seem more natural, and it sets off rock plants very well.

Greenhouse

●**Uses.** A greenhouse can be put to many uses and makes it possible to grow a wide range of plants, but only if the garden owner is interested in plants. There are thousands of empty, or at least grossly under-utilised, greenhouses in the country.

Roses,
though beautiful, are demanding of attention.

Spots of colour with informal bedding.

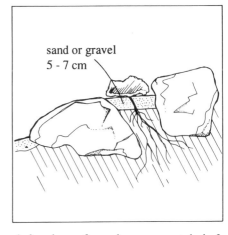

A deep layer of gravel saves a great deal of weeding.

Greenhouse tomatoes — are they really worth the bother?

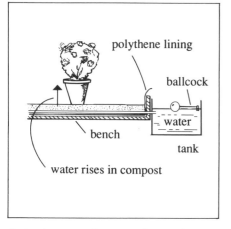

polythene lining

ballcock

water

bench

tank

water rises in compost

A simple system for automatic watering.

Containers, though attractive, need regular watering.

Before getting a greenhouse, consider carefully what it is to be used for. Many greenhouses play host to a few tomato plants each year and a collection of ailing houseplants. Although a greenhouse can be used to grow a wide range of fruit, vegetables and flowers, there is considerable time and effort involved in using a greenhouse to even a fraction of its potential.

Plants in a greenhouse are completely dependent on the gardener, which is fine if the gardener wants the burden of caring for them. There is watering, feeding and ventilation to be considered, as well as potting up, pest control and some weeding.

However, it is possible to use a greenhouse effectively with very little effort. The most minimal use for a greenhouse is to plant it with long-lived plants like Ivy-leaved geraniums, Agaves, Clivias, Epiphyllums, Abutilons, Jasmine, Hibiscus, even Camellias and Hydrangeas if there is enough space. These will get by in the ordinary soil and will survive winter cold unless it is very severe. Leave the vents open all summer, and water heavily perhaps once a week.

●**Watering.** Watering is by far the biggest part of the work of a greenhouse. During the summer, tomatoes, for example, need watering every second day, perhaps even every day during very hot weather. This can be most interesting fun, or a real nuisance, depending on your point of view.

There a number of ways to make greenhouse watering easier. To avoid carrying water, have the water supply close to hand, ideally piped into the greenhouse itself. A lazy, but effective, way to water a greenhouse quickly is to take a hose and spray over the whole lot. Plants which do not need much water tend to get over-watered with this method. There are various proprietary watering systems available involving drip watering and wet-mat watering.

A very effective wet-mat system can be installed with a little effort. It consists of a layer of wet sand laid on heavy gauge polythene and topped up every few days. Alternatively, a reservoir with a ballcock can be fitted to make watering automatic. Once installed, this system makes the watering of miscellaneous pots very easy indeed.

Containers

●**Number.** Containers are a very useful way of adding ornamental interest to the garden. In recent years, they have become extremely popular. However, there is a tendency to over-use containers, placing window-boxes on every windowsill, hanging baskets at every corner, and tubs and planters on every path and paved area.

Remember that the more containers planted up, the more watering will be necessary during the summer. It is best to restrict the number of containers to the minimum necessary and concentrate on looking after those properly. In any garden, there are a few key locations for containers. These are usually associated with entrances, paths, paved areas and corners of buildings. Pick out the important locations, by moving containers around if necessary, and plant up that number only.

●**Size.** The size of the container, and its shape, have a very significant effect on how easy it is to water. Large containers hold a greater volume of compost, and a larger reserve of water and plant nutrients. Deep containers dry out more slowly because they have less compost surface area relative to their volume. If containers are too deep, however, they look ungainly; their proportions are not pleasing.

The material of which the container is made has a bearing on drying out, too. Clay and concrete containers look good but they dry out quickly. They can be lined with polythene sheeting to keep the moisture in. Metal urns look well, especially lead and cast iron, and they dry out more slowly. Plastic holds in the moisture but does not look great.

●**Compost.** The compost used in containers should have the capacity to hold moisture. Any form of organic material, especially peat, is useful in this regard. A compost containing half peat, half good garden soil with some fertiliser added is a suitable mixture. It costs less than using peat-based compost alone. If it dries out, it is easier to wet than peat-based compost, and there is a small reserve of nutrients in the soil if feeding is neglected. Do not use garden soil on its own; it tends to become compacted with regular watering and the plant roots are starved of air.

●**Watering.** Watering, including liquid feeding, is the only work attached to growing container plants, once they are planted. Various ways to reduce the frequency of watering have already been mentioned, but another important tactic is to accustom the plants, from the beginning, to getting by on less water. If container plants are watered each day, they will grow luxuriantly but wilt very quickly if watering is missed for any reason.

If they are watered every four or five days, they will become less leafy, probably carry more flowers, and they will certainly be able to stand up to water shortage much better. All plants are to some extent adaptable to the conditions in which they find themselves. Plants grown in adequate, but less generous, regimes are tougher, with more wax on their leaves and better root systems.

Hedges

●**Size.** Hedges are a most important garden feature for their dual functions of decoration and division. They provide structure within the garden, and a good boundary and privacy from the outside. They also shelter less robust plants and make a good backdrop to more decorative kinds. However, they are also among the most labour-intensive garden features. The amount of work is directly related to the size of the hedge.

The first consideration is the total length of hedges in the garden. Very often hedges are planted without taking into account subsequent maintenance. Is a hedge really necessary? The choice for a boundary division is between hedges, walls and fences. Hedges are cheaper than walls and fences, but the latter provide better boundaries, and usually the best design solution too.

Hedges are sometimes planted unnecessarily beside a garden wall to hide the bare concrete. Disguise can be achieved more successfully, for less expense and with less maintenance, by using climbers, shrubs and standard trees.

The other major aspect of the size of a hedge is height; the higher the hedge, the more clipping and the more difficult the clipping. A hedge of 5 feet (1.5m) has twenty per cent less clipping than one of 6 feet (1.8m) metres. Tall hedges might be needed in a garden that is overlooked but, for privacy on a level site, a hedge does not need to be more than 5.5 feet (1.65m) high. Any hedge higher than this cannot be clipped without using a stepladder. Higher hedges need higher ladders, or some kind of scaffolding. This adds greatly to the work because it is more difficult to clip a hedge from a ladder, and the ladder will need to be moved.

A wide hedge takes up more garden space and makes more work in reaching across to clip the top. All hedges grow most vigorously at the top and the wider the hedge the more top-clipping necessary. All hedges should be trained to a wedge-shape, in cross-section, to keep the top narrow and allow light down to the sides.

●**Type.** The species of hedge has a big influence on the amount of clipping work. Some kinds like Privet, Lonicera, Cotoneaster lacteus, Leyland cypress, and Monterey cypress are very rapid growers, capable of making a decent hedge in four or five years. It is not surprising that these are among the most common hedges, but they are also the ones that need most maintenance. Because they grow fast, they need clipping more often. Lonicera and Privet need to be clipped at least twice and as often as four times each year to stay neat.

Slower-growing hedges like Beech, Yew, Griselinia, Thuya, Lawson cypress, Hawthorn, Hornbeam, Berberis, Olearia and Holly hold their neat look with a single clipping each year. Feeding has an influence on the growth rate of hedging. These slower-growing kinds can be speeded up in the initial years of establishment by feeding and watering. If this is done, they lose nothing in speed of establishment to the faster-growing kinds, but have the distinct advantage of easier maintenance for life.

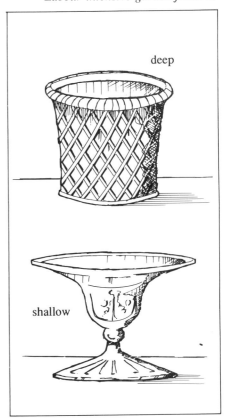

Some containers need less frequent watering.

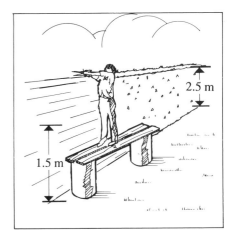

High hedges are more difficult to clip.

Box hedges, though fashionable, demand attention.

●**Clipping.** Clipping should be done before the young shoots begin to get woody. This process begins in July and by mid-August the job of clipping will be much more difficult. At the same time, clipping too early will encourage new growth and necessitate a second clip later.

Powered hedgetrimmers make the work much easier, but they also need care in handling to get a neat finish. Petrol-engined trimmers cope more easily with long runs of hedge, large hedges and tougher material. The cables of electric trimmers can be awkward over long runs of hedge, but they are cheaper. Laying out polythene or similar sheeting before clipping makes tidying up much easier. Alternatively, if the clippings fall onto a lawn area, and they are not too plentiful, a rotary mower with a grass-bag can be used to chew them up and collect them.

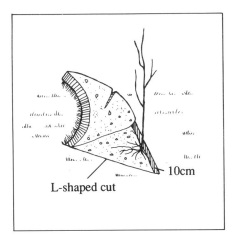

L-shaped cut
10cm

An easy way to plant 'whips'.

Good weed control is essential around young trees.

Labour-Saving Garden Features

The time and effort spent on any garden, new or existing, can be reduced by increasing the area given to labour-saving features. Some of these, like paving, and walls, are more expensive than their labour-intensive alternative, but that is not necessarily the case. For example, perennial flowers are less expensive over their long life than an equivalent area of bedding plants which must be replaced twice a year.

Trees

●**Advantages.** Trees are the most successful plants because their height allows them to intercept light before it reaches the ground, and their deep root system affords them access to supplies of soil moisture and nutrients that smaller plants cannot reach. We can use the success of trees to our own advantage.

Because trees grow large, they can be used to fill space. In large gardens, the more space filled by trees the less work of maintenance. Trees can look after themselves. Once they get above the grassy layer, they are away. As time passes, their competitive advantage becomes so great that grass and weeds find it difficult to grow. The ground layer beneath trees becomes dominated by plants which tolerate shade.

●**Planting.** Trees are best planted as young plants two or three years old. The smaller plants establish more successfully and produce better anchor roots for the future. But they are also easier to plant than larger sizes; they do not need staking, and they are cheaper.

Detailed information on the general techniques of Planting, Watering, Feeding, Weed control and Pruning of trees is given on pages 8–11. In the establishment of large areas of trees, using small plants, a number of short-cuts can be used. Although it is desirable to dig, plough or rotavate the area to be planted, it is not essential. The existing grass and weeds can be controlled by two applications of Round-up, Tumbleweed or Greenscape. Planting should be carried out in late autumn or early spring. The dead sod can be simply cut in an L-shape with a spade, and the sod lifted. The young tree is slotted into the hole and the sod firmed back in place. Using this method, it is possible to plant several hundred trees in a single day.

Weed control must be kept up for the first few years. After that, the trees themselves will be able to keep control. Only elder, briars and large perennial weeds will need control. Feeding the young trees in the early years will result in quicker establishment and bring forward the day when weed control can be abandoned.

●**Thinning.** In a natural situation, a surplus of young trees attempts to colonise a free piece of ground. In time, some will dominate the rest, and there will be losses. Similarly, in establishing garden woodland planting, it is desirable to slightly over-plant to start with. Planting at a random spacing averaging two metres apart will ensure a quicker cover of the soil surface, and will provide for early losses.

After eight or ten years, it will be necessary to reduce the number of trees by about half, choosing the poorer specimens to go. These can be cut down and removed, or simply killed in situ by using Roundup or Brushwood killer in an axe wound low down on the stem. Further thinning, again by about half the number of trees, can be carried out twenty or twenty-five years after planting.

Garden woodland can be established to cover very small areas — as little as a few hundred square metres. Smaller trees like Birch, Alder, Hazel and Holly could be used in smaller gardens. Where there is plenty of space to fill, the large forest trees like Oak, Ash, Beech, Elm, Lime, Pine, Horse chestnut, Spruce and Sweet chestnut are ideal. Established woodland has an extremely low maintenance demand, needing only the occasional control of woody weeds and ivy. The life of such a garden feature will range from one hundred years for Birch to several hundred years for Oak and Spanish chestnut.

Shrubs that are clothed to ground level need less weeding.

Some shrubs, such as Rhododendrons, need no pruning.

Shrubs

●**Advantages.** Shrubs can be used in small gardens to fill space in the same way that trees can be used in large gardens. Many of them are fast-growing and quickly fill a considerable area. A piece of ground planted with shrubs has a much lower maintenance requirement than a similar area of lawn. Therefore, the conversion of part of the garden area to accommodate shrubs reduces effort.

Many shrubs clothe themselves with foliage down to ground level, which increases their competitive ability over non-woody weeds. A distinct advantage in favour of woody plants in general, and shrubs in particular, is their immunity to the chemical weedkiller, Simazine. Although not all shrubs are immune, the majority are.

●**Planting.** Most shrubs are grown in containers and sold as container-grown stock with their full root system intact. This means that they are much easier to get established. When planted during the late autumn or early spring, they are unlikely to need any subsequent watering, except possibly during drought spells. This is a considerable saving of effort. Because they have their full root system, container-grown shrubs can be planted during the growing season. However, this means losing the advantage of reduced effort because they must be kept watered until well established. The general technical details of Planting, Feeding, Watering, Weed control and Pruning are given on pages 8–11.

Shrubs may be planted through dead sod, as described for trees above, but each shrub must have a proper planting hole dug out. This should be 6–8 inches (15–20cm) wider all round than the rootball from the pot.

●**Pruning.** Shrubs vary greatly in their requirement for pruning; some kinds never need pruning, some need occasional thinning to keep them neat. However, no shrub need necessarily be pruned as a matter of course. Where there is space, they can be let grow as they please.

However, space is a limiting factor in most gardens; the main reason for pruning shrubs is to keep them within bounds. If you prune out roughly the amount of growth the plant puts on each year, then it will stay the same size, or only slowly get bigger.

No pruning is necessary at all for the first five or six years, or until the shrub is flowering well, if it is a flowering kind. Then, remove about one in five of the plant's branches each year, choosing the oldest ones to go. Most shrubs flower best on young growth so this will not upset flowering.

Do not remove part of all the branches because this interferes with flowering. Never trim a shrub with a hedge-clippers unless it has fine foliage like that of Broom, Heather or Lavender. The principle is to thin out the shoots, not shorten them all back.

Some shrubs like Rhododendrons, Magnolias, Pieris, Enkianthus, and most evergreens are best not pruned at all. Pruning applies mainly to bushy, twiggy shrubs which produce a lot of new growth each year, particularly from ground level or near it. Choose shrubs that rarely, if ever, need pruning, and give them adequate space. This approach can reduce, or remove, the necessity to prune shrubs at all. (*See the List of Shrubs That Need No Pruning. Page 106–7*).

●**Weed control.** Although shrubs are competitive against weeds, in most cases they are not as competitive as trees. Whereas trees only need a high level of weed control for the first five or six years after planting, there will be a need to maintain proper weed control throughout the life of a shrub planting.

Hoeing is a good method of weed control among young shrubs. It is not time-consuming if the ground is completely free of perennial weeds before planting, and if the seedling weeds are controlled before they reach 2 inches (5cm).

Mulching can provide a major saving of effort as an alternative to hoeing. Bark mulch is the best choice because it is free of weed seeds. It must be laid on weed-free soil to an even depth of 2½–3 inches (6–8cm). Grass mowings are very effective too, but not deeper than 2 inches (5cm) at a time. Garden compost is not really suitable for this purpose because it contains weed seeds.

Straw to a depth of about 8 inches (20cm) is effective but only on large areas because it looks untidy. It may contain cereal seeds. Black polythene is effective for a year or so until it breaks down and cracks. It tends to be messy and not as successful as organic mulches. If mulches are used to control weeds, they must be topped up every couple of years. Otherwise, the cover is not adequate to block out the light and the weeds grow in the gaps. In addition, it will be necessary to remove weeds that manage to establish themselves on the mulch, either by pulling, or by directed spray of Tumbleweed, Greenscape or Roundup.

Hoeing can be continued as the main method of weed control but it involves a lot of effort. Mulching is a good alternative but tends to be a bit expensive. Weed control with Simazine is an option which is effective and cheap. This chemical prevents the germination of weed seedlings. It will not control existing weeds and must be applied to weed-free, moist soil. Some shrubs are susceptible to damage by Simazine such as Rhododendrons, Cherries and Heathers.

Perennial flowers

●**Advantages.** Perennial flowers have a number of very significant advantages over other non-woody plants. Unlike bedding plants which must be planted each year, the perennial flowers need only be planted once. This is a big saving of effort; the more garden space given over to perennial flowers instead of annuals, the better.

Even though they are perennial, these non-woody plants die down at the end of each season. Effectively therefore, they are self-pruning. Perennial flowers are very quick to get established, requiring little watering, and some kinds are very good at competing with weeds. With each passing year, the original plant spreads outwards to form a clump and claim more ground for itself. This is ground denied to weeds.

●**Planting.** Unlike trees and shrubs which can be planted into dead sod, perennial flowers must have the soil dug over and cultivated before planting. It is essential to get these plants off to a good start. Otherwise, their ability to compete with weeds will be much reduced and they will not regain the advantage. For the first two or three years, it is worth dividing, and re-planting, the original plants. This technique, which initially requires more effort, results in a quicker filling-in of the ground area and subsequently reduces the work of weed control.

The complete control of perennial weeds in the ground where perennial flowers are to be planted will save endless effort later. There is no possibility of using weed-killers once the perennial flowers have been planted, and control of perennial weeds will become extremely difficult and time-consuming. At least two applications of Tumbleweed, Greenscape or Roundup will be necessary to kill off all existing vegetation. If chemical control is ruled out, meticulous digging of the roots of perennial weeds, though not wholly effective, is one way to remove perennial weeds in advance of planting. Alternatively, old carpet laid over the ground for about twelve months provides a relatively easy and effective, if slow, method of control.

Weed control following establishment is made more easy by selecting perennial flowers which cover the soil surface. The less soil left bare, the fewer weeds come through. Hoeing is relatively easy if the weeds are not allowed to grow taller than 2 inches (5cm) and certainly never allowed to go to seed. Hand-weeding is much slower but will probably be necessary close to the plants. A mulch of bark chippings is very effective around perennial flowers, especially in the early years until the plants begin to cover the soil.

●**Aftercare.** Perennial flowers need relatively little regular care and attention. They need far less effort than annual flowers and Roses, for example. In fact, if some care is taken to avoid the ones which need dividing and staking, most kinds need no more work than shrubs. (*See the List of Flowers That Need No Staking. Page 108–9*).

The lifting and division of perennial flowers to keep the plants vigorous is often advised. It involves lifting, dividing and re-planting every three or four years.

Chopped bark provides a good mulch and an attractive dark background.

Perennial flowers need very little care.

Very many perennial flowers need no staking or tying up.

A mixed border is most ornamental and easiest to keep.

Though relatively expensive, paving saves effort.

However, this work is not at all necessary for many species, and some positively dislike being shifted.

Because the stems of perennial flowers are not woody, some kinds tend to be easily blown over by wind, and need to be staked. Many others, however, do not need staking. The problem is greatly increased by growing perennial flowers in large groups in herbaceous borders. When they are provided with shelter by shrubs and trees, the problem is lessened. Heavy feeding with manures, while encouraging bigger displays, also contributes to the problem of floppy stems.

When perennial flowers die back in autumn, many books advise the removal of the dead flower stalks. However, these are best left in place until early spring, because most kinds are ornamental through the winter. They also provide over-wintering shelter for many beneficial animals. When they are cut down in spring, it is a good idea to remove the stems to only half their height. The remainder is often quite stiff and will provide a measure of support for the new shoots. The top half of the dead shoots can be removed by clipping with a hedge-clippers. The debris can be removed to a compost heap, or chopped up and left to rot down around the plants. Removing only part of the stems reduces the amount of effort involved and makes it possible to tidy up a large area of perennial flowers very quickly.

Mixed borders

●**Ornament.** Planting trees, shrubs and flowers together in a mixed border confers a number of advantages. The overall ornamental impact of using the various plant types together is much greater than restricting the types to their own kind, as in herbaceous borders and shrub borders. Trees, even just one or two, can be used at the back of such borders with shrubs to fill in beneath, and in front of them. Around the shrubs and in front of them in turn, the perennial flowers provide colour and lush foliage to contrast with the hard stiffness of the woody plants. Annual flowers, bulbs and even Roses can be used at the front of mixed borders to add further interest.

●**Weed control.** It is possible to have two layers of foliage covering the soil over most of the area of a mixed border, with resultant suppression of weeds. This reduces the work of weeding. Shrubs and perennial flowers can be used to hide areas of bare ground beneath trees at the back of mixed planting. Simazine can be used to keep down weeds around trees and shrubs where there is no under-planting of perennial flowers. Where there are perennial flowers, bark mulch is a good alternative.

A mixed border has in common with other borders that they have only one side that requires edging. In small gardens, it is usual for borders to back onto the boundary. In large gardens, they might back onto internal boundaries or areas of tree planting. Borders with gentle curves have the advantage over straight borders that the edging need not be so frequently attended to without looking unkempt.

Paving

●**Advantages.** Apart from its ornamental value and conceding that it is relatively expensive, paving has the major advantage of requiring very little maintenance. By increasing the area of garden under paving, a resultant reduction in labour requirement can be achieved. Relative to any other garden feature, paving of any kind needs practically no work. This is especially true of paving slabs and concrete, somewhat less so of tarmac.

●**Maintenance.** All kinds of paving requires to be swept of debris and dust occasionally to prevent a build-up that would allow moss and weeds to grow, but this is a very light task compared with maintaining a similar area of lawn, for example. Where there are cracks, or joints in the case of concrete slabs, weeds are likely to get established. These can be difficult to remove physically but there are many excellent products for their control. These include Hytrol, Pathclear,

Murphy Superweedex, Path Weedkiller, Root Out, Path and Drive Weedkiller, and Casoron. Tarmac has a more porous surface and is more prone to moss and weed infestation than solid concrete, or paving slabs.

Gravel beds

●**Advantages.** Gravel beds are sometimes used to reduce the proportion of the garden covered by lawn, the idea being to reduce the work of mowing. Gravel areas need practically no maintenance compared with lawns, flower beds or borders, and they compare well with solid paving. They have the advantage over paving of being cheaper and easier to install. Gravel sets off many plants very nicely. However, the location of gravel areas, and whether or not they contain plants, can affect their value for reduced effort.

●**Maintenance.** Gravel beds are easy to maintain if they contain few or no plants. If the gravel is sufficiently deep — 3–4 inches (8–10cm) — very few weeds will come through. These can usually be pulled by hand. The weedkiller Simazine can also be used, except around non-woody plants. All gravel areas need to be raked over occasionally to leave the surface even, but this is relatively light work. Gravel beds close to trees tend to suffer badly from falling leaves and germinating tree seedlings, typically Sycamore and Ash. Unless removed, leaves rot down to provide excellent rooting material for weeds. Although Simazine can be used where there are no non-woody plants, it will not control tree seedlings.

As time passes, gravel beds tend to sink into the soil and must be topped up. A lining of polythene, or woven polypropylene, beneath the gravel can reduce sinking but tends to encourage the accumulation of debris among the gravel, and consequently more weed growth.

Walls, fences

●**Advantages.** Like paving, walls and fences are relatively expensive but, when built, require practically no attention. In comparison with hedges, they never require clipping; they do not take up as much space and they have no invasive roots.

●**Maintenance.** Fences are usually made of wood or metal, both of which need painting occasionally. Walls may also be painted, or they can be left as bare bricks or concrete. In the latter case, an aging process will eventually help the wall to blend better with plants. This can be speeded up by spraying the wall with a little milk, liquid fertiliser or cowdung diluted in water.

●**Plants.** Climbing plants and other wall plants can be used to decorate walls and fences, taking the bareness off them, and turning the otherwise blank space to good advantage. Most are easy enough to look after, some more so than others. Some climbing plants can creep up walls and fences by means of suckers and aerial roots but most need some support to cling onto, or to be tied onto. Choosing the ones that creep by their own means, such as Ivy and Virginia creeper, avoids the need for tying-in.

Constant tying-in of wall plants can be very time-consuming, and usually it boils down to having an inadequate support system to start with. The easiest way to approach the task is to wire the whole wall first, or at least that part of it where plants are to grow. It is by no means necessary, or even desirable, to cover an entire wall with climbing plants, but the aim should be to wire the area which the climber will fill.

Wires can be placed in horizontal lines about 12 inches (30cm) apart, from about 24 inches (60cm) off the ground right to the top of the wall. Galvanised steel wire is best, attached to brass screws at about 16 inch (40cm) centres along each length. If a wall needs painting, these screws can be removed and the plants taken down. An easier way is simply to trim back the wall plants a little, paint the wall as close as possible to them, and allow them to grow out again.

A gravel bed sets off plants beautifully.

Blank walls provide opportunity to grow wall plants and climbers.

A large pool looks well and needs little attention.

Pools

●**Maintenance.** Garden pools vary considerably in their maintenance requirements. Generally, large pools require less attention than smaller ones. A larger body of water is more stable than smaller volumes which tend to get polluted and overgrown more quickly. If a pool can be fed naturally by a small trickle of water, it makes maintenance much easier.

A large pool takes up space that might otherwise be sown down to grass, usually. Only requiring the clearing out of surplus plant growth every few years, such a pool is easy to maintain. It takes a great deal of effort to put in place but relatively little subsequently. Because they are generally deeper, large pools contain relatively more water and a natural balance is more easily achieved and maintained.

A small pool tends to warm up more quickly, goes green more readily and becomes contaminated with leaves and debris more easily. Plants fill the space of a small pool more quickly and need reduction more frequently. If fish are kept, they need feeding regularly. In terms of ornamental value, a small pool is far more effort than a large one, and probably best avoided if the aim is to reduce effort.

Wildflower meadows

●**Advantages.** Compared to a conventional lawn, a wildflower area has considerable advantages, the most important being the reduction in mowing. Mowing requirements can be cut to a fraction of that required for a good lawn. Another significant advantage is the removal of any necessity to apply fertilisers or weed-killers. A wildflower area makes a change from manicured lawns; it is a beautiful feature in itself, and very appropriate for a certain kind of garden.

●**Maintenance.** There is a big reduction in effort when a lawn area is turned over to wildflower meadow. Instead of mowing once a week from April to September, no mowing at all is done before the end of June, or early July, just like a traditional hay-meadow. After cutting, the grass is left for a few days to shed seed and then removed to a compost area. Subsequently, the regrowth of grass is mown every four or five weeks to keep it tidy.

The cut grass must be removed to reduce the fertility of the soil. This, in turn, reduces the vigour of grass growth and encourages wildflowers — the exact opposite of looking after a quality lawn. For the same reasons, no fertiliser is ever given, or lawn weedkiller applied, to a wildflower area.

Mown boundary to an area of bulbs naturalised in grass.

The process of creating a successful wildflower area takes a few years. The reduction of fertility and the build-up of wildflowers takes some time. It can be speeded up by removing some of the top-soil, and by planting wildflower seedlings raised in pots. However, if the object in converting to a wildflower area is to reduce effort, these tactics are unlikely to be adopted.

The single big cut in July can involve considerable effort. For a small wildflower area, the grass can be cut with a strimmer and raked off. For larger areas, a rough grass mower, or mowing machine will be required. However, the job of mowing gets easier as the meadow settles down, and infertility increases. Even in the early years, it is still a lot easier than weekly mowing. This feature suits large gardens best because it can look a bit messy in a small garden. A close-mown boundary where wildflower meadow meets paths and driveways helps to tame an otherwise unkempt look.

Banks, cuttings

●**Problems.** Very many houses on large sloping sites require earthmoving to level the house site. This invariably leaves the garden with one or more banks, or cuttings. These may be close to the house running along one or more sides, or they may run alongside a driveway entrance. They may rise back from the house, or fall away. In either case, they present a serious problem. The usual approach is to plant these banks with shrubs of various kinds. The result is nearly always an unsatisfactory garden feature that does not fit in very well with the rest of the garden but requires considerable maintenance effort to control weeds.

●**Solutions.** There are three possible solutions that will reduce the effort involved in maintaining banks. The most obvious answer is simply to reduce the grade of the bank further. In the case of a slope away from the house, this may involve filling the slope. Then it can be grassed over, usually just extending the adjoining lawn area.

If the slope is too steep to be reduced, or a boundary is in the way, the alternative option is to build a retaining wall and fill in behind. Then a terrace of lawn, paving or shrubs can be installed, as appropriate.

If it is not possible to soften the slope or to retain it, the third option is to plant it with suitable plants. Trees, shrubs and perennial flowers are the plants of choice for a bank. These should be planted up just as a full-scale mixed border would be, not just relying on ground-cover plants and low-growing plants. If the bank is near a boundary, the bank/border should run back to the boundary with trees filling the back. The advantage of mixed planting is that it is easier to maintain than a motley scatter of low shrubs or ground-cover alone, and it looks much better. The slope is lost among taller plants whereas low plants just mirror the slope.

Steep bank disguised with a variety of plants.

LIST OF WIND-RESISTANT TREES

Name	Common name	deciduous/evergreen	height in metres	flower colour	flower season	soil preference
Acer 'Brilliantissimum'	*Pink sycamore*	d	3m	fl	sp	or
Acer pseudoplatanus	*Sycamore*	d	15m	fl	au	or
Acer platanoides	*Norway maple*	d	15m	fl	au	or
Alnus glutinosa	*Common alder*	d	8m	ck	sp	mt
Alnus incana	*Grey alder*	d	8m	ck	sp	mt
Araucaria araucana	*Monkey puzzle*	e	20m	fl	-	or
Betula pendula	*Silver birch*	d	15m	fl	au	or
✻**Cordyline australis**	*Cabbage palm*	e	6m	wh	su	or
Crataegus monogyna	*Hawthorn*	d	6m	wh	sp	or
Fraxinus excelsior	*Ash*	d	20m	fl	au	or
Fraxinus ornus	*Manna ash*	d	8m	fl	au	or
✻**Genista aetnensis**	*Mt. Etna broom*	e	5m	yl	su	dr
Hippophae rhamnoides	*Sea buckthorn*	d	6m	ft	wi	dr
Ilex 'JC Van Tol'	*Holly*	e	6m	ft	wi	or
Ilex aquifolium	*Holly*	e	6m	ft	wi	or
Laburnum anagyroides	*Laburnum*	d	5m	yl	sp	or
Larix decidua	*European larch*	d	20m	fl	au	or
Larix kaempferi	*Japanese larch*	d	20m	fl	au	or
✻**Olearia macrodonta**	*New Zealand holly*	e	5m	wh	su	or
✻**Olearia paniculata**	*New Zealand holly*	e	7m	wh	su	or
Picea abies	*Norway spruce*	e	20m	fl	-	or
Picea sitchensis	*Sitka spruce*	e	25m	fl	-	mt
Pinus contorta latifolia	*Lodgepole pine*	e	15m	fl	-	mt
Pinus mugo 'Gnom'	*Dwarf pine*	e	2m	fl	-	or
Pinus radiata	*Monterey pine*	e	15m	fl	-	or
Pinus sylvestris	*Scots pine*	e	20m	fl	-	dr
✻**Pittosporum tenuifolium**	*Pittosporum*	e	5m	fl	-	or
Populus alba	*White poplar*	d	15m	fl	au	mt
Populus nigra 'Italica'	*Lombardy poplar*	d	20m	fl	au	or
Populus 'Serotina'	*Poplar*	d	15m	fl	au	mt
Populus tremula	*Aspen*	d	12m	fl	au	or
Prunus spinosa	*Blackthorn*	d	5m	wh	sp	or
Quercus cerris	*Turkey oak*	d	20m	fl	au	or
Quercus ilex	*Evergreen oak*	e	15m	fl	-	or
Quercus petraea	*Sessile oak*	d	15m	fl	au	or
Quercus robur	*Common oak*	d	15m	fl	au	or
Salix alba	*White willow*	d	20m	fl	au	mt
Sorbus 'Joseph Rock'	*Yellow rowan*	d	5m	wh	sp	or
Sorbus 'Sheerwater Seedling'	*Mountain ash*	d	4m	wh	sp	or
Sorbus aria	*Whitebeam*	d	10m	wh	sp	or
Sorbus aucuparia	*Mountain ash*	d	10m	wh	sp	or
Tilia cordata	*Small-leaved lime*	d	15m	fl	au	or

✻ = frost susceptible   d = deciduous: e = evergreen   sn = sun: sh = shade
fl = foliage: ck = catkins: ft = fruit: wh = white: yl = yellow: bl = blue: pk = pink: pr = purple: gr = green: rd = red: lc = lilac: or = orange: mx = mixed
sp = spring: su = summer: au = autumn: wi = winter   or = ordinary: mt = moist: dr = dry: ac = acid

LIST OF SHADE-TOLERANT SHRUBS

Name	Common name	deciduous/evergreen	height in metres	flower colour	flower season	soil preference
Aucuba japonica	Japanese laurel	e	3m	ft	au	or
Buxus sempervirens	Common box	e	4m	fl	-	or
Buxus sempervirens 'Suffruticosa'	Edging box	e	1m	fl	-	or
✳Camellia 'Alba Simplex'	White camellia	e	4m	wh	sp	ac
✳Camellia 'Donation'	Camellia	e	3m	pk	sp	ac
✳Camellia 'J.C. Williams'	Camellia	e	3m	pk	wi	ac
✳Camellia 'St. Ewe'	Camellia	e	3m	pk	sp	ac
✳Corylopsis pauciflora	Winter hazel	d	2m	yl	sp	ac
✳Corylopsis spicata	Winter hazel	d	2m	yl	sp	ac
Eleagnus ebbingei	Eleagnus	e	3m	fl	-	or
Euonymus 'Emerald Gaiety'	Euonymus	e	1m	fl	-	or
✳Fatsia japonica	Fatsia	e	3m	wh	su	or
Gaultheria procumbens	Gaultheria	e	.2m	wh	su	ac
✳Hydrangea 'Mme Emile Mouilliere'	Hydrangea	d	2m	wh	su	or
✳Hydrangea aspera	Hydrangea	d	3m	wh	su	or
✳Hydrangea serrata 'Preziosa'	Hydrangea	d	1m	rd	su	or
Hypericum calycinum	Creeping hypericum	d	.4m	yl	su	or
Ilex crenata 'Golden Gem'	Dwarf holly	e	.4m	fl	-	or
✳Leycesteria formosa	Pheasant berry	d	2m	rd	su	or
Lonicera pileata	Lonicera	e	1m	fl	-	or
Mahonia aquifolium	Oregon grape	e	1m	yl	sp	or
Mahonia japonica	Mahonia	e	2m	yl	wi	or
✳Osmanthus burkwoodii	Osmanthus	e	3m	wh	sp	or
✳Osmanthus delavayii	Osmanthus	e	3m	wh	sp	or
Pachysandra terminalis	Japanese spurge	e	.2m	fl	-	or
Philadelphus coronarius 'Aureus'	Yellow philadelphus	d	3m	wh	sp	or
✳Pieris 'Forest Flame'	Pieris	e	3m	wh	sp	ac
✳Pieris formosa 'Wakehurst'	Pieris	e	3m	wh	sp	ac
Prunus 'Otto Luyken'	Dwarf laurel	e	1m	wh	sp	or
Rhododendron 'Susan'	Rhododendron	e	2m	pr	sp	ac
Rhododendron kaempferi	Japanese azalea	e	2m	rd	sp	ac
Rhododendron mollis	Deciduous azalea	d	2m	or	sp	ac
Rhododendron schlippenbachii	Deciduous azalea	d	2m	pk	sp	ac
Rhododendron williamsianum	Rhododendron	e	1m	pk	sp	ac
Ribes alpinum	Alpine currant	d	2m	fl	au	or
Rubus tricolor	Rubus	e	.5m	fl	-	or
Rubus 'Tridel'	Flowering bramble	d	2m	wh	su	or
Sambucus 'Plumosa Aurea'	Golden elder	d	2m	fl	sp	or
✳Sarcococca humilis	Sweet box	e	1m	wh	wi	ac
Skimmia japonica	Skimmia	e	1m	wh	sp	or
Sasa veitchii	Bamboo	e	1m	fl	-	mt
Symphoricarpus 'Hancock'	Pink snowberry	d	1m	ft	au	or
Symphoricarpus albus	Snowberry	d	2m	ft	au	or
Viburnum tinus	Lauristinus	e	3m	wh	wi	or
Vinca minor	Periwinkle	e	.2m	bl	sp	or

✳ = frost susceptible   d = deciduous: e = evergreen   sn = sun: sh = shade
fl = foliage: ck = catkins: ft = fruit: wh = white: yl = yellow: bl = blue: pk = pink: pr = purple: gr = green: rd = red: lc = lilac: or = orange: mx = mixed
sp = spring: su = summer: au = autumn: wi = winter   or = ordinary: mt = moist: dr = dry: ac = acid

LIST OF SHADE-TOLERANT FLOWERS

Name	Common name	height in cms	flower colour	flower season	soil preference
Acanthus mollis	*Bears breeches*	120cm	wh	su	or
Anemone nemorosa	*Wood anemone*	20cm	wh	sp	or
Astilbe arendisii	*Astilbe*	50cm	pk	su	mt
Bergenia cordifolia	*Elephant ears*	50cm	pk	sp	or
Brunnera macrophylla	*Siberian bugloss*	40cm	bl	sp	mt
Campanula latifolia	*Tall bellflower*	120cm	bl	su	dr
Convallaria majalis	*Lily of the valley*	20cm	wh	sp	mt
Dicentra eximia	*Ladys locket*	30cm	pk	sp	or
Dicentra spectabilis	*Ladys locket*	60cm	pk	sp	or
Digitalis purpurea	*Foxglove*	150cm	pr	su	or
Dryopteris felix-mas	*Male fern*	90cm	fl	su	mt
Epimedium rubrum	*Barrenwort*	30cm	fl	-	mt
Eupatorium ageratoides	*Hemp agrimony*	100cm	wh	au	mt
Euphorbia robbiae	*Milkweed*	40cm	gr	sp	dr
Filipendula ulmaria	*Meadowsweet*	90cm	wh	su	mt
Geranium macrorhizum	*Hardy geranium*	40cm	pk	su	or
Helleborus corsicus	*Corsicus hellebore*	60cm	gr	wi	or
Helleborus foetidus	*Stinking hellebore*	50cm	gr	wi	or
Helleborus niger	*Christmas rose*	30cm	wh	wi	or
Heuchera sanguinea	*Coral flower*	40cm	rd	su	or
Hosta 'Halcyon'	*Hosta*	50cm	lc	su	mt
Hosta 'Royal Standard'	*Hosta*	60cm	wh	su	mt
Hosta fortuneii	*Hosta*	60cm	lc	su	mt
Hosta sieboldiana	*Hosta*	100cm	lc	su	mt
Iris foetidissima	*Stinking iris*	60cm	pr	su	mt
Kirengshoma palmata	*Kirengshoma*	90cm	yl	au	mt
Lamium maculatum 'White Nancy'	*Deadnettle*	20cm	wh	su	or
Lunaria rediviva	*Perennial honesty*	60cm	lc	sp	or
Luzula sylvatica	*Great woodrush*	40cm	br	su	or
Malva moschata alba	*Musk mallow*	60cm	wh	su	mt
Milium effusum aureum	*Wood millet*	90cm	fl	sp	or
Omphalodes verna	*Navelwort*	15cm	bl	sp	or
Polygonatum hybridum	*Solomon's seal*	120cm	wh	sp	or
Polystichum setiferum	*Soft shield fern*	60cm	fl	su	mt
Primula japonica	*Candelabra primula*	40cm	pr	su	mt
Primula vulgaris	*Primrose*	20cm	yl	sp	or
Pulmonaria saccharata	*Lungwort*	30cm	bl	sp	or
Saxifraga urbium	*London pride*	40cm	pk	su	or
Smilacina racemosa	*False spikenard*	90cm	wh	sp	mt
Symphytum grandiflorum	*Comfrey*	30cm	wh	sp	mt
Tellima grandiflora	*Fringecups*	50cm	wh	sp	or
Tiarella cordifolia	*Foamflower*	25cm	wh	sp	or
Trillium grandiflorum	*Wake robin*	40cm	wh	sp	mt
Uvularia grandiflora	*Bellwort*	50cm	yl	sp	mt
Viola labradorica 'Purpurea'	*Labrador violet*	15cm	bl	sp	mt

✤ = frost susceptible   d = deciduous: e = evergreen   sn = sun: sh = shade
fl = foliage: ck = catkins: ft = fruit: wh = white: yl = yellow: bl = blue: pk = pink: pr = purple: gr = green: rd = red: lc = lilac: or = orange: mx = mixed
sp = spring: su = summer: au = autumn: wi = winter   or = ordinary: mt = moist: dr = dry: ac = acid

LIST OF PLANTS FOR DRY SOIL

Name Shrubs	Common name	deciduous/evergreen	height in metres	flower colour	flower season	sun/shade
Berberis thunbergii	*Berberis*	d	2m	yl	sp	sn
✳ **Cistus purpureus**	*Sunrose*	e	1m	pr	su	sn
Cytisus albus	*White broom*	e	1m	wh	sp	sn
Cytisus praecox	*Early broom*	e	1m	yl	sp	sn
Daphne mezereum	*Mezereon*	d	1m	pr	sp	sn
Daphne retusa	*Daphne*	e	.5m	pk	sp	sn
Genista 'Lydia'	*Dwarf broom*	e	.5m	yl	su	sn
Helianthemum nummularium	*Rockrose*	e	.2m	pk	su	sn
Lavandula angustifolia 'Hidcote'	*Lavender*	e	.7m	bl	su	sn
Rosmarinus officinalis	*Rosemary*	e	1m	bl	sp	sn
Salvia officinalis 'Purpurascens'	*Purple sage*	e	.5m	bl	su	sn
Tamarix pentandra	*Summer tamarisk*	d	3m	pk	su	sn
Tamarix tetrandra	*Spring tamarisk*	d	3m	pk	sp	sn
Yucca filamentosa	*Yucca*	e	1m	wh	su	sn

Name Flowers	Common Name	height in cms	flower colour	flower season	sun/shade
Acanthus mollis	*Bears breeches*	120cm	wh	su	sh
Achillea ptarmica 'The Pearl'	*Achillea*	50cm	wh	su	sn
Alchemilla alpina	*Lady's mantle*	20cm	gr	su	sn
Anaphallis triplinervis	*Pearl everlasting*	50cm	wh	su	sn
Anemone 'Prinz Heinrich'	*Japanese anemone*	100cm	pk	su	sh
Artemisia 'Lambrook Silver'	*Artemisia*	80cm	fl	-	sn
Bergenia cordifolia	*Elephant ears*	50cm	pk	sp	sh
Centranthus ruber	*Red valerian*	60cm	pk	su	sn
Corydalis cheilantifolia	*Yellow fumitory*	30cm	yl	sp	sn
Crambe cordifolia	*Giant kale*	200cm	wh	su	sn
Crambe maritima	*Seakale*	50cm	wh	su	sn
Dianthus 'Doris'	*Pink*	25cm	pk	su	sn
Erigeron alpinus	*Fleabane*	30cm	pk	su	sn
Eryngium alpinum	*Sea holly*	80cm	bl	su	sn
Euphorbia characias wulfenii	*Milkweed*	100cm	gr	sp	sn
Euphorbia myrsinites	*Milkweed*	15cm	gr	sp	sn
Euphorbia polychroma	*Milkweed*	30cm	yl	sp	sn
Euphorbia robbiae	*Milkweed*	40cm	gr	sp	sh
Festuca glauca	*Blue fescue*	20cm	fl	-	sn
Geranium 'Johnson's Blue'	*Hardy geranium*	40cm	bl	su	sn
Geranium endressii	*Hardy geranium*	30cm	pk	su	sn
Gypsophila 'Bristol Fairy'	*Gypsophila*	100cm	wh	su	sn
Helleborus corsicus	*Corsicus hellebore*	60cm	gr	wi	sh
Heuchera sanguinea	*Coral flower*	40cm	rd	su	sh
Linaria purpurea	*Purple toadflax*	70cm	pr	su	sn
Nepeta faasenii	*Catmint*	40cm	bl	su	sn
Polygonatum hybridum	*Solomon's seal*	120cm	wh	sp	sh
Verbascum bombyciferum	*Mullein*	150cm	yl	su	sn

Note: See also the Lists for Seaside Areas, Pages 103-5.

✳ = frost susceptible   d = deciduous: e = evergreen   sn = sun: sh = shade
fl = foliage: ck = catkins: ft = fruit: wh = white: yl = yellow: bl = blue: pk = pink: pr = purple: gr = green: rd = red: lc = lilac: or = orange: mx = mixed
sp = spring: su = summer: au = autumn: wi = winter   or = ordinary: mt = moist: dr = dry: ac = acid

LIST OF PLANTS FOR MOIST SOIL

Name Shrubs	Common Name	deciduous/evergreen	height in metres	flower colour	flower season	sun/shade
Cornus alba 'Elegantissima'	*Variegated dogwood*	d	2m	fl	au	sn
Cornus alba 'Sibirica'	*Dogwood*	d	2m	fl	au	sn
Salix lanata	*Woolly willow*	d	1m	wh	sp	sn
Sinarundinaria nitida	*Bamboo*	e	4m	fl	-	sn
✳Hydrangea macrophylla	*Hydrangea*	d	2m	pk	su	sh
Sorbaria sorbifolia	*Spirea*	d	2m	wh	su	sn

Name Flowers	Common name	height in cms	flower colour	flower season	sun/shade
Astilbe arendisii	*Astilbe*	50cm	pk	su	sh
Brunnera macrophylla	*Siberian bugloss*	40cm	bl	sp	sh
Caltha palustris	*Marsh marigold*	30cm	yl	sp	sn
Campanula lactiflora	*Bellflower*	120cm	bl	su	sn
Cimicifuga simplex	*Bugbane*	150cm	wh	au	sh
Convallaria majalis	*Lily of the valley*	20cm	wh	sp	sh
Dicentra spectabilis	*Ladys locket*	60cm	pk	sp	sh
Dryopteris felix-mas	*Male fern*	90cm	fl	su	sh
Epimedium rubrum	*Barrenwort*	30cm	pk	sp	sh
Eupatorium ageratoides	*Hemp agrimony*	100cm	wh	au	sh
Filipendula rubra	*Red meadowsweet*	200cm	rd	su	sn
Gunnera manicata	*Gunnera*	200cm	fl	su	sn
Hemerocallis 'Golden Chimes'	*Day lily*	60cm	yl	su	sn
Hemerocallis flava	*Day lily*	60cm	yl	su	sn
Hosta fortuneii	*Hosta*	60cm	lc	su	sh
Hosta sieboldiana	*Hosta*	100cm	lc	su	sh
Iris sibirica	*Siberian iris*	90cm	bl	su	sn
Kirengshoma palmata	*Kirengshoma*	90cm	yl	au	sh
Ligularia 'The Rocket'	*Ligularia*	150cm	yl	su	sn
Lysichiton americanus	*Skunk cabbage*	100cm	yl	sp	sn
Lysimachia clethroides	*White loosestrife*	75cm	wh	su	sn
Lysimachia punctata	*Yellow loosestrife*	60cm	yl	su	sn
Lythrum salicaria	*Purple loosestrife*	100cm	pr	su	sn
Phalaris arundinacea	*Gardeners garters*	90cm	fl	su	sn
✳Phormium 'Purpureum'	*Phormium*	200cm	bl	su	sn
✳Phormium 'Yellow Wave'	*Phormium*	100cm	bl	su	sn
✳Phormium tenax	*New zealand flax*	200cm	bl	su	sn
Polygonum bistorta	*Bistort*	50cm	pk	su	sn
Polygonum campanulatum	*Knotweed*	80cm	pk	su	sh
Polystichum setiferum	*Soft shield fern*	60cm	fl	su	sh
Primula denticulata	*Drumstick primula*	30cm	pr	sp	sn
Primula japonica	*Candelabra primula*	40cm	pr	su	sh
Rodgersia aesculifolia	*Rodgersia*	100cm	wh	su	sn
Smilacina racemosa	*False spikenard*	90cm	wh	sp	sh
Symphytum grandiflorum	*Comfrey*	30cm	wh	sp	sh
Trollius europaeus	*Globeflower*	50cm	yl	sp	sn

✳ = frost susceptible   d = deciduous: e = evergreen   sn = sun: sh = shade
fl = foliage: ck = catkins: ft = fruit: wh = white: yl = yellow: bl = blue: pk = pink: pr = purple: gr = green: rd = red: lc = lilac: or = orange: mx = mixed
sp = spring: su = summer: au = autumn: wi = winter   or = ordinary: mt = moist: dr = dry: ac = acid

LIST OF SHRUBS FOR SEASIDE AREAS

Name	Common name	deciduous/evergreen	height in metres	flower colour	flower season	sun/shade	soil preference
✻**Artemisia 'Powis Castle'**	*Artemisia*	e	2m	yl	su	sn	or
Ballota pseudodictamnus	*Ballota*	e	1m	fl	-	sn	or
Berberis darwinii	*Darwins barberry*	e	4m	or	sp	sn	or
Berberis stenophylla	*Barberry*	e	3m	yl	sp	sn	or
Berberis thunbergii atropurpurea	*Purple barberry*	d	2m	yl	sp	sn	or
Buddleia 'Royal Red'	*Butterfly bush*	d	4m	rd	su	sn	or
Buddleia alternifolia	*Butterfly bush*	d	4m	lc	sp	sn	or
✻**Bupleurum fruticosum**	*Bupleurum*	e	2m	yl	su	sn	dr
✻**Callistemon citrinus**	*Bottle brush*	e	3m	rd	su	sn	or
Caryopteris clandonensis	*Blue spirea*	d	1m	bl	au	sn	or
✻**Ceanothus 'Autumnal Blue'**	*Californian lilac*	e	2m	bl	au	sn	or
✻**Ceanothus 'Gloire de Versailles'**	*Californian lilac*	d	2m	bl	au	sn	or
✻**Ceanothus impressus**	*Californian lilac*	e	2m	bl	sp	sn	or
✻**Ceratostigma willmottianum**	*Hardy plumbago*	d	.5m	bl	au	sn	or
✻**Choisya ternata**	*Choisya*	e	2m	wh	sp	sn	or
✻**Cistus corbariensis**	*Sunrose*	e	1m	wh	su	sn	dr
✻**Cistus ladanifer**	*Sunrose*	e	1m	wh	su	sn	dr
✻**Cistus purpureus**	*Sunrose*	e	1m	pk	su	sn	dr
✻**Convolvulus cneorum**	*Convolvulus*	e	.5m	wh	su	sn	dr
✻**Corokia cotoneaster**	*Wire netting bush*	e	1m	yl	sp	sn	or
✻**Coronilla glauca**	*Coronilla*	e	1m	yl	sp	sn	dr
Cotoneaster 'Skogholm'	*Cotoneaster*	e	.5m	wh	su	sn	or
Cotoneaster congestus	*Cotoneaster*	e	.2m	wh	su	sn	or
Cotoneaster dammerii	*Cotoneaster*	e	.5m	wh	su	sn	or
Cotoneaster horizontalis	*Cotoneaster*	d	1m	wh	su	sn	or
Cotoneaster lacteus	*Cotoneaster*	e	4m	ft	au	sn	or
Cytisus albus	*White broom*	e	1m	wh	sp	sn	dr
Cytisus praecox	*Early broom*	e	1m	yl	sp	sn	dr
Eleagnus commutata	*Silver berry*	d	3m	fl	-	sn	or
Eleagnus ebbingei	*Eleagnus*	e	4m	fl	-	sn	or
✻**Erica erigena**	*Tree heather*	e	1m	pk	su	sn	or
✻**Escallonia 'Apple Blossom'**	*Escallonia*	e	2m	pk	su	sn	or
✻**Escallonia 'Donard Seedling'**	*Escallonia*	e	3m	pk	su	sn	or
✻**Escallonia 'Iveyi'**	*White escallonia*	e	4m	wh	su	sn	or
Euonymus 'Emerald Gaiety'	*Euonymus*	e	1m	fl	-	sh	or
Euonymus japonicus	*Japanese spindle*	e	4m	fl	-	sn	or
Euonymus 'Silver Queen'	*Euonymus*	e	1m	fl	-	sn	or
✻**Fuchsia 'Mrs. Popple'**	*Fuchsia*	d	2m	rd	su	sn	or
✻**Fuchsia 'Riccartonii'**	*Fuchsia*	d	3m	rd	su	sn	or
✻**Fuchsia magellanica 'Versicolor'**	*Variegated fuchsia*	d	1m	rd	su	sn	or
✻**Garrya elliptica**	*Tassel tree*	e	5m	gr	wi	sn	or
Genista 'Lydia'	*Dwarf broom*	e	.5m	yl	su	sn	dr
Genista hispanica	*Spanish gorse*	e	1m	yl	sp	sn	dr
Hebe 'Autumn Glory'	*Veronica*	e	2m	pr	su	sn	or
Hebe 'Mid-summer Beauty'	*Veronica*	e	2m	lc	su	sn	or

✻ = frost susceptible d = deciduous: e = evergreen sn = sun: sh = shade
fl = foliage: ck = catkins: ft = fruit: wh = white: yl = yellow: bl = blue: pk = pink: pr = purple: gr = green: rd = red: lc = lilac: or = orange: mx = mixed
sp = spring: su = summer: au = autumn: wi = winter or = ordinary: mt = moist: dr = dry: ac = acid

LIST OF SHRUBS FOR SEASIDE AREAS
(continued)

Name	Common name	deciduous/evergreen	height in metres	flower colour	flower season	sun/shade	soil preference
✳ Hebe 'Mrs Winder'	Hebe	e	2m	fl	-	sn	or
✳ Hebe 'Pageii'	Hebe	e	.5m	wh	su	sn	or
✳ Hebe salicifolia	Willow hebe	e	3m	lc	su	sn	or
Helianthemum 'Wisley Pink'	Rockrose	e	.2m	pk	su	sn	dr
Helianthemum 'Wisley Primrose'	Rockrose	e	.2m	yl	su	sn	dr
Helianthemum 'Wisley White'	Rockrose	e	.2m	wh	su	sn	dr
✳ Helichrysum petiolare	Helichrysum	e	1m	wh	su	sn	or
✳ Hydrangea 'Blue Wave'	Lacecap hydrangea	d	2m	bl	su	sn	or
✳ Hydrangea macrophylla	Mophead hydrangea	d	2m	bl	su	sn	or
Hypericum 'Elstead'	Hypericum	d	1m	ft	au	sn	or
Hypericum 'Hidcote'	Hypericum	d	2m	yl	su	sn	or
Hypericum calycinum	Creeping hypericum	d	.4m	yl	su	sh	or
Iberis sempervirens	Candytuft	e	.4m	wh	sp	sn	or
Lavandula angustifolia 'Hidcote'	Lavender	e	.7m	bl	su	sn	dr
✳ Lavatera thuringiaca 'Rosea'	Tree mallow	e	2m	pk	su	sn	dr
✳ Lupinus arboreus	Yellow tree lupin	e	2m	yl	su	sn	dr
✳ Olearia haastii	Daisybush	e	2m	wh	su	sn	or
✳ Olearia traversii	Olearia	e	4m	wh	su	sn	or
✳ Ozothamnus ledifolius	Ozothamnus	e	2m	wh	su	sn	or
Perovskia atriplicifolia	Russian sage	d	1m	bl	au	sn	or
✳ Phlomis fruticosa	Jerusalem sage	e	1m	yl	sp	sn	dr
Potentilla 'Abbotswood'	Potentilla	d	.6m	wh	su	sn	or
Potentilla 'Katherine Dykes'	Potentilla	d	1m	yl	su	sn	or
Potentilla 'Primrose Beauty'	Potentilla	d	.7m	yl	su	sn	or
Rosa 'Ballerina'	Shrub rose	d	1m	pk	su	sn	or
Rosa 'Canarybird'	Shrub rose	d	2m	yl	su	sn	or
Rosa 'Fruhslingsgold'	Shrub rose	d	2m	yl	sp	sn	or
Rosa 'Nevada'	Shrub rose	d	2m	wh	su	sn	or
Rosa rugosa	Shrub rose	d	1m	pr	su	sn	or
Rosa rubrifolia	Shrub rose	d	2m	pk	su	sn	or
Rosmarinus officinalis	Rosemary	e	1m	bl	sp	sn	dr
Ruta graveolens	Rue	e	.5m	yl	su	sn	or
Salix lanata	Woolly willow	d	1m	wh	sp	sn	mt
Salvia officinalis 'Purpurascens'	Purple sage	e	.5m	bl	su	sn	dr
✳ Santolina chamaecyparissus	Cotton lavender	e	.8m	yl	su	sn	dr
✳ Senecio 'Sunshine'	Senecio	e	1m	yl	su	sn	or
✳ Spartium junceum	Spanish broom	e	2m	yl	su	sn	dr
Spiraea japonica 'Goldflame'	Spirea	d	.7m	pk	su	sn	or
Spiraea 'Anthony Waterer'	Spirea	d	1m	pk	su	sn	or
Spiraea arguta	Spring spirea	d	2m	wh	sp	sn	or
Tamarix pentandra	Summer tamarisk	d	3m	pk	su	sn	dr
Tamarix tetrandra	Spring tamarisk	d	3m	pk	sp	sn	dr
✳ Teucrium fruticans	Teucrium	e	2m	bl	su	sn	dr
Viburnum tinus	Lauristinus	e	4m	wh	sp	sh	or
Yucca filamentosa	Adams needle	e	1m	wh	su	sn	or

✳ = frost susceptible   d = deciduous: e = evergreen   sn = sun: sh = shade
fl = foliage: ck = catkins: ft = fruit: wh = white: yl = yellow: bl = blue: pk = pink: pr = purple: gr = green: rd = red: lc = lilac: or = orange: mx = mixed
sp = spring: su = summer: au = autumn: wi = winter   or = ordinary: mt = moist: dr = dry: ac = acid

LIST OF FLOWERS FOR SEASIDE AREAS

Name	Common name	height in cms	flower colour	flower season	sun/shade	soil preference
✳Agapanthus campanulatus	African lily	100cm	bl	su	sn	or
Alchemila mollis	Lady's mantle	40cm	gr	su	sn	or
Anaphallis triplinervis	Pearl everlasting	50cm	wh	su	sn	or
Anemone japonica	Japanese anemone	100cm	pk	su	sh	or
✳Anthemis cupaniana	Chamomile	20cm	wh	su	sn	or
Anthemis tinctoria	Chamomile	60cm	yl	su	sn	or
Artemisia 'Lambrook Silver'	Artemisia	80cm	fl	-	sn	dr
Campanula poscharskyana	Bellflower	25cm	bl	su	sn	or
Centranthus ruber	Red valerian	60cm	pk	su	sn	or
✳Cheiranthus 'Bowles Mauve'	Purple wallflower	80cm	pr	sp	sn	or
Coreopsis verticillata	Tickseed	50cm	yl	su	sn	or
Cortaderia selloana	Pampas grass	200cm	wh	au	sn	or
Crambe maritima	Seakale	50cm	wh	su	sn	or
Dianthus 'Doris'	Pink	25cm	pk	su	sn	or
✳Diascia 'Ruby Field'	Diascia	30cm	pk	su	sn	or
✳Diascia rigescens	Diascia	60cm	pk	su	sn	or
✳Dierama pulcherrimum	Wandflower	100cm	pk	su	sn	or
Erigeron alpinus	Fleabane	30cm	pk	su	sn	or
Eryngium alpinum	Sea holly	80cm	bl	su	sn	or
Euphorbia characias wulfenii	Milkweed	100cm	gr	sp	sn	or
Euphorbia myrsinites	Milkweed	15cm	gr	sp	sn	or
Euphorbia polychroma	Milkweed	30cm	yl	sp	sn	or
Festuca glauca	Blue fescue	20cm	fl	-	sn	or
Geranium 'Johnson's Blue'	Hardy geranium	40cm	bl	su	sn	or
Geranium endressii	Hardy geranium	30cm	pk	su	sn	or
Hemerocallis flava	Day lily	60cm	yl	su	sn	mt
Kniphofia uvaria	Red hot poker	150cm	rd	su	sn	or
Lathyrus latifolius 'White Pearl'	Everlasting pea	100cm	wh	su	sn	or
✳Libertia formosa	Libertia	60cm	wh	su	sn	or
Lychnis flos-jovis	Flower of Jove	40cm	pk	sp	sn	or
Nepeta faasenii	Catmint	40cm	bl	su	sn	or
Oenothera missouriensis	Evening primrose	15cm	yl	su	sn	or
Origanum vulgare aureum	Golden marjoram	25cm	fl	su	sn	or
✳Osteospermum ecklonis	Dimorphotheca	30cm	wh	su	sn	or
Papaver nudicaule	Iceland poppy	40cm	mx	su	sh	or
✳Phormium 'Dazzler'	Phormium	200cm	fl	-	sn	mt
✳Phormium 'Maori Chief'	Phormium	150cm	fl	-	sn	mt
✳Phormium 'Purpureum'	Phormium	200cm	fl	-	sn	mt
✳Phormium tenax	New zealand flax	200cm	fl	-	sn	mt
Salvia superba	Salvia	60cm	bl	su	sn	or
Sedum spectabile	Iceplant	50cm	pk	au	sn	or
Sisyrinchium striatum	Pigroot	50cm	yl	su	sn	or
Stachys 'Silver Carpet'	Lambs ear	25cm	fl	-	sn	or
Stipa gigantea	Golden oats	200cm	fl	su	sn	or
Teucrium chamaedrys	Germander	30cm	pk	su	sn	or

✳ = frost susceptible   d = deciduous: e = evergreen   sn = sun: sh = shade
fl = foliage: ck = catkins: ft = fruit: wh = white: yl = yellow: bl = blue: pk = pink: pr = purple: gr = green: rd = red: lc = lilac: or = orange: mx = mixed
sp = spring: su = summer: au = autumn: wi = winter   or = ordinary: mt = moist: dr = dry: ac = acid

LIST OF SHRUBS THAT NEED NO PRUNING

Name	Common name	deciduous/evergreen	height in metres	flower colour	flower season	sun/shade	soil preference
Aucuba japonica	Japanese laurel	e	3m	ft	au	sh	or
Berberis thunbergii 'Aurea'	Golden barberry	d	1m	yl	sp	sn	or
✳Callistemon citrinus	Bottle brush	e	3m	rd	su	sn	or
Calluna vulgaris	Heather	e	.5m	pk	au	sn	or
✳Camellia 'Alba Simplex'	White camellia	e	4m	wh	sp	sh	ac
✳Camellia 'Donation'	Camellia	e	3m	pk	sp	sh	ac
✳Camellia 'J.C. Williams'	Camellia	e	3m	pk	wi	sh	ac
✳Ceratostigma willmottianum	Hardy plumbago	d	.5m	bl	au	sn	or
✳Chimonanthus praecox	Winter sweet	d	2m	yl	wi	sn	or
✳Cistus ladanifer	Sunrose	e	1m	wh	su	sn	dr
✳Cistus purpureus	Sunrose	e	1m	pk	su	sn	dr
Clerodendron trichotomum	Glory tree	d	3m	wh	au	sn	or
✳Convolvulus cneorum	Convolvulus	e	.5m	wh	su	sn	dr
✳Coronilla glauca	Coronilla	e	1m	yl	sp	sn	dr
Corylopsis pauciflora	Winter hazel	d	2m	yl	sp	sh	ac
Cotoneaster 'Skogholm'	Cotoneaster	e	.5m	wh	su	sn	or
Cotoneaster congestus	Cotoneaster	e	.2m	wh	su	sn	or
Cotoneaster dammerii	Cotoneaster	e	.5m	wh	su	sn	or
Cotoneaster horizontalis	Cotoneaster	d	1m	wh	su	sn	or
Cryptomeria 'Elegans Nana'	Japanese cedar	e	3m	fl	-	sn	or
Daboecia cantabrica	Daboecs heath	e	.5m	pr	su	sn	ac
Daphne mezereum	Mezereon	d	1m	pr	sp	sn	dr
Daphne retusa	Daphne	e	.5m	pk	sp	sn	dr
Eleagnus commutata	Silver berry	d	3m	fl	-	sn	or
Eleagnus 'Limelight'	Eleagnus	e	3m	fl	-	sn	or
Enkianthus campanulatus	Pagoda bush	d	3m	pk	sp	sh	ac
Erica carnea 'King George'	Winter heather	e	.2m	pk	wi	sn	or
Erica carnea 'Myretoun Ruby'	Winter heather	e	.2m	pk	wi	sn	or
Euonymus 'Emerald Gaiety'	Euonymus	e	1m	fl	-	sh	or
Euonymus 'Silver Queen'	Euonymus	e	1m	fl	-	sn	or
Euonymus alatus	Chinese spindle	d	3m	ft	au	sn	or
Fothergilla monticola	Fothergilla	d	2m	wh	sp	sn	ac
Gaultheria procumbens	Gaultheria	e	.2m	wh	su	sh	ac
Genista 'Lydia'	Dwarf broom	e	.5m	yl	su	sn	dr
Genista hispanica	Spanish gorse	e	1m	yl	sp	sn	dr
✳Hebe 'Pageii'	Hebe	e	.5m	wh	su	sn	or
✳Hebe buxifolia nana	Hebe	e	.5m	fl	-	sn	or
✳Hebe hulkeana	Hebe	e	.5m	lc	sp	sn	or
Helianthemum nummularium	Rockrose	e	.2m	yl	su	sn	dr
Hypericum 'Elstead'	Hypericum	d	1m	ft	au	sn	or
Hypericum calycinum	Creeping hypericum	d	.4m	yl	su	sh	or
Iberis sempervirens	Candytuft	e	.4m	wh	sp	sn	or
Ilex crenata 'Golden Gem'	Dwarf holly	e	.4m	fl	-	sh	or
Juniperus 'Blue Carpet'	Dwarf juniper	e	.2m	fl	-	sn	or
Juniperus 'Blue Star'	Dwarf juniper	e	.4m	fl	-	sn	or

✳ = frost susceptible   d = deciduous: e = evergreen   sn = sun: sh = shade
fl = foliage: ck = catkins: ft = fruit: wh = white: yl = yellow: bl = blue: pk = pink: pr = purple: gr = green: rd = red: lc = lilac: or = orange: mx = mixed
sp = spring: su = summer: au = autumn: wi = winter   or = ordinary: mt = moist: dr = dry: ac = acid

LIST OF SHRUBS THAT NEED NO PRUNING (continued)

Name	Common name	deciduous/evergreen	height in metres	flower colour	flower season	sun/shade	soil preference
Juniperus 'Depressa Aurea'	*Dwarf juniper*	e	.4m	fl	-	sn	or
Juniperus communis 'Compressa'	*Dwarf juniper*	e	1m	fl	-	sn	or
Juniperus communis 'Hibernica'	*Pillar juniper*	e	3m	fl	-	sn	or
Juniperus communis 'Repanda'	*Prostrate juniper*	e	.2m	fl	-	sn	or
Mahonia aquifolium	*Oregon grape*	e	1m	yl	sp	sh	or
Mahonia japonica	*Mahonia*	e	2m	yl	wi	sh	or
❊**Myrtus communis**	*Myrtle*	e	2m	wh	sp	sn	or
❊**Olearia haastii**	*Daisybush*	e	2m	wh	su	sn	or
❊**Osmanthus delavayii**	*Osmanthus*	e	3m	wh	sp	sh	or
Pachysandra terminalis	*Japanese spurge*	e	.2m	fl	-	sh	or
Paeonia lutea	*Tree paeony*	d	2m	yl	sp	sn	or
❊**Parahebe catarractae**	*Parahebe*	e	.4m	pr	sp	sn	or
Pernettya mucronata	*Pernettya*	e	1m	ft	au	sn	ac
Picea abies 'Nidiformis'	*Dwarf spruce*	e	1m	fl	-	sn	or
❊**Pieris 'Forest Flame'**	*Pieris*	e	3m	wh	sp	sh	ac
❊**Pieris formosa 'Wakehurst'**	*Pieris*	e	3m	wh	sp	sh	ac
Pinus mugo 'Gnom'	*Dwarf pine*	e	2m	fl	-	sn	or
❊**Pittosporum 'Tom Thumb'**	*Dwarf pittosporum*	e	1m	fl	-	sn	or
Potentilla fruticosa	*Potentilla*	d	.6m	yl	su	sn	or
Prunus 'Otto Luyken'	*Dwarf laurel*	e	1m	wh	sp	sh	or
Prunus cistena	*Dwarf cherry*	d	1m	pk	sp	sn	or
❊**Pseudowintera colorata**	*Drimys*	e	1m	fl	-	sh	or
Prunus tenella 'Fire Hill'	*Siberian almond*	d	1m	pk	sp	sn	or
Rhododendron 'Elizabeth'	*Rhododendron*	e	1m	rd	sp	sh	ac
Rhododendron 'Hinomayo'	*Evergreen azalea*	e	1m	pk	sp	sh	ac
Rhododendron 'Susan'	*Rhododendron*	e	2m	pr	sp	sh	ac
Rhododendron 'Vuyks Scarlet'	*Evergreen azalea*	e	.7m	rd	sp	sh	ac
Rhododendron impeditum	*Evergreen azalea*	e	.6m	bl	sp	sn	ac
Rhododendron kaempferi	*Japanese azalea*	e	2m	rd	sp	sh	ac
Rhododendron luteum	*Deciduous azalea*	d	2m	yl	sp	sn	ac
Rhododendron mollis	*Deciduous azalea*	d	2m	or	sp	sh	ac
Rhododendron williamsianum	*Rhododendron*	e	1m	pk	sp	sh	ac
Ruta graveolens	*Rue*	e	.5m	yl	su	sn	or
Salix lanata	*Woolly willow*	d	1m	wh	sp	sn	mt
❊**Sarcocca humilis**	*Sweet box*	e	.6m	wh	wi	sh	mt
Sinarundinaria nitida	*Bamboo*	e	4m	fl	-	sn	mt
Skimmia japonica 'Foremanii'	*Skimmia*	e	2m	wh	sp	sh	or
Syringa velutina	*Korean lilac*	d	2m	lc	sp	sn	or
Thuya 'Ericoides'	*Dwarf thuya*	e	1m	fl	-	sn	or
Thuya 'Rheingold'	*Dwarf thuya*	e	2m	fl	-	sn	or
Thuya orientalis 'Aurea Nana'	*Dwarf thuya*	e	1m	fl	-	sn	or
Viburnum carlesii	*Viburnum*	d	1m	pk	sp	sn	or
Viburnum davidii	*Viburnum*	e	1m	wh	sp	sn	or
Yucca filamentosa	*Adams needle*	e	1m	wh	su	sn	or

❊ = frost susceptible　d = deciduous: e = evergreen　sn = sun: sh = shade
fl = foliage: ck = catkins: ft = fruit: wh = white: yl = yellow: bl = blue: pk = pink: pr = purple: gr = green: rd = red: lc = lilac: or = orange: mx = mixed
sp = spring: su = summer: au = autumn: wi = winter　or = ordinary: mt = moist: dr = dry: ac = acid

LIST OF FLOWERS THAT NEED NO STAKING

Name	Common name	height in cms	flower colour	flower season	sun/shade	soil preference
Acanthus mollis	Bears breeches	120cm	wh	su	sh	or
✳ Agapanthus campanulatus	African lily	100cm	bl	su	sn	or
Alchemila mollis	Lady's mantle	40cm	gr	su	sn	or
Anemone japonica	Japanese anemone	100cm	pk	su	sh	or
✳ Anthemis cupaniana	Chamomile	20cm	wh	su	sn	or
Aquilegia vulgaris	Columbine	60cm	pk	su	sn	or
Astilbe japonica	Astilbe	50cm	pk	su	sh	mt
Bergenia cordifolia	Elephant ears	50cm	pk	sp	sh	or
Brunnera macrophylla	Siberian bugloss	40cm	bl	sp	sh	mt
Caltha palustris	Marsh marigold	30cm	yl	sp	sn	mt
Carex 'Evergold'	Variegated sedge	30cm	fl	-	sn	or
Carex comans 'Bronze Form'	Bronze sedge	40cm	fl	-	sn	or
Centranthus ruber	Red valerian	60cm	pk	su	sn	or
✳ Cheiranthus 'Bowles Mauve'	Purple wallflower	80cm	pr	sp	sn	or
Chrysanthemum parthenium aureum	Golden feverfew	30cm	wh	su	sn	or
Convallaria majalis	Lily of the valley	20cm	wh	sp	sh	mt
Cortaderia selloana	Pampas grass	200cm	wh	au	sn	or
Corydalis cheilantifolia	Yellow fumitory	30cm	yl	sp	sn	or
Dianthus 'Doris'	Pink	25cm	pk	su	sn	or
✳ Diascia 'Ruby Field'	Diascia	30cm	pk	su	sn	or
Dicentra spectabilis	Ladys locket	60cm	pk	sp	sh	or
✳ Dierama pulcherrimum	Wandflower	100cm	pk	su	sn	or
Digitalis purpurea	Foxglove	150cm	pr	su	sh	or
Dryopteris felix-mas	Male fern	90cm	fl	su	sh	mt
Epimedium grandiflorum	Barrenwort	30cm	pk	sp	sh	mt
Erigeron alpinus	Fleabane	30cm	pk	su	sn	or
Eryngium alpinum	Sea holly	80cm	bl	su	sn	or
Euphorbia myrsinites	Milkweed	15cm	gr	sp	sn	or
Euphorbia polychroma	Milkweed	30cm	yl	sp	sn	or
Euphorbia robbiae	Milkweed	40cm	gr	sp	sh	dr
Festuca glauca	Blue fescue	20cm	fl	-	sn	or
✳ Francoa sonchifolia	Bridal wreath	60cm	pk	su	sn	or
Geranium endressii	Hardy geranium	30cm	pk	su	sn	or
Geranium macrorhizum	Hardy geranium	40cm	pk	su	sh	or
Gunnera manicata	Gunnera	200cm	fl	su	sn	mt
Hakonechloa 'Aureola'	Ornamental grass	40cm	fl	-	sn	or
Helleborus niger	Christmas rose	30cm	wh	wi	sh	or
Helleborus orientalis	Lenten rose	50cm	pr	sp	sh	or
Hemerocallis 'Golden Chimes'	Day lily	60cm	yl	su	sn	mt
Hemerocallis flava	Day lily	60cm	yl	su	sn	mt
Heuchera 'Palace Purple'	Purple coral flower	40cm	wh	su	sh	or
Heuchera sanguinea	Coral flower	40cm	rd	su	sh	or
Hosta fortuneii	Hosta	60cm	lc	su	sh	mt
Hosta sieboldiana	Hosta	100cm	lc	su	sh	mt
Iris germanica	Bearded iris	90cm	bl	su	sn	or

✳ = frost susceptible   d = deciduous: e = evergreen   sn = sun: sh = shade
fl = foliage: ck = catkins: ft = fruit: wh = white: yl = yellow: bl = blue: pk = pink: pr = purple: gr = green: rd = red: lc = lilac: or = orange: mx = mixed
sp = spring: su = summer: au = autumn: wi = winter   or = ordinary: mt = moist: dr = dry: ac = acid

LIST OF FLOWERS THAT NEED NO STAKING (continued)

Name	Common name	height in cms	flower colour	flower season	sun/shade	soil preference
Iris unguicularis	Winter iris	25cm	lc	wi	sn	or
Kniphofia 'Little Maid'	Red hot poker	50cm	yl	su	sn	or
Lamium maculatum 'White Nancy'	Deadnettle	20cm	wh	su	sh	or
Liatris spicata	Gay feather	50cm	pr	su	sn	or
✳Libertia formosa	Libertia	60cm	wh	su	sh	or
Liriope muscari	Lilyturf	25cm	bl	au	sn	or
Luzula sylvatica	Great woodrush	40cm	br	su	sh	or
Lychnis flos-jovis	Flower of Jove	40cm	pk	sp	sn	or
Lysichiton americanus	Skunk cabbage	100cm	yl	sp	sn	mt
Lysimachia punctata	Yellow loosestrife	60cm	yl	su	sn	mt
Milium effusum aureum	Wood millet	90cm	fl	sp	sh	or
✳Mimulus luteus	Yellow musk	30cm	yl	su	sn	mt
Miscanthus sinensis	Silver grass	200cm	wh	su	sn	mt
Nepeta faasenii	Catmint	40cm	bl	su	sn	or
Oenothera missouriensis	Evening primrose	15cm	yl	su	sn	or
Omphalodes verna	Navelwort	15cm	bl	sp	sh	or
Origanum vulgare aureum	Golden marjoram	25cm	fl	su	sn	or
Osmunda regalis	Royal fern	150cm	fl	su	sn	wt
✳Osteospermum barberiae	Dimorphotheca	40cm	pr	su	sn	or
✳Phormium 'Bronze Baby'	Phormium	75cm	br	su	sn	mt
✳Phormium 'Dazzler'	Phormium	200cm	br	su	sn	mt
Phyllitis scolopendrium	Harts tongue fern	50cm	br	su	sh	mt
Polemonium coeruleum	Jacob's ladder	50cm	bl	su	sn	or
Polystichum setiferum	Soft shield fern	60cm	fl	su	sh	mt
Primula pulverulenta	Candelabra primula	60cm	pr	su	sh	mt
Primula vulgaris	Primrose	20cm	yl	sp	sh	or
Pulmonaria saccharata	Lungwort	30cm	bl	sp	sh	or
Rheum palmatum	Ornamental rhubarb	200cm	rd	su	sn	or
Salvia superba	Salvia	60cm	bl	su	sn	or
Saxifraga urbium	London pride	40cm	pk	su	sh	or
✳Schizostylis 'Mrs Hegarty'	Kaffir lily	50cm	pk	au	sn	or
Sedum 'Aurantiacum'	Sedum	25cm	yl	su	sn	or
Sedum spectabile	Iceplant	50cm	pk	au	sn	or
Sisyrinchium striatum	Pigroot	50cm	yl	su	sn	or
Stachys 'Silver Carpet'	Lambs ear	25cm	fl	-	sn	or
Stachys macrantha 'Superba'	Stachys	30cm	pr	su	sn	or
Stipa gigantea	Golden oats	200cm	br	su	sn	or
Tellima grandiflora	Fringecups	50cm	wh	sp	sh	or
Teucrium chamaedrys	Germander	30cm	pk	su	sn	or
Tiarella cordifolia	Foamflower	25cm	wh	sp	sh	or
Valeriana phu 'Aurea'	Valeriana	40cm	fl	sp	sn	or
Veronica spicata	Spiked speedwell	50cm	bl	su	sn	or
Viola 'Nellie Britten'	Viola	15cm	lc	su	sn	or
Viola labradorica 'Purpurea'	Labrador violet	15cm	bl	sp	sh	mt
✳Zantedeschia 'Crowborough'	Arum lily	120cm	wh	su	sn	mt

✳ = frost susceptible   d = deciduous: e = evergreen   sn = sun: sh = shade
fl = foliage: ck = catkins: ft = fruit: wh = white: yl = yellow: bl = blue: pk = pink: pr = purple: gr = green: rd = red: lc = lilac: or = orange: mx = mixed
sp = spring: su = summer: au = autumn: wi = winter   or = ordinary: mt = moist: dr = dry: ac = acid

Weeds

Weeds are plants in the wrong place — grass is o.k. in a lawn, but not in the flower beds! Weeds compete with garden plants for space, light, water and nutrients.

Weed types

●**Annual weeds.** These are wild plants with remarkable ability to produce seed quickly, and in large quantities. They grow fast, reach flowering size in a matter of weeks and shed seed — each new generation can take as little as 8 or 10 weeks to appear. They are weeds of cultivated ground, taking advantage of the soil being broken up for crop plants.

It is essential to prevent them getting big enough to produce seed. They have no other means of survival or spread, so the cycle is easily broken. There is a reservoir of weed seed in the soil which is added to each season. If seed production is prevented, the reservoir declines as the weed seeds get older and lose their ability to germinate. There is a lot of truth in the saying — 'one year's seeding is seven years weeding'. Common annual weeds include groundsel, shepherd's purse, chickweed, annual meadow grass and speedwell.

●**Perennial weeds.** These are persistent weeds which, once established, spread until they take over a piece of ground. They survive by dying down in winter to a network of thick, fleshy storage roots, or a tight rosette of leaves. Each year the storage root network becomes more extensive, and this is the main method by which these weeds spread. They may be controlled by removing the root system completely, or by killing it with weedkiller. Removal is difficult, since even small pieces of root may be enough for the weed to regenerate. Ground made free of perennial weeds is reasonably easy to keep clear. Hoeing will prevent establishment from seed, and if the rootball of new plants is checked for the presence of weed roots, there is no other way of introducing them.

Perennial weeds infest both cultivated and uncultivated ground. They prefer relatively uncultivated ground such as a shrub border, where their root systems will be undisturbed. Only a few, such as bindweed and scutch, are vigorous enough to tolerate continuous disturbance. Other common perennial weeds include nettles, docks, bishop weed, creeping thistle and dandelion. Many lawn weeds are perennials too. *(See the Section on Lawns. Page 29).*

Killing weeds

●**Hand weeding.** Pulling up weeds from among garden plants is the simplest way of separating good and bad. It is very effective, but slow, and suitable only in close to plants where hoeing might cause damage. An old kitchen knife is a useful aid to hand-weeding.

●**Hoeing.** A quick, effective and cheap way of controlling weeds, with little or no drainage to crop plants, hoeing must be done while the weeds are small. The ideal stage is when they have one or two 'true' leaves, and are an inch or two high. The hoe separates the top from the root, and the weed seedling dies. Earlier hoeing may only move the seedlings, as the root may not be deep enough to be caught by the hoe. Hoeing at the right stage will kill perennial weed seedlings before they get a chance to develop their storage root survival system. Hoe on a warm, breezy day, so that the weeds dry out before they get a chance to root again.

Annual meadow grass, shepherd's purse, and groundsel — three very common annual weeds, note the small root systems.

Bindweed or convolvulus — a common and difficult perennial weed, note the thick storage root system.

●**Digging.** Perennial weeds which have developed their storage roots will not be controlled by hoeing — they simply grow new leaves. Instead, they must be dug out. Use a fork or spade, and make sure to get the entire storage root system. Leave the lifted weeds on a hard surface to die.

●**Chemical weedkillers.** These work by scorching the foliage, or by poisoning the internal system. Weedol, Gramoxone and Basta scorch the weed's foliage, and if they are annuals without storage roots, they die. Perennial weeds survive Weedol, Gramoxone and Basta in the same way as they survive hoeing.

Tumbleweed, Weed Out, and Nettlex Brushwood Killer work by poisoning the weed's internal system which means they have the ability to kill perennial weeds. These chemicals are taken in by the foliage and then passed right down into the storage root system. This makes them more effective than digging for disposing of perennial weeds. They are very specific though in the way they work, and in what they kill. Tumbleweed (Roundup is the same thing for large areas) kills both grasses and broadleaved weeds. It needs six hours without rain, after application.
Weed Out kills grasses, but not broadleaved weeds or plants. Grass weeds beyond a certain stage of growth will survive. Nettlex Brushwood Killer kills broadleaved weeds only and growth must be active.
Repeat applications of the first two may be necessary. Read the instructions carefully.

Preventing weeds

●**Mulches.** The application of a layer of material free from weeds or weed seeds is very effective in preventing weeds. Weed seeds germinate but die for lack of light. Loose mulches, such as compost, manure, bark, grass clippings, peat or gravel must be thick enough to block out light. They only work when applied to weed-free soil, and in the case of manure and compost must be well-rotted and weed-free themselves. The organic mulches have to be topped up every couple of years, because they break down, themselves providing excellent rooting conditions for blown-in weeds. Gravel must be kept free of fallen leaves, for the same reason. Thick black polythene is an excellent mulch, and may even be used to kill existing weeds, but it tends to split and break up after a few years. A combination of polythene and gravel is long-lasting, the gravel shielding the polythene from the sun.

●**Ground cover plants.** Living plants act in the same way as mulches to prevent weeds — by blocking access to light. Any low-growing, spreading plant, either woody or herbaceous, can be used, some being better than others. A few weeds will always appear through gaps — especially in the early years. On occasion, the ground cover itself may become a nuisance. Commonly used ground cover plants include St. John's wort, Vinca, Ivy, Rubus tricolor, Ajuga, Lamium, Acaena and Bergenia.

●**Chemical weed prevention.** There are several chemicals which may be used to stop weed seeds from germinating, but only two are available in garden packs. Simazine works by killing the weed seedling as it germinates. It is absorbed by the top inch or two inches of soil (2.5-5cm) and creates a weed-free layer which must not be broken. Simazine controls nearly all types of weeds at germination, but not beyond, so it must only be applied to weed-free soil; and it must be applied to moist soil, or it will not be absorbed properly. It gives control for about six months, if applied properly, and is best applied in early spring, to give season-long control.

Simazine must only be applied to areas without plants and where no plants are to be grown, or to areas which contain only well-established trees, shrubs, roses or fruit trees. It should not be used on plums, cherries including Flowering cherries or Rhododendron. It is easy to overdose with Simazine, particularly on sandy soil. Follow the instructions accurately. Simazine must never be applied to an area where a lawn is to be laid.

Weed control options

●**Vegetable area and flower beds or borders.** These should first be made weed-free by removing perennial weeds while digging, or by using Tumbleweed or Roundup in early summer, if the ground has been neglected. Early digging in the vegetable area buries weeds before seed formation. Cultivated soil may be kept free of weeds before the vegetables or flowers are sown or planted, by hoeing, or spraying with Weedol, when the weeds are still small. Where vegetables or flowers have been sown or planted, only hoeing and hand-weeding may be used.

●**Established shrub borders, rose beds and fruit plantations.** New planting should be treated as above, for a year or two. After that, hoeing and Weedol may be used to dispose of annual weeds. Tumbleweed, Casoron G or Nettlex Brushwood Killer may be used to carefully 'spot-treat' perennial weeds. Weed Out can be used overall, on grass weeds among woody plants. It does not damage the woody plants. Tumbleweed may be used overall, to kill weeds in plantations of needle conifers, such as shelter belts. It does not damage the needle conifers. When existing weeds have been controlled, Simazine may be used overall to provide continuing control.

●**Paths, driveways, patios.** Where there are no plants which might be damaged, chemical weed killers and preventers are ideal. It is often difficult to hoe or handweed in these situations because weeds have their roots between slabs or cracks in concrete. Special 'cocktails' of weed-killing and weed-preventing chemicals are sold for use on these areas. They are used as a single dose solution to both existing weeds and germinating weed seeds and are applied in spring or early summer. The available products include Hytrol, Pathclear, Path Weedkiller and Superweedex. Casoron G is a granular weedkiller which has the dual ability to kill existing weeds and prevent weed seed germination. Moss and algae may be killed on paths, walls or tarmac by spraying with Taroil, Clean Up, Mosgo or mosskillers. Sweeping paths and drives to prevent debris building up helps to prevent moss and algae. If tree seedlings or briars need to be killed, use Nettlex Brushwood Killer. Asulox will kill bracken.

**Lawn weeds are dealt with in
the Section on Lawns.**

Pests

Plants are food for many types of animal — from microscopic eelworms to large mammals — but very few of these could be called pests.

Unless an animal causes damage great enough to destroy the feature for which the plant is grown, it cannot be termed a pest, for example, carrot root fly maggots bore in the roots of carrots, making them useless; codling moth grubs feed inside apples causing them to fall prematurely; greenfly, by their presence render lettuce inedible. The simplest way to solve a particular pest problem is not to grow the pest's food plant, but, if it is decided to grow the plants, and there are pests in the vicinity, control measures will be necessary.

Plant defence mechanisms

Plants are not totally helpless against pests — they have their own defence arrangements. The most obvious ones are thorny leaves or stems to deter grazing animals. Scaled-down versions of these are hairy stems — some plant hairs can be quite sharp and cause skin irritation. Other plants, such as Butterfly flower and Petunia, have sticky plant hairs which act as miniature fly traps, making difficult the passage of greenfly and other small insects. Some plants rely on being unpalatable or poisonous. For example, plants with milky sap do not seem to suffer so much from greenfly, and the well-known insecticides — derris, pyrethrum, nicotine and quassia are all of plant origin. Even common plants have ways of dissuading feeding animals — rhubarb is a strong laxative, the leaves containing large quantities of poisonous oxalic acid. Ragwort, bracken and yew are poisonous to grazing animals. Laburnum, Daphne, Cotoneaster, Laurel and Monkshood are examples of cultivated plants which are poisonous to a greater or lesser degree.

Natural enemies

Pests have their own 'pests' in the form of predators and parasites. Predators are usually larger, killing and eating the pest species. Obvious examples are birds, bats, hedgehogs, field mice, frogs and foxes which dispose of considerable numbers of insects and other pests. Less well-known examples are the insect predators which include ladybirds, lacewings, ground beetles, hoverflies, capsid bugs, spiders and earwigs. Most of these live off greenfly, suckers, leaf-hoppers and red spider mites.

Parasites are usually smaller than the insect parasitised and the pest is usually kept alive for some time before dying. Many kinds of tiny flies, wasps and midges parasitise the eggs and larvae of pest species, especially greenfly and caterpillars. Pests are attacked by diseases which play an important role in limiting their populations. For example, myxomatosis disease greatly reduced the rabbit population, although it has recovered somewhat.

The equilibrium of nature

Nature tends to balance itself. If, because of favourable weather, huge numbers of a pest appear, and plant defences are overwhelmed, there are two consequences. The plants under attack fail to produce as much seed, so there will be fewer plants the following year. This means less food for the pest, causing numbers to decrease. At the same time, the predators and parasites would quickly increase in numbers, there being a large population of pests to feed off. In time, the two factors would bring pest numbers back to the former level.

Natural pest control could be relied upon if the garden had nothing but wild plants. In a garden of cultivated plants, artificial plant populations are created. Plants are grown in groups or rows, simply inviting pest attack. Weeds and debris are removed, destroying the shelter of predators. A garden is an artificial situation and natural balancing systems will not get it right, unaided. However, the natural systems go a long way towards keeping the balance right. Correct pest control in the garden should concentrate on encouraging, or at least not damaging, the natural systems. In commercial horticulture it is possible to introduce natural predators to control pests but, as yet, these have not been made available to home gardeners. Only when the natural control systems prove inadequate, because of the artificiality of the garden, should they be assisted by physical or chemical control methods.

Physical pest control methods

These consist of separating the pest from its food source. They are the most effective and health-safe way of dealing with a pest problem. The pest may be actually removed physically from the vicinity of the food plant, as in removing snails near young plants or picking caterpillars off cabbage; or the pest may be excluded by a physical barrier, for example, birds may be excluded by netting and rabbits by fencing. Scaring may be effective too. Physical control does not interfere with natural control systems which is a major advantage. It may be more costly and time-consuming than chemical control but there are no residues to consider. The removal of old crops and debris which harbour pests is an important method of physical control, as is early digging to expose over-wintering pests to the weather, and to predators.

Chemical pest control methods

These consist of killing the pest with chemical poisons. It appears to be a simple solution to pest problems but there are serious disadvantages — chemicals getting onto plants may damage them or leave residues on a food crop; harmless, potentially beneficial insects may be killed. To make chemical control more acceptable, the chemicals now offered for sale are less poisonous and less persistent, meaning it is less likely there will be residues and, if there are, they will be less dangerous. Chemical control is cheap and easy — perhaps too easy. Because of the disadvantages, it should be used only when there is no other solution. Routine spraying is to be avoided. Except in a few well-defined, exceptional situations, it is unnecessary, leaves excess residues, damages the natural balance and eventually renders the chemical useless when resistant strains of the pest are selected by a process of elimination.

Ants

Ants are not strictly a pest because they do not damage plants. However, their presence in large numbers may be a nuisance. Ants are social insects, living in nests in dry soil under stones and paving. They actually farm colonies of greenfly for the honeydew they excrete and they often move greenfly to new plants. Burrowing by ants while building nests sometimes undermines small shrubs, leaving them high and dry and prone to wilting in a warm summer.

There is no effective method of physical control. Pouring hot water into the nests does not work. If the nest can be got at, to soak it with Hexyl is effective. If the nest is hard to find, leave some sugar in a little heap where the ants have been seen and a couple of days later there will be a trail of ants back to the nest. Apply ant-killers at the entrance to the nest. These include Anti-ant Powder, Murphy's Antkiller, ICI Antkiller, Nippon Ant Destroyer and Panant. They may need to be renewed several times until the ants are no longer seen.

Big bud mite

Tiny mites feed inside the buds of blackcurrants, causing the tissues to swell. The bud, normally elongated, takes on a rounded shape. Swollen buds are most noticeable in winter. In spring, they usually fail to open. The direct damage — reducing the number of fruiting buds — is usually not too serious. However, the mites spread reversion, the most serious virus disease of blackcurrants, by migrating from the swollen buds at around flowering time. Leaving a bush with the virus disease and moving to a healthy one, they bring particles of virus with them.

The best way of controlling them is to pick off all swollen buds during the winter and burn them. Over a few years, this will achieve control. There is no chemical control, but if Benlate is used for disease control, it also suppresses the mites.

Birds

Many different bird species cause damage to plants. Fruit and vegetables are the main targets, being good food sources. Pigeons are major pests of all Cabbage family plants, peas, raspberries, gooseberries and blackcurrants. Crows attack peas in rural areas. Bullfinches and sparrows strip out the buds of fruit trees and bushes. Blackbirds, thrushes and redwings eat strawberries, cherries, apples, pears and any sort of red berries such as Cotoneaster, Mountain ash and Pyracantha. Starlings eat cherries and, along with crows, may peck at lawns to get leather jacket grubs but this is at least as beneficial as damaging.

Netting is the most effective solution to bird damage. Crops are only vulnerable for a part of the year and may be netted at those times. Damage to Cabbage family plants usually ceases when they are about 8 inches (20 cm) tall. Scaring devices such as strips of foil or plastic work quite well, but the birds may get used to them eventually.

Cabbage root fly

The damage is done by the grubs as they feed on the roots of Cabbage family plants, including radish and turnip. Wallflowers and Cleome may also be attacked. Sometimes in a wet season, the sprouts of brussels sprouts may be attacked as well as the roots. When the small white grubs reach an half-inch (1 cm), they pupate in the soil, emerging as adults after a few weeks, or else the following spring. The adults are like houseflies and may be seen hovering around young cabbage plants prior to laying eggs in the soil. If the attack comes early in the life of the plant, it is usually severely stunted and killed by wilting in a hot spell. The main roots will have been destroyed. If the plant is fairly big when attacked, it often grows on after the initial check.

Early digging and the removal of old crops are important in reducing the numbers of adult flies which emerge. However, they can fly considerable distances, so others will appear. Discs or squares of polythene, about a foot (30cm) across, can be placed around the stem of the plants at planting out to prevent egg-laying. However, to protect the seedlings before planting out, and to prevent damage to radish and turnip, it will be necessary to use Bromophos or ICI Sybol, as directed on the pack. *(See Page 42)*.

Capsid bug

These insects are both friend and foe! Most types of capsid bug are beneficial predators, especially in fruit trees. However, a few species cause damage to plants. Apples may have rough patches and bumps due to capsids feeding on the developing fruit but this is rarely significant. Dahlias and Asters are often damaged quite seriously by capsids feeding on the shoot tips as they emerge — the damage only becoming apparent later on when it is too late to control the pest. Either grow something else or spray the plants, a few days after planting out, with Malathion, Sybol, Fentro or Fenitrothion.

Carrot root fly

Tiny white or yellowish maggots tunnel into carrots. If the attack takes place early on, the plants will be completely stunted. Later, the roots may be made useless if the attack is severe. After feeding in the roots, the maggots pupate in the soil, emerging as adults after a few weeks, or the following spring. Parsnips are often attacked in the southern part of the country, and occasionally elsewhere. Parsley and celery are sometimes attacked too. The symptoms are the same as carrots — stunting and reddening of foliage, and small, rusty mines in the roots.

Control is quite difficult. The adult flies rarely fly above two feet (60cm), so that a barrier of polythene 30 inches (75cm) high will keep most of them out. The barrier must have no gaps, especially at ground level. Sowing onions and carrots together to confuse the fly does not work. Chemical control is not very successful unless it is repeated at 7 or 8 week intervals. Apply ICI Sybol or Bromophos at sowing and again 8 weeks later. A third application will be necessary to protect maincrop carrots which should be lifted when mature — not left in the ground. Delaying sowing to May does not work in the garden because there is considerable overlap in the emergence of generations of the flies. *(See Page 42).*

Caterpillars

These are the larvae of butterflies and moths. Typically, caterpillars feed on the shoots and leaves of plants for a few weeks before pupating in the soil, or in a dry place, and emerge as adults some weeks later, or the following spring. They vary considerably in size. Some are only a fraction of an inch long; others can reach 3 inches (7.5 cm). The damage they cause is easily recognised — irregular holes of various sizes, often bounded by leaf veins. Some types burrow into plant tissues, such as heads of cabbage and cauliflower. Practically every plant — trees, flowers, fruit or vegetables — has its own caterpillar pest, but they usually do not cause damage serious enough to warrant control measures. Cabbage caterpillars are the major exception — they almost always cause considerable damage.

Caterpillars may be picked or knocked off the plants, and killed. Batches of yellow or white eggs, often visible on the undersides of leaves, should be destroyed. If small holes appear on houseplants, a careful search will uncover a single, small caterpillar which can then be removed. Chemical control is not usually necessary, except on the Cabbage family. Suitable insecticides include Derris, Malathion, Hygeia Caterpillar Spray, Sybol, Picket, Crop Saver, Fentro and Fenitrothion.

Celery fly

The maggot of this fly is so tiny that it can tunnel between the upper and lower surfaces of celery leaves, earning for itself the alternative name of celery leaf miner. If the attack comes early and in numbers, the foliage may be destroyed and growth stopped. A late attack only damages some leaves and is of no great concern.

If the attack is light — just a couple of mines per plant — it is possible to pick off parts of the affected leaves. If this is not possible Murphy's Systemic Insecticide, Hygeia Greenfly Spray, Bio Longlast or Sybol could be used.

Codling moth

This is a common pest of apples in some parts of the country, especially in town gardens. Pears are occasionally attacked. The caterpillar bores into the centre of the fruit, destroying it and often causing it to fall early. The caterpillar pupates in a cocoon and emerges the following year. *(See Page 49).*

Destroying fallen apples, and using bands of sacking to trap the pest in the cocoons, helps to reduce numbers but control will not be good because the adults fly in from neighbouring gardens. Spray with Picket, Hygeia Caterpillar Spray, Fentro or Fenitrothion as blossoming finishes, and again three weeks later, to kill the caterpillars before they enter the fruit. Plum sawfly and plum fruit moth have a similar life cycle and may be controlled in the same way.

Cutworms

This pest is a type of caterpillar — the larvae of night-flying moths — but they are unusual among caterpillars in that they live just below the soil surface, attacking young plants just at, or below, soil level. Lettuce and young Cabbage family plants are those most commonly damaged. The seedlings are usually eaten right through at soil level, fall over and wither — hence the name. Cutworms can be brown, green or yellowish, and often work their way along a row of seedlings, eating as they go.

Search in the top inch (2.5cm) of soil near the most recently damaged plants for the caterpillar and remove it. Controlling weeds helps too, as fewer eggs are laid. Generally, no chemical control is necessary but Bromophos or ICI Sybol may be used if it is a regular occurrence.

Dogs and Cats

Considerable damage is caused to lawns, by female dogs, and to small shrubs, by male dogs, urinating on them. Keep gates closed and fence off the garden. Solutions of strong-smelling disinfectant, Scent-off or Pepper Dust have a temporary effect. Dogs often wear tracks on lawns and may be diverted by placing obstacles such as dead, leafless boughs, in their path. The same deterrents apply to cats, but in addition water freshly cultivated soil to stop them scratching at it.

Earwigs

These are not really pests, only occasionally eating parts of the petals of flowers such as Dahlias, Delphiniums and Pansies. They are often responsible for 'mystery' damage to flowers, but this is generally so slight as not to need control, besides, they are beneficial predators of certain kinds of greenfly.

The removal of debris reduces their hiding places. Upturned pots with wood-wool or dry leaves make good traps and the earwigs may then be removed. Tapping flower heads is usually enough to dislodge them.

Eelworms

This pest attacks a wide range of plants, especially Chrysanthemums, onions, strawberries, potatoes and Tulips. The tiny worms get into the leaf, stem and root tissue of plants and feed in the sap, the plants often taking on a swollen or 'bloated' look.

Affected plants should be lifted and destroyed.

Flea beetle

These are small, black or striped beetles which jump away from Cabbage family seedlings when touched. They eat small round holes in the seed leaves. Usually, the plants grow out of it and no control is necessary.

If damage is severe, growth may be checked. A seed dressing, such as Murphy's Seed Dressing, or a shake of BHC Dust along the rows of seedlings, give good control.

Greenfly

A major pest of plants, both indoor and outdoor, greenfly may be black, brownish, reddish or blue instead of green. There is a type of greenfly for nearly every kind of plant. Weakening plants by sucking out the sap, they are also the main distributors of virus diseases. Leaves and shoots often curl up when infested, the greenfly usually feeding on the undersides.

They have many natural enemies, both predators and parasites, and very often these can be left to control the greenfly population. However there are a limited number of plants which usually need to be sprayed for greenfly and these include strawberries, raspberries, apples, plums, blackcurrants, gooseberries, lettuce, beans, cabbage, brussels sprouts, roses, honeysuckle, any greenhouse or indoor plant, and herbs. Even then, the natural control systems need to be supplemented only when populations look like building up early in the summer. Controlling the first attack is usually enough to return to balance.

The best product to use is Rapid, because it kills only greenfly and not the natural predators. Other products which may be used are non-persistent chemicals like Derris, Picket, Bio Sprayday and Tumblebug. These are more suitable close to harvest than Rapid which is active for about two weeks. Systemic insecticides that get into the plant sap are used where the leaves are rolled up and the greenfly are safely hidden. These include Hygeia Greenfly Spray, Bio Longlast and Murphy's Systemic Insecticide. Soap solutions, including the proprietary one, Savona, are quite effective against greenfly, and not harmful to predators. Hosing greenfly off with a jet of water may be tried too. Winter wash, with tar-oil, is effective against greenfly eggs on fruit trees, but is harmful to predators. *(See Page 49)*.

Leaf miners

Many trees and shrubs, especially apples, plums, Lilac, Holly and Flowering cherry, are attacked by tiny flies, the maggots of which tunnel between the surfaces of leaves. Little twisting, and widening, tracks may be seen. Damage is rarely severe, or worth controlling. If Holly is badly attacked, and losing a lot of leaves, Hexyl could be sprayed in June.

Leatherjackets

These brown, legless maggots are the larvae of daddy-long-legs. They eat the roots of many plants, including grass, weeds, vegetables and strawberries. They are usually only a problem in lawns and ground newly-broken out of grass and weeds, especially after wet summers, and near existing meadows. Treading heavily on affected patches of lawn gives some control. The application of Draza slug pellets is effective too.

Mealy bugs and scale insects

These, like greenfly, are sap-suckers. Being covered with wax or scale, they are difficult to control. Mealy bugs are mainly pests of indoor plants, especially cacti and succulents. Scale insects affect both indoor and outdoor plants, usually woody types, for example, Beech and Bay laurel.

The main control method indoors is to avoid introducing them on new plants. Otherwise, brush them off with some methylated spirits or use systemic insecticides such as Hygeia Greenfly Spray, Murphy's Systemic Insecticide and Bio Longlast. Test these on a part of the plant first, to see if they are safe. They may be used to control scale insects too, applied early in summer. Tar oil winter wash may be used on dormant trees to kill scale insects.

Millipedes

These are soil-living insects which normally eat dead plant tissue. However, they may attack living plants too, especially seeds and seedlings of peas and beans, potatoes, strawberries and bulbs. Millipedes have two pairs of legs per body segment, compared with centipedes which have one. Centipedes are beneficial predators.

Millipedes are most common on wet soils and in wet seasons, especially on soils high in organic material. Remove debris or incorporate it thoroughly into the soil to rot quickly. Use Seed Dressing on early sown peas and beans.

Onion bulb fly

The larvae of this insect bores into onion bulbs, destroying them. It is not common but may be a problem in some localities. Destroy wilted plants and cultivate before winter to expose the pupating maggots. Use Bromophos or ICI Sybol at sowing, if there has been a recurrent problem.

Pea and bean weevils

These little beetles are difficult to find on the plant but the damage they cause is obvious — U-shaped, bite-like pieces are eaten from the edges of the leaves of peas and beans.

They are not worth controlling unless the young seedlings are seriously damaged. Derris Dust or BHC Dust are suitable insecticides.

Pear midge

The tiny grubs of this pest feed inside developing pears, causing the fruitlets to swell and blacken. Each fruitlet may contain several grubs when they fall off the tree prematurely in June.

Pick up the fallen fruitlets and burn them. This usually gives control of this not-so-common pest.

Rabbits and hares

These are major pests of trees and shrubs in rural gardens, also damaging fruit trees and vegetables.

The only complete remedy is to fence the garden with a 3 feet (90 cm) high fence of netting wire, sunk 6 inches (15 cm) down and 6 inches (15 cm) towards the outside in an L-shape underground. Sleeves of strong polythene stapled together around the trunks of young trees give good protection. Around flower beds, string dipped in creosote and suspended on 6 inch (15 cm) high pegs is a useful, temporary deterrent.

Raspberry beetle

This is a familiar pest of raspberries, blackberries and loganberries, being the maggots often found in wild blackberries. The grub enters through the stem end which will be brown instead of white on an affected berry. It is more common in rural areas.

If the pest has attacked in the past, spray after flowering finishes, with Fenitrothion, Fentro, Malathion or Derris. This spray is timed to prevent the grubs entering the fruit.

Red spider mite

These are very tiny mites, just visible to the naked eye. Various types attack flowers, fruit, vegetables, trees, greenhouse plants and house plants. Cucumbers, melons, peppers, peaches, apples, strawberries, Blackeyed susan, Busy lizzie and Ageratum seem to be especially attractive but more or less any plant may be attacked, even potatoes. The sap-sucking of teeming thousands of mites causes stunting and yellowing of plant leaves. The most obvious symptom is small, yellow flecks on the upper surface of the leaf, although the pest feeds beneath.(See page 64).

Control is difficult to achieve. First, be careful to avoid buying plants which are infested. Healthy, strong plants are fairly resistant, so feed and water indoor plants properly. Spraying twice a day with clear water helps to control the mites but this is impractical. Outdoors, the mites have many predators, usually becoming troublesome only in warm summers. Benlate used on apple trees for apple scab disease helps to control them. If colonies begin to build up, indoors or outdoors, a spray of Derris, Malathion, Hygeia Greenfly Spray, Murphy's Systemic Insecticide, Bio Longlast or Sybol gives some control but may need to be repeated. Some of the sprays mentioned may damage certain plants so test them on a few leaves first. Also, red spider mite has built up resistance to certain chemicals, for instance Malathion, in some places.

There is a very efficient predator which may be introduced deliberately to control the pest in greenhouses but it is not commercially available to home gardeners.

Slugs and snails

Essentially the same kind of animal, snails have shells; slugs do not. They attack many kinds of plants, especially young plants and the soft, succulent growth of herbaceous perennials and vegetables. They eat a lot of dead plant tissue and are more prevalent on soils with high organic matter where manure and compost have been applied. They are more active in wet years.

Slugs and snails can be collected in the garden and disposed of. Collection is made easier by laying out traps of old cabbage leaves or fruit skins. Stale beer is attractive too and a shallow dish at soil level allows them to enter and drown. Some people simply walk on every slug or snail they see. Apart from this general control, it is particularly important to protect young plants and strawberries. A barrier of soot is reasonably effective. Otherwise, chemical slug-killers may be used. These include Draza, Hygeia Slug Pellets, Tumbleslug, Slugit, ICI Miniblue Slug Pellets, Slug Mini-pellets and Fertosan. Some of these are liquids or powders with the advantage that birds or pets cannot eat them. Mini-pellets are smaller and more difficult for birds and pets to find than large pellets. These should be covered by a slate supported on a few stones. The slugs will find them all right.

Vine weevil

Both the grubs and adults of this beetle cause damage. The adults take bite-shaped pieces from the edge of leaves of shrubs, especially Rhododendron and Pieris. This damage, usually near the ground, is not significant except as an indication of the presence of the pest and the likelihood that the white, C-shaped grubs are active below soil level. These cause severe damage to many different plants by eating the roots, especially Rhododendron, strawberries, grapes, Cyclamen, Primula, Begonia, Sempervivums, Saxifrages, Camellias and any potted plant. They are more active in pots because the soil is warm. Virtually unknown ten years ago, they have been spread by nursery containers in recent years. Affected plants show little or no growth and often wilt, though well supplied with moisture, before dying.

Check the roots of new plants for grubs. Clear all debris to reduce hiding places for the flightless, nocturnal-feeding, adult weevils. BHC Dust is effective when incorporated into the compost at potting, or into the soil when planting small rockery plants. If large areas, such as peat beds, are to be treated, use GammaCol or Cudgel, both of which are available only in litre packs and may have to be specially ordered.

Whitefly

This tiny fly — about the size of a grain of sugar — is often confused with the skins shed by greenfly when they moult. They are easy to tell apart — the whitefly has white wings and it flies out of the plant when the foliage is touched. Though small, they are quite serious pests of greenhouse plants and houseplants. They weaken the plants, and excrete sticky honeydew on which black moulds grow, rendering the plants very unsightly.

Avoid buying plants which are infested — this is the usual method of spread. Spray two or three times, at weekly intervals, with Picket, PY Spray, Sybol, Derris, Bio Sprayday, Malathion, or Hygeia Greenfly Spray.

Wireworm

These are hard, reddish or yellowish grubs about half an inch (1cm) long. They are usually only a problem in new gardens which have been broken out of old grassland. Potatoes are often used as a 'cleaning' crop in these situations, and the resulting tubers are sometimes tunnelled by wireworm. Usually the problem solves itself but, in heavy infestations, and where the old sods are slow to break down, Bromophos or ICI Sybol might be used.

Diseases

When a plant malfunctions because it has been attacked by a fungus, bacterium or virus, it has a disease. The malfunction is the disease, not the organism causing it.

Fungi are like very tiny plants with no chlorophyll. To stay alive, they must feed off dead, or living, organic material. They cause the majority of plant diseases.

Bacteria consist of a single cell, so small as to be visible only with a microscope. They can move independently — a characteristic of animals. There are not many major bacterial plant diseases.

Viruses are even more radical. Smaller than cells, they consist mainly of the genetic code for their own production.

Plant defence mechanisms

The main defence of plants is their outer surface — bark, skin or wax layer. If this is damaged, and the plant is too weak to heal the injury, fungi, bacteria and viruses can get in. Many diseases are specific to the plants they attack, other plants being resistant. Some varieties of a particular plant have resistantce to certain diseases. Very often this was bred into the variety by a plant breeder.

Physical disease control

Moist conditions generally favour fungal diseases, although mildew likes dry air. Do not splash water about indoors, and outdoors, position susceptible plants so that they dry out quickly. Take care not to buy diseased plants and do not leave old plants as sources of infection. Removing diseased plant parts gives good control in some cases.

Chemical disease control

Most of the modern fungicides act by preventing the fungal spores — the equivalent of seeds — from germinating. Many of them form a protective layer on the plant's surface, and some of them actually enter the sap of the plant, giving it systemic protection.

Bacterial diseases are affected by some of the same chemicals, but to a lesser extent. Antibiotics used to kill bacteria in human and animal medicine are much too costly to be used on plants.

Viruses cannot be treated by chemicals at all. They operate within the plant cells and any chemical which kills them damages the plant.

Apple scab

This very common disease is caused by a fungus which attacks the young leaves as soon as they emerge in spring. It grows on the leaves, producing spores. When the fruits form they are attacked too, small brown or black scabs being the result. (See page 50). Apart from direct damage to the fruit, apple scab seriously weakens the tree, predisposing it to apple canker disease. Pears are affected by a similar scab disease, but less frequently.

Spray at bud-burst, in late March or early April, with Benlate, Systemic Fungicide or Supercarb. Repeat the spray at least three times between then and the end of June. In a wet year, and in wet localities, more spraying may be necessary.

Bacterial canker

This is one of the few serious bacterial diseases. It causes members of the Cherry and Plum family to fail gradually, and die. The signs are; branches dying; foliage with little holes — 'shothole'; and gum exuding from the main limbs. The bacteria being prevalent in winter, it is most important to prevent injury to these trees in that season. For that reason, pruning is done only in summer.

Brown rot

This is a fungus disease of plums and occasionally cherries, apples and pears. It causes a brown rot, often with white spots, which destroys the affected fruit. It is rarely a very serious problem, destroying only a few fruits usually.

Pick off all old 'mummified' fruits left on the trees in the autumn. These are the main sources of infection. The sprays for apple scab are a big help in prevention.

Cane diseases

Three separate fungi cause the canes of raspberry and loganberry to die back. Cane blight kills entire canes by invading at ground level. Spur blight causes individual spurs on the canes to die. Cane spot causes purple spots on canes and leaves, and parts of canes may die in a bad attack.

Spray at bud-burst for cane spot; when the new canes are 6 inches (15cm) high for spur blight. Suitable chemicals are Benlate, Supercarb and Hexyl. For cane blight, avoid injury, and, if the small white grubs of cane midge are found beneath the bark providing an entry point, spray with Fenitrothion, Fentro or Sybol, twice in May.

Canker and dieback

These are general names given to the damage caused by the fungal and bacterial diseases which kill twigs and branches. The bark often dies with a sunken, cracked appearance. Very many trees and shrubs may be affected by these diseases which are most common in wet localities, and in over-sheltered gardens. Apples, Roses, Beech, Ash, Laburnum and Clematis are commonly affected.

Prune out cankers, and twigs that have died-back. An application of potash fertiliser helps to toughen the wood.

Clubroot

This fungal disease causes finger-like swellings on the roots of the members of the Cabbage family — hence the alternative name, 'finger-and-toe'. It occurs frequently on wet, acid soils but very seldom on limy soils. Affected plants are stunted and fail to develop. Spores can survive in the soil for many years.

Improving drainage, and applying lime, are two ways to reduce the disease. Clubroot preventers, such as Clubroot Control used as directed, or one ounce of Benlate or Systemic Fungicide in 5 pints of water (10g/litre), gives a good measure of control.

Fairy rings

The most serious disease of lawns, this is caused by a soil fungus feeding off the roots of the lawn grasses. A ring of vigorous green grass may surround a broken ring of bare spots. The rings expand slowly outwards, producing on occasion a few pale brown, small mushrooms. It occurs most frequently on good lawns, and can be very disfiguring. Toadstools or inkcap mushrooms are not lawn diseases and should just be removed.

Control may be obtained by digging out the top 6 inches of soil and breaking up the soil below. Apply Basamid as directed. In removing the soil, do not contaminate other parts of the lawn. Fill the hole with good soil and re-seed the area.

Gooseberry mildew

A fungal disease causing a white or brownish deposit on the leaves, shoots and fruit of gooseberries, it also attacks the leaves and shoots of currants and Flowering currants. The bushes may be seriously weakened.

Prune gooseberries to keep the centre of the bush open, allowing air to circulate. Prune out any affected shoots in summer and to prevent fruit mildew, spray gooseberries with Benlate, Nimrod, Systemic Fungicide, or pbi Supercarb when the first flowers open, and again when the fruit is the size of a pea. *(See Page 40).*

Grey mould

The name describes the masses of grey spores produced on the rotted parts of plants affected by this fungal disease. The fungus involved is mainly a decomposer of dead plant tissue but it can invade living tissue as well. Any plant which has some dead tissue attached, such as withered flowers or leaves, may develop this disease. Old plants in cool, damp conditions are very susceptible. Most common in a wet season, it often affects soft fruit, french beans, celery, lettuce, cucumbers and tomatoes.

Avoid damp situations for indoor plants, especially in the dull months. Remove dead plant parts before they are invaded. The only routine sprays against this disease are those given to soft fruit. Strawberries and raspberries should be sprayed at least twice, starting when the first flowers open, with Benlate, Systemic Fungicide, or Supercarb. *(See Page 44).*

Gummosis

This is a disorder of rhubarb caused by changeable growing conditions. Gum exudes from the stems, but the plant recovers. Use the unaffected stalks. Apply some potash fertiliser.

Honey fungus

This is the most serious fungal disease of trees and shrubs. It moves through the soil between woody plants, invading them through the roots. These growths in the soil are like black boot-laces, hence the alternative name 'boot-lace fungus'. Affected plants have their root systems destroyed, causing them to wilt and die. Yellowish mushrooms are sometimes produced at soil level beside the trunk. The fungus spreads from old stumps to living plants and it is very common in old woodland and ditches. Trees and shrubs die off in ones and twos over a period of years.

Remove old stumps and do not plant too near the site of old ditches for a few years. Susceptible plants include Privet, Apple, Griselinia, Cypresses, Lilac and Willow. Reasonably resistant plants include Hawthorn, Yew, Ash, Beech, Laurel, Box, Clematis, Honeysuckle and Holly. A barrier of heavy polythene might be placed vertically in a 2 feet (60cm) deep trench between an infected area and new planting. If a plant dies in a hedge, remove it together with the plant on either side; remove 12 inches (30cm) of soil; drench the hole with Jeyes' Fluid or ICI Clean Up; fill the hole with fresh soil and plant again.

Leaf spots

Almost every plant has a leaf spot disease. Most are not very damaging, being no more than curiosities like sycamore tar spot, but blackcurrants, celery, beans and Rhododendrons are among the plants which suffer serious leaf spot diseases. If these recur each year, weakening the plants, a spray or two with Benlate or Supercarb in late spring and early summer will help.

Neck rot

This is a serious fungal disease of onions, causing them to rot in store. The fungus gets into the bulb during its period of growth and only causes the rot later. It is worst in wet years.

Destroy all rotted onions — do not simply dump them. Dress seed and sets with a dusting of Benlate before sowing.

Potato blight

This disease spreads from old, dumped potatoes to new plants in mid-summer. The foliage quickly rots with brown spots appearing. The fungus needs moist conditions; so it is worse in a wet year. The spores spread rapidly from plant to plant, sometimes causing all the leaves to rot. Apart from stopping growth, the spores get into the soil to affect the tubers which develop a bronze rot, and become unusable.

Spraying is essential in most years, except for early crops. Spray with Dithane, Bordeaux Mixture, Brestan, or Liquid Copper. Old potatoes should be buried deeply, not just dumped in a corner.

Powdery mildew

These are common diseases affecting a wide range of plants. The symptoms are obvious — a chalky, dust-like coating on the leaves, flower buds or stems, and sometimes the fruit as well. The most seriously affected garden plants are Apples, Roses, Clematis, Asters, Forget-me-nots, Sweet pea, Foxglove, courgettes, swede turnips, strawberries and grapevines. These plants may be seriously weakened by the feeding of the fungus; leaves destroyed; flowering and fruiting stopped or spoiled. Plants growing in greenhouses, and on light, dry soils in a sunny position, are much more prone to mildew attack. It is common in dry seasons, but may also make a strong attack in dull seasons when plants have grown quickly and are soft as a result. (See page 50).

Apple mildew may be controlled by pruning out the affected shoots in early summer. Otherwise, consider spraying any plant which has been attacked in the past. Suitable chemicals include Benlate, Supercarb, Systemic Fungicide, Nimrod, and Sulphur Dust. Sulphur may damage some kinds of fruit and should be tested first. Apply these chemicals in late spring and early summer, twice or three times. Swede turnip mildew is not controlled by these but late sowings usually escape damage.

Root rot

Several types of soil-living fungi attack the roots of a wide range of plants, causing the root system to rot. The plant above ground first stops growing, then leaves may go yellow and wilt, and finally total collapse occurs. Commonly affected plants include Geraniums, Primulas, tomatoes, cucumbers, lettuce, Lawson's cypress, Heathers, Rhododendrons and fruit trees. When seedlings die of root rot, it is called damping-off.

The root rot fungi are moisture-lovers which thrive in conditions of water-logging outdoors, and over-watering indoors. Use clean trays, compost and water when raising plants from seed. Cheshunt Compound may be used to reduce damping-off. Outdoors, drainage should be improved and plants kept growing strongly by using adequate fertiliser. Affected plants should be disposed of.

Rose blackspot

This fungal disease is the most serious problem of roses. It overwinters on dead leaves and infected shoots. In spring the emerging leaves are infected and the cycle completed. It causes black or brown spots on the leaves which often turn yellow and fall off. The plant is seriously weakened after a few years of this.

Collect and burn affected leaves in the autumn. Spray in late March or early April, with Supercarb, Benlate, Systemic Fungicide, Roseclear, Multirose, or Nimrod to break the cycle. Continue spraying, at least once a month, until July, and longer in a wet summer. Some varieties are more susceptible. *(See the List of Rose Varieties on page 35).*

Rust

Very many plants have a rust disease caused by a specific fungus. Brown, yellow or reddish spots appear on the undersides of the leaves, often with a 'shadow' on the upper surface. Most of these diseases are not fatal to the plants affected, but usually spoil the foliage and reduce flowering. Commonly attacked plants include Roses, leeks, Hollyhocks,

Carnations, beans, Geraniums, Mint, Poplars and Willows. Rust diseases have a curious habit of appearing every few years for just one season. If they appear more frequently, and the plants are weakened, spraying might be considered. Usually only Roses and Willows need to be sprayed.

Suitable chemicals include Dithane, Liquid Copper, Bordeaux Mixture and Tumbleblite. Use these sprays as indicated above, in early summer, when the disease is first noticed — not as a routine. Repeat the spray twice. Rusts are more common in hot years.

Silver leaf

This fungal disease is the major killer of plums and cherries, including Flowering cherries. The fungus gets in through wounds during the cool, wet part of the year and gradually kills the tree by blocking its water-carrying vessels — the tree wilts. Usually a single branch is first affected and dies. The disease spreads until the whole tree dies.

Never prune these trees in winter. Prune away any sick-looking branches in summer, and immediately seal all pruning cuts or injuries.

Virus diseases

These diseases may affect any type of garden plant. They cause stunting, mottling and curling of foliage, and reduce flowering and fruiting. Commonly affected plants are strawberries, raspberries, potatoes, courgettes, cucumbers, spinach, Tulips and blackcurrants. But many other plants are affected too.

There is no cure. Affected plants must be removed and destroyed. Virus diseases are spread by greenfly, and eelworms and on pruning tools. Controlling greenfly helps, especially on strawberries, and to avoid the use of secateurs or knives on healthy plants after infected ones is important, for example, when harvesting courgettes. *(See Page 44).*

White blister

This is a fairly 'new', but now common, disease of the Cabbage family. It causes raised yellow bumps about an inch across on the upper surface of the leaves, and white spots on the underside. It spoils the foliage but does not greatly weaken the plant. Since it usually affects old leaves, the crops are generally edible. Remove old crops.

White rot

This is a serious disease of onions in some gardens. It is soil-borne, rotting the roots and making the bulbs unusable. On a badly infected site, every plant will be lost. *(See Page 41).*

To keep out the disease, avoid planting onion sets — use seed instead. If the disease is already in a part of the garden do not grow onions there, and avoid transferring soil on tools and boots to other parts. Clubroot Control gives reasonable results as does a seed dressing with Benlate but the best solution is to avoid infected ground. Destroy all affected plants by burning.

Weather and Timing

For best results in gardening, it is important to get things done on time. Daylength varies considerably between the start, middle and end of the growing season. It has a very big influence on the growth, flowering and fruiting of plants, and because it does not vary from year to year, it might be supposed that it would be possible to go by the calendar for the main cultural operations — sowing, planting, spraying, pruning and so on. However, this is not so. The growing season varies greatly from year to year because of the influence of weather.

The main influencing weather factors are rainfall and temperature. Cold weather and a lot of rain early in the year delays the start of growing season because it keeps down soil temperature — the key factor in early growth. Equally, the wetter parts of the country are more likely to have a delayed start to the growing season, and an earlier finish, than the drier parts. Frost plays a big part too. Late frost in the spring affects many plants and effectively dictates the planting-out dates for tender plants. Early frost in autumn brings the growing season to a close because soil temperatures fall — apart from the damage to tender plants.

Generally speaking, things should be done as early as possible to get the longest time to develop, but not too early just the same. There is always some leeway. In using the calendars on the following pages, allowance should be made for local factors. There is about a month's difference in the growing season between the southern and northern counties— a fortnight at each end.

Annual rainfall (cm)

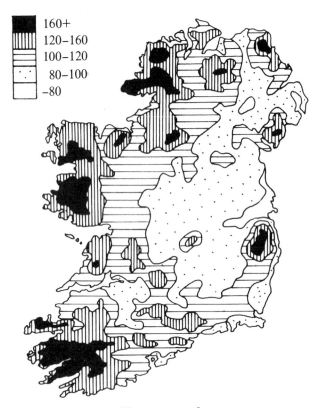

160+
120–160
100–120
80–100
–80

Last spring frost

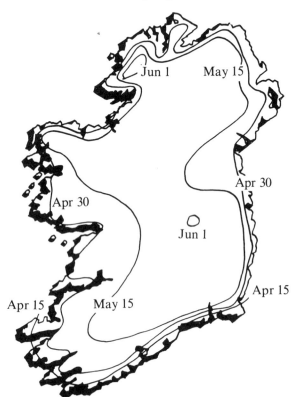

First autumn frost

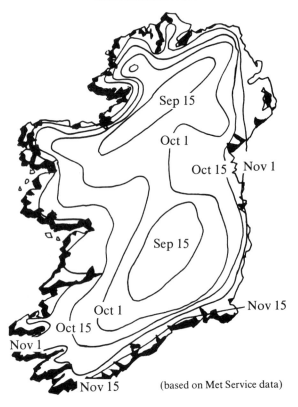

(based on Met Service data)

Trees and shrubs through the year . . .

January   Continue planting dormant deciduous trees and shrubs in good weather. Carry out any general pruning of deciduous trees and remove damaged, or diseased branches, painting the pruning cuts.

February   Continue planting deciduous trees and shrubs. Firm the soil around shrubs planted in autumn. Finish general pruning. Clear out weeds and briars under hedges, spot-treating ivy with Brushwood Killer.

March   Finish planting deciduous trees and start planting evergreens. Apply fertilisers, or mulches, to young trees and shrubs. Apply Weedol and Simazine for weed control. Prune Hypericum, Spirea, Hydrangea and Fuchsia.

April   Finish planting evergreens. Apply weedkillers and mulches, if not applied yet. Plant out rooted cuttings of shrubs into nursery beds. Apply Sequestrene to lime-haters. Prune Butterfly Bush.

May   Watch all newly planted trees and shrubs for water shortage. Give Privet and Lonicera hedges a first trim. Prune Forsythia, Flowering currant, Kerria and Broom, after flowering.

June   Water newly planted shrubs and trees if a dry spell occurs. Watch Honeysuckle for greenfly. Remove Rhododendron flowers as they go over. Prune Orange ball tree, Deutzia and Weigela when they finish flowering.

July   Water any trees or shrub which is short of water, especially close to walls. Layer Clematis and Wisteria. Begin taking semi-hardwood cuttings. Prune shrubs that have flowered, if necessary.

August   Watch for water shortage. Loosen tree ties that have tightened. Prune the Plum family, if necessary. Take semi-hardwood cuttings of most flowering shrubs. Trim all hedges, especially Beech before it gets too tough.

September   Prepare for autumn planting. Take semi-hardwood cuttings of shrubs and conifers. Apply weedkillers around trees and shrubs, if necessary, but be careful not to over-dose with Simazine.

October   Plant evergreen trees and shrubs. Take hardwood cuttings of Forsythia, Flowering currant, Willow, Poplar, Butterfly bush, Escallonia, Griselinia. Check ties on wall-trained shrubs and tie in new shoots, using soft string.

November   Plant deciduous trees and shrubs. Consider windbreak protection for newly planted conifers. Sow chestnuts, acorns, beechmast and other tree seeds and stratify fleshy seeds in pots of sand.

December   Generally, tidy up. Remove over-grown shrubs or surplus trees. Rake up leaves for the compost heap. Any major lopping or pruning should be carried out now when the branches can be seen.

Roses through the year. . .

January   Dig ground for new rose beds. Top up old beds with new soil if they have sunk, and the plants are loose.

February   Begin pruning bush roses and continuous-flowering climbers. Plant new roses of all kinds.

March   Finish planting and pruning. Tidy up rose beds. Apply Simazine. Apply fertilisers and mulches.

April   Spray against blackspot. Finish tidying and straightening rose bed edges, and applying weedkiller.

May   Spray against blackspot and watch out for greenfly. Water newly planted roses in dry weather.

June   Spray against blackspot, and mildew on wall-trained roses. Remove suckers as soon as they appear.

July   Spray for greenfly if they appear. Apply fertiliser to encourage late blooms.

August   Remove flower heads as they go over. Remove suckers that have appeared since June.

September   Prune climbers and ramblers which flower once and have finished. Tie in new shoots.

October   Prepare new rose beds. Take cuttings of all types of roses for rooting outdoors.

November   Plant roses of all types. Remove part of the top of tall roses, if wind rocking is likely.

December   Continue planting, if the weather is good. Remove all dead rose leaves and burn them.

Flowers through the year . . .

January   Generally tidy up flower beds and borders. Continue digging lightly around perennial flower clumps. Sow Geraniums for bedding in gentle heat indoors or in a propagator.

February   Finish off tidying and digging. Prepare ground for planting perennial flowers. Sow Snapdragons and Busy lizzies under protection — they are slow developers. Watch for damping-off disease.

March   Divide and plant perennial flowers and apply general fertiliser around them. Sow half-hardy annual summer bedding plants under protection. Sow hardy annual flowers outdoors, if the soil is in good condition.

April   Finish sowing hardy annual flowers outdoors. Apply mulches, or grass cuttings, around perennial flowers after removing weeds. Finish planting perennial flowers. Plant Gladiolus and unsprouted Dahlias in mixed borders.

May   Harden off boxes of half-hardy annuals and start planting them after the middle of the month. Plant sprouted Dahlias. Thin out and weed hardy annual flowers. Stake perennial flowers, if necessary, before they get too big.

June   Finish planting out half-hardy summer bedding. Sow Wallflowers and other spring bedding plants. Sow perennial flower seeds outdoors, or under protection. Stake tall flowers. Line out Tulips and Polyanthus from spring bedding displays.

July   Weed and water bedding plants, if necessary. Remove flower heads which have faded, if practical. Transplant Wallflowers to the nursery bed. Watch for pests, especially greenfly, which can severely check flower plants.

August   Tidy up perennial flowers that have finished. Build rockeries, alpine beds, patios, etc. Transplant perennial flower seedlings into the nursery bed and watch them for water shortage for the first week.

September   Prepare new ground for planting. Continue tidying perennial flowers. Sow some hardy annual flowers such as Calendula, California Poppy, Cornflower and Limnanthes. Pot up bulbs for flowering at Christmas.

October   Remove summer bedding and plant spring bedding. Plant spring flowering bulbs. Plant perennial flowers. Divide old perennial flower clumps if necessary. Plant Lilies in a sheltered position.

November   Lift Dahlias, Gladiolus and Begonias and store them over winter in a dry shed or garage. Finish planting spring bedding and bulbs. Bring Christmas bulbs into a warm room to flower.

December   Tidy away perennial flower stalks that have died back, using the stems on the compost heap. Lightly dig over perennial flower borders, removing weeds in the process.

Greenhouse through the year. . .

January   Bring in strawberry plants in pots. Plant grapevines. Water plants very lightly, if necessary.

February   Start potted Fuchsias, Hydrangeas and Geraniums into growth by watering. Trim greenhouse shrubs.

March   Pollinate peach flowers. Sow tomato, pepper, cucumber and melon seeds. Pot up Begonias and Gloxinias.

April   Increase watering and begin feeding. Take Fuchsia and Geranium cuttings. Ventilate strawberries.

May   Plant out the greenhouse vegetables. Pinch out grape laterals. Ventilate on hot days.

June   Watch carefully for pests, especially greenfly and red spider mite. Take Christmas cherry cuttings.

July   Continue feeding, watering and training plants as necessary. Sow Primula and Cineraria seeds.

August   Take Geranium, Fuchsia, Campanula cuttings, and sow Cyclamen seeds. Pot up strawberries.

September   Continue taking cuttings. Sow Schizanthus seeds. Reduce feeding of all plants.

October   Stop feeding and reduce watering. Ventilate on dry days. Pot up rooted cuttings.

November   Remove all old, diseased and pest-ridden plants and fumigate the house. Wash pots and trays.

December   Make sure to stop draughts and leaks. Wash the glass to let in full light.

Vegetables through the year . . .

January   Complete digging, if not already done. Apply lime if necessary. Plant rhubarb stools. Sow early cabbage and cauliflower, under protection. Sow onion seed under protection for large onions.

February   Put seed potatoes in trays for sprouting. Sow early peas and broad beans, using a seed dressing. Remove weeds around asparagus, rhubarb, globe artichoke and spray with Simazine. Apply fertiliser to these vegetables.

March   Make first sowings of the salad vegetables. Sow parsnips, onions and brussels sprouts. Sow cabbage and cauliflower for late summer use. Sow early potatoes. Sow seed for outdoor tomatoes, under protection. Sow lettuce seed for planting out later.

April   Plant out early cabbage and cauliflower. Protect against cabbage root fly. Sow maincrop vegetables and herbs. Make successional sowings of salad vegetables. Plant onion sets and maincrop potatoes.

May   Sow sweet corn, courgette and runner bean seed early in the month under protection. Sow winter cabbage, cauliflower and broccoli. Make further sowings of salad crops. Thin, weed and transplant crops sown earlier.

June   Plant outdoor tomatoes, sweet corn, courgettes and runner beans early in the month. Sow swede turnips carrots and french beans. Watch for pests. Control weeds by hoeing regularly while they are still small.

July   Plant out winter cabbage, cauliflower and broccoli early in the month. Make late sowings of beetroot, lettuce and peas. Water crops showing signs of drought. Sow spring cabbage late in the month.

August   Remove crops as they go over and dig the ground. Sow Japanese onions. Spray autumn cabbage, cauliflower and broccoli against cabbage moth caterpillars. Sow hardy lettuce varieties. Lift garlic.

September   Lift early potatoes. Plant spring cabbage. Check brussels sprouts for cabbage greenfly. Freeze surplus vegetables before they get over-mature. Lift and dry bulb onions for storage, using 'thick-necks' immediately.

October   Lift and store maincrop potatoes and carrots. Dig the ground as it is cleared; apply compost before digging. Ripen outdoor tomatoes indoors. Plant more spring cabbage for an extended supply.

November   Finish the tidying and removal of old crops as an important part of the control of weeds, pests and diseases. Put plant waste on the compost heap which could now be turned and tidied before winter.

December   Finish off digging, leaving the soil fairly rough to expose overwintering pest larvae and diseases to birds and the winter weather. Frost breaks down the rough surface by penetrating the lumps.

Houseplants through the year. . .

January   Make sure plants get whatever light is available. Keep plants out of cold positions.

February   Water and feed only plants in flower. Keep all others slightly dry.

March   Increase watering when the weather improves. Begin re-potting plants that need it.

April   Begin regular watering and feed plants once a fortnight. Spring clean plant leaves.

May   Continue watering and feeding. Take cuttings, divide plants and root runners to get new plants.

June   Continue watering and feeding. Be careful that plants in sunny windows do not scorch.

July   Continue watering and feeding. Watch closely for pests, especially red spider mites.

August   Continue watering and feeding. Water plants before holidays and make arrangements.

September   Ease off watering and stop feeding. Control pests, if necessary, before winter.

October   Further reduce watering. Keep plants a little on the dry side. Give full light.

November   Move plants where they will get full light. Check that plants are not getting too much water.

December   Feed and water flowering Christmas plants as necessary, but not too much.

Fruit through the year . . .

January	Continue planting fruit trees and bushes if the weather is good. Prune apple and pear trees and blackcurrrant and gooseberry bushes. Take shoots for grafting in April.
February	Finish off any remaining pruning. Dig out, or spot-treat perennial weeds with Casoron G. Spray wall — trained peach trees with Dithane, or Liquid Copper against peach leaf curl.
March	Finish off any remaining planting of new fruit trees. Plant strawberry runners. Apply fertiliser to all fruit trees. Spray apple trees at bud-burst against apple scab. Prune young plum trees and Morello cherry.
April	Apply Simazine around fruit trees and bushes growing in bare ground, also to strawberries. Continue spraying apple and pear trees against scab. Watch these and all other fruits for greenfly and caterpillars.
May	Continue spraying apple and pear trees. Spray strawberries with Benlate against grey mould. Watch newly planted fruit bushes for signs of water shortage. Spray raspberries against raspberry beetle.
June	Continue spraying apple and pear trees. Watch for greenfly build-up on plums and cherries. Pin down strawberry runners for new plants. Train in new loganberry shoots. Spray apples against codling moth.
July	Thin apple and pear fruits if too many have set. Begin summer pruning of dwarf tree forms of apple and pears, and also, over-vigorous trees. Water all fruits if there is a long, dry spell. Tie-down young apple shoots.
August	Prune raspberries after picking is finished. Continue summer pruning of apples, pears and plums. Prune peaches and tie-in new replacement shoots. Remove unwanted strawberry runners and weed the rows.
September	Prune plum trees after picking. Plant strawberry runners. Finish summer pruning of apples, pears and plums. Prune loganberries and tie-in the new canes, or simply wrap them around the wires. ·
October	Prepare ground for planting new fruit trees. Finish planting strawberry runners. Spray plum, cherries and peaches, at leaf-fall, with Dithane or Liquid Copper against bacterial canker and peach leaf curl.
November	Plant all fruit trees and bushes — this is the best month. Pick and store apples in open polythene bags. Prune blackberries and tie-in new canes. Spray apple trees with Liquid Copper against canker and apple scab.
December	Winter prune apples, pears, blackcurrants and gooseberries. Spray all fruit trees and bushes with tar-oil winter wash against pests and diseases, except where red spider mite is a problem. Cut down old trees.

Lawns through the year . . .

January	Rake off fallen leaves. In good weather, prepare ground for new lawns.
February	Continue ground preparation. Apply moss control prodructs, if necessary, especially in shady areas.
March	Begin regular mowing. Apply a spring lawn fertiliser. Apply general fertiliser to ground for new lawns.
April	Continue mowing. Sow new lawn areas. Apply lawn weedkillers, if necessary. Re-seed worn patches.
May	Mowing, at least once a week is necessary. Apply ½ ounce per square yard of sulphate of ammonia.
June	Continue mowing. Apply weedkillers, if necessary. Keep lawn edges trimmed.
July	Ease off mowing if the weather is dry and consider watering. Raise the blades a little.
August	Continue mowing and finish applying weedkillers. Prepare new lawn areas for sowing next month.
September	Continue mowing. Sow new lawn areas — this is the best month for sowing.
October	Continue mowing. Apply an autumn lawn fertiliser. Repair worn patches by re-seeding or turfing.
November	Give a final cutting. Finish applying autumn fertiliser. Get the lawn mower serviced.
December	Rake off fallen leaves and put them on a compost heap — much better than burning.

List of Further Reading

Garden Style. Gerry Daly.

The Tree and Shrub Expert. Dr. D.G. Hessayon. pbi Publications.

The Flower Expert. Dr. D.G. Hessayon. pbi Publications.

The Lawn Expert. Dr. D.G. Hessayon. pbi Publications.

The Rose Expert. Dr. D.G. Hessayon. pbi Publications.

The Vegetable Expert. Dr. D.G. Hessayon. pbi Publications.

The Houseplant Expert. Dr. D.G. Hessayon. pbi Publications.

The Fruit Garden Displayed. The Royal Horticultural Society.

The Vegetable Garden Displayed. The Royal Horticultural Society.

Hillier's Manual of Trees and Shrubs. Hillier Nurseries Ltd.

The Climate of Ireland. The Stationery Office, Dublin.

The Gardening Year. The Reader's Digest Association Ltd.

Reader's Digest Encyclopaedia of Garden Plants and Flowers.

Pests, Diseases, and Disorders of Garden Plants. Collins.

Gardener's Encyclopaedia of Plants and Flowers. Dorling Kindersley.

Index